Vocabula
NEW SCIENCE STANDARDS

Robert J. Marzano
Katie Rogers
Julia A. Simms

MARZANO
—Research—

555 North Morton Street
Bloomington, IN 47404
888.849.0851
FAX: 866.801.1447
email: info@marzanoresearch.com
marzanoresearch.com

Visit **marzanoresearch.com/reproducibles** to download the reproducibles in this book.

Printed in the United States of America

Library of Congress Control Number: 2014916718

ISBN: 978-0-9913748-9-2

18 17 16 15 14   1 2 3 4 5

Cover and Text Designer: Rian Anderson
Compositors: Rachel Smith
            Abigail Bowen

Marzano Research Development Team

Director of Publications

Julia A. Simms

Production Editors

Katie Rogers

Laurel Hecker

Editorial Assistant/Staff Writer

Ming Lee Newcomb

Marzano Research Associates

Tina Boogren

Bev Clemens

Jane Doty Fischer

Jeff Flygare

Tammy Heflebower

Mitzi Hoback

Jan K. Hoegh

Russell Jenson

Jessica Kanold-McIntyre

Sonny Magaña

Margaret McInteer

Diane E. Paynter

Kristin Poage

Salle Quackenboss

Cameron Rains

Ainsley B. Rose

Tom Roy

Gerry Varty

Phil Warrick

Kenneth C. Williams

Visit **marzanoresearch.com/reproducibles** to download the reproducibles from this book.

Table of Contents

PART I

Vocabulary Instruction for the New Science Standards 3

PART II

PART III

About the Authors

 **Robert J. Marzano, PhD,** is the cofounder and CEO of Marzano Research in Denver, Colorado. During his forty years in the field of education, he has worked with educators as a speaker and trainer and has authored more than thirty books and 150 articles on topics such as instruction, assessment, writing and implementing standards, cognition, effective leadership, and school intervention. His books include *The Art and Science of Teaching, Leaders of Learning, On Excellence in Teaching, Effective Supervision, The Classroom Strategies Series, Using Common Core Standards to Enhance Classroom Instruction and Assessment, Vocabulary for the Common Core, Teacher Evaluation That Makes a Difference,* and *A Handbook for High Reliability Schools.* His practical translations of the most current research and theory into classroom strategies are known internationally and are widely practiced by both teachers and administrators. He received a bachelor's degree from Iona College in New York, a master's degree from Seattle University, and a doctorate from the University of Washington.

 **Katie Rogers** is a production editor for Marzano Research in Denver, Colorado, where she writes and edits books, research reports, and website materials. She is coauthor of *Teaching Argumentation: Activities and Games for the Classroom* and has experience teaching and mentoring at the middle school and college levels, respectively. She holds a bachelor of arts degree in sociology from Colorado College, where she developed a strong interest in social theory and education research.

 **Julia A. Simms** is director of publications for Marzano Research in Denver, Colorado. She has worked in K–12 education as a classroom teacher, gifted education specialist, teacher leader, and coach, and her books include *Coaching Classroom Instruction, Using Common Core Standards to Enhance Classroom Instruction and Assessment, Vocabulary for the Common Core, Questioning Sequences in the Classroom, A Handbook for High Reliability Schools,* and *Teaching Argumentation: Activities and Games for the Classroom.* She has led school- and district-level professional development on a variety of topics, including literacy instruction and intervention, classroom and schoolwide differentiation, and instructional technology. She received her bachelor's degree from Wheaton College in Wheaton, Illinois, and her master's degrees in educational administration and K–12 literacy from Colorado State University and the University of Northern Colorado, respectively.

About Marzano Research

Marzano Research is a joint venture between Solution Tree and Dr. Robert J. Marzano. Marzano Research combines Dr. Marzano's forty years of educational research with continuous action research in all major areas of schooling in order to provide effective and accessible instructional strategies, leadership strategies, and classroom assessment strategies that are always at the forefront of best practice. By providing such an all-inclusive research-into-practice resource center, Marzano Research provides teachers and principals with the tools they need to effect profound and immediate improvement in student achievement.

Introduction

In 2009, the National Research Council (NRC), American Association for the Advancement of Science (AAAS), Achieve, and the National Science Teachers Association (NSTA) teamed up to develop the Next Generation Science Standards* (NGSS; NGSS Lead States, 2013). Their goal was to update previous standards documents and to clearly describe progressions of learning in four dimensions of science understanding:

- Physical science

- Life science

- Earth and space science

- Engineering, technology, and applications of science

As with any set of standards, educators are faced with the significant challenge of designing instruction that allows students to meet the standards' requirements. We believe that an important element of effective science instruction involves a comprehensive program of direct vocabulary instruction.

As Marco Bravo and Gina Cervetti (2008) stated, "Content areas expose students to a large corpus of challenging and often abstract words, many of which require the use of other equally challenging words to define and exemplify them" (p. 130). Understanding science content in particular requires familiarity with precise and specialized language and vocabulary terms. Consider a term such as *tissue*. Many students might be familiar with a number of common meanings for it: a disposable handkerchief, a piece of thin paper used for wrapping presents, and so on. However, the scientific term *tissue* has a precise and specialized meaning: it refers to the material that composes living things and is made of different types of cells. This example highlights the significance of direct vocabulary instruction in science: terms are the labels for important concepts. Knowing the labels for concepts allows students to connect one understanding to another, forming networks of knowledge. As Bravo and Cervetti (2008) explained:

> In science, social studies, and mathematics, words index important concepts and those concepts are organized in thematically related networks. . . . This web of concepts affords students a rich context from which they can learn the new technical terminology offered by content areas. Yet, students must be challenged to consider the semantic relationship among the core set of words. Under this approach, a term like *organism* would be semantically introduced as referencing such living things as plants and animals. An example of such is an *isopod*, an animal characterized by its seven pairs of legs, flattened body, and existence in forest floor *habitats*, which is the place where it gets what it needs to *survive*, including *shelter, food, protection, moisture,* and so forth. These italicized words tied semantically together assemble a structure of knowledge within the life science domain. (p. 139)

---

* *"Next Generation Science Standards" is a registered trademark of Achieve. Neither Achieve nor the lead states and partners that developed the Next Generation Science Standards was involved in the production of, and does not endorse, this product.*

In other words, vocabulary is the medium that allows students to learn new concepts, work with the ones they know, and expand their understanding of foundational scientific ideas and theories.

Although some might question whether the time spent on vocabulary instruction is worthwhile, Judith Scott, Dianne Jamieson-Noel, and Marlene Asselin (2003) explained that "when conceptual understanding is central, the time devoted to understanding the vocabulary is well worth the effort. . . . When students understand vocabulary and concepts more completely at the beginning, reading and comprehension of subsequent materials will improve" (p. 283). Additionally, understanding vocabulary (which leads to improved conceptual understanding) gives students the linguistic tools they need to produce higher-quality oral and written products, as noted by Olga Maia Amaral, Leslie Garrison, and Michael Klentschy (2002).

This book includes three parts. Part I contains chapters 1–4. In chapter 1 we explain the importance of vocabulary knowledge, give evidence for the efficacy of direct vocabulary instruction, and highlight critical elements of effective vocabulary instruction. Chapter 2 outlines a six-step research-based process for vocabulary instruction. It also gives teachers explicit, concrete guidance about how to introduce and explain new terms, prompt students to create descriptions and graphic representations of new terms, and facilitate activities, discussions, and games to deepen their knowledge by using new terms in a wide variety of contexts. In chapter 3 we narrow our focus to the menu of science terms in parts II and III, explaining how we analyzed the NGSS and other standards documents to identify terms and then organized them into categories that facilitate teaching and learning in the classroom. Finally, chapter 4 walks teachers and school leaders through the process of building a classroom, schoolwide, or districtwide vocabulary program.

Part II contains two lists of terms: (1) vocabulary pertaining to crosscutting practices and concepts in science and (2) cognitive verbs. These are terms from the science standards that are not necessarily specific to science (for example, *investigate*, *measurement*, and *complex*), but are essential for students to understand if they are to interact effectively with scientific content. The terms pertaining to crosscutting practices and concepts are organized into seventeen categories, and the cognitive verbs are organized into twenty-two categories.

Part III contains the domain-specific terms from the science standards—organized into forty-seven categories called measurement topics—and is followed by an appendix. The appendix lists all of the terms in the book alphabetically and directs readers to their specific entries in parts II and III so readers can easily find specific words.

PART I

Vocabulary Instruction for the New Science Standards

1

The Importance of Vocabulary

There is a clear and urgent need for vocabulary instruction in schools. Loren Marulis and Susan Neuman (2010) stated that "vocabulary is at the heart of oral language comprehension and sets the foundation for domain-specific knowledge and later reading comprehension" (p. 300). Teaching students new vocabulary terms expands their world by helping them access new concepts and the network of ideas connected to those concepts. A student who knows the terms *photosynthesis*, *carbon dioxide*, and *oxygen* thinks about plant-related concepts differently than a child who only knows *leaves*, *soil*, and *water*. Similarly, a student who understands *galaxy*, *comet*, *planet*, *light year*, and *interstellar* has a significantly wider scope than a student who only grasps *sun*, *moon*, *sky*, and *star*. As Katherine Stahl and Steven Stahl (2012) explained, "To expand a child's vocabulary is to teach that child to think about the world, and in a reciprocal fashion, more refined vocabulary indicates that child's degree of knowledge about his or her world" (p. 73). Words are the medium through which ideas are formulated and communicated; the more words a person comprehends, the more ideas he or she will be able to ponder and express.

Beyond conceptual learning, a person's vocabulary also communicates information about him or her to other individuals during social interactions. As Stahl (2005) pointed out:

> To a large extent, the words we know and use are who we are. Words can define, to the outside world (and maybe even to ourselves), how smart we are (or think we are), what kinds of jobs we do, and what our qualifications for jobs might be. . . . Words are not just tokens that one might memorize to impress others. Instead, the words that make up one's vocabulary are part of an integrated network of knowledge. (p. 95)

This integrated network of vocabulary terms allows a person to talk about the world, share information with others, and expand his or her knowledge by connecting new concepts to existing ones. More words extend the network and enhance one's ability to expand it further. More words also facilitate greater precision (*crystalline* versus *sparkly*) and complexity (*cells* and *chromosomes* versus *looking like my mom*) of thought. In short, a person's vocabulary plays an enormously important role in his or her life and future possibilities (Beck & McKeown, 2007; Neuman & Dwyer, 2011). To begin, we explore several areas that are affected by, and which have an effect on, students' vocabulary knowledge.

Vocabulary Knowledge and Learning to Read

At a very basic level, vocabulary knowledge is a critical factor in the process of learning to read. Keith Stanovich (1986) explained that understanding how letters and sounds combine to form words is largely useful because "it allows children to recognize words that are in their vocabulary but have not been taught or encountered before in print" (p. 375). As students learn the sounds for individual letters and gain an understanding of how to string those sounds together to read words (decoding), their oral vocabulary (the words they understand when heard or spoken) allows them to match the string of sounds to words they already know.

For example, imagine a student sounding out the word *material*. Beginning with the first chunk, /mat/, the student might also identify /er/ as a chunk, then /i/, and /al/ as the final part of the word. The critical moment occurs when the student says the sounds of each chunk, stringing them together either aloud or in his or her head. A student who is familiar with the term *material* will likely be able to match the string of sounds to the term he or she knows, and therefore comprehend it. However, a student who has never heard (or is otherwise unfamiliar with) the term *material* may not be able to match the sounds of /mat/, /er/, /i/, and /al/ to a meaning, even if the student is able to pronounce the word correctly. As the National Reading Panel (2000) stated, "Benefits in understanding text by applying letter-sound correspondences to printed material come about only if the target word is in the learner's oral vocabulary. When the word is not in the learner's oral vocabulary, it will not be understood when it occurs in print" (chapter 4, p. 3). In other words, vocabulary knowledge is the critical link between decoding and reading comprehension (Biemiller & Slonim, 2001).

Vocabulary Knowledge and Reading Comprehension

In support of this idea, many researchers have found a strong and persistent relationship between vocabulary knowledge and reading proficiency (Anderson & Freebody, 1979, 1985; Beck & McKeown, 2007; Beck, Perfetti, & McKeown, 1982; Cain, Oakhill, Barnes, & Bryant, 2001; Cunningham & Stanovich, 1997; Davis, 1942, 1944, 1968; Farkas & Beron, 2004; Just & Carpenter, 1987; McKeown, Beck, Omanson, & Perfetti, 1983; McKeown, Beck, Omanson, & Pople, 1985; Mezynski, 1983; National Reading Panel, 2000; Scarborough, 2002; Singer, 1965; Stahl, 1983; Stahl & Nagy, 2006; Stanovich, Cunningham, & Feeman, 1984; Storch & Whitehurst, 2002; Thurstone, 1946; Whipple, 1925). Specifically, Andrew Biemiller (1999) found a correlation of 0.81 between vocabulary size and reading comprehension. A correlation of 1.00 indicates a perfect positive relationship between two variables; as one variable increases, so does the other. A correlation of zero indicates no relationship between two variables, and a correlation of -1.00 indicates a perfect negative relationship between two variables; as one variable increases, the other decreases. Therefore, a correlation of 0.81 indicates a strong positive relationship between vocabulary size and reading comprehension: the more vocabulary terms a student knows, the better she is able to understand what she reads.

In many studies (Beck & McKeown, 2007; Biemiller & Boote, 2006; Cunningham & Stanovich, 1997; Davis, 1944, 1972; Pearson, Hiebert, & Kamil, 2007; Scarborough, 1998, 2002), students' vocabulary knowledge actually predicted their reading proficiency later in life. For example, in a meta-analysis of sixty-one studies, Hollis Scarborough (1998) found a significant correlation of 0.46 between the complexity of kindergarten students' vocabularies and their reading achievement in second grade. In other words, the more complex a student's vocabulary was in kindergarten, the more likely he was to be proficient in reading by second grade. Anne Cunningham and Keith Stanovich (1997) reported that the size of first-grade students' vocabularies strongly predicted their reading comprehension a decade later (in eleventh grade). Other studies have also found that vocabulary size consistently predicted later reading comprehension, with positive correlations between 0.60 and 0.80 (Pearson et al., 2007).

Even more interestingly, Biemiller (2005, 2012; Biemiller & Slonim, 2001) found that after third grade, most students could decode (on average) 25–30 percent more words than they could understand: "From third grade on, the main limiting factor for the majority of children is vocabulary, not reading mechanics (i.e., decoding print into words)" (Biemiller, 2012, p. 34). Therefore, students with smaller vocabularies in third grade experienced declining reading comprehension in subsequent years (Biemiller & Boote, 2006; Chall & Jacobs, 2003). The work of Biemiller and his colleagues highlights a critical issue in the discussion of vocabulary in schools—certain subgroups of students are particularly hindered by limited vocabulary knowledge.

Vocabulary and Socioeconomic Status

Extensive research (Becker, 1977; Coyne, Simmons, & Kame'enui, 2004; Hart & Risley, 1995; Templin, 1957; White, Graves, & Slater, 1990) has found that students from lower-income families typically begin school with smaller vocabularies than students from higher-income families. In one of the best-known studies, Betty Hart and Todd Risley (1995, 2003) followed young children from forty-two families for two and one-half years. Thirteen of the families were of a higher socioeconomic status (SES), ten were middle SES, thirteen were lower SES, and six families were on welfare. Hart and Risley found that "the three year old children from families on welfare not only had smaller vocabularies than did children of the same age in professional families, but they were also adding words more slowly" (2003, p. 7). To illustrate, figure 1.1 shows the vocabulary growth of children from different SES families.

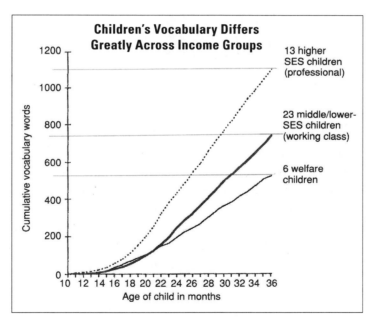

Source: Hart & Risley, 2003, p. 7. Used with permission.

Figure 1.1: Vocabulary growth for children from different SES families.

Perhaps most importantly, the trends shown in figure 1.1 are persistent. Hart and Risley found that children's rate of vocabulary growth at age three (thirty-six months) was strongly associated with their scores on measures of vocabulary, language skill, and reading comprehension at ages nine through ten.

In sum, students with smaller vocabularies began school at a disadvantage that was still evident six to seven years later.

These data raise an important question: Why do children from lower-income families have smaller vocabularies? Hart and Risley (1995) observed each of the forty-two families they studied over the course of two years, recording the quantity and quality of language used in each household. Although they found that the quality of language was fairly consistent from family to family, they found that students from lower-income families simply heard fewer words each day:

> The average child on welfare was having half as much experience per hour (616 words per hour) as the average working-class child (1,251 words per hour) and less than one-third that of the average child in a professional family (2,153 words per hour). . . . In four years of such experience, an average child in a professional family would have accumulated experience with almost 45 million words, an average child in a working-class family would have accumulated experience with 26 million words, and an average child in a welfare family would have accumulated experience with 13 million words. (Hart & Risley, 2003, p. 8)

Based on their observations, Hart and Risley asserted that students from families on welfare enter school having heard approximately thirty million fewer words than students from professional families. This puts them at an immediate disadvantage. Perhaps more importantly, this disadvantage is likely to become increasingly detrimental to low-income students' success in school because it affects the volume and scope of their independent reading.

Vocabulary Growth Through Wide Reading

As explained previously, vocabulary knowledge plays a critical role in the process of learning to read. When a reader encounters a word in print and decodes it (sounds it out), comprehension usually occurs if that word is already in the reader's oral vocabulary. If not, comprehension often fails to occur. Therefore, students with larger vocabularies understand more of the words they read, making reading generally easier.

However, the advantage of students with large vocabularies extends even further. Research has found that a large portion of vocabulary growth during the elementary and middle school years can be attributed to learning unknown words by inferring their meanings from context (Nagy & Anderson, 1984; Nagy, Herman, & Anderson, 1985; Sternberg, 1985). For example, a student reading the following sentence might encounter the unfamiliar term *metallic*: "As John examined the rock samples, he saw the metallic glint he was searching for." A reader who understood other vocabulary in the passage, such as *samples*, *examined*, or *glint*, could probably infer that the meaning of *metallic* had something to do with metal. However, a reader who did not understand other key terms might experience more difficulty in discerning the meaning of *metallic*.

This type of contextual inference is the key to rapid vocabulary growth for students who are already proficient decoders. Therefore, having a large vocabulary facilitates wide reading, and wide reading expands one's vocabulary. William Nagy (2005) put it this way:

> There is every reason to believe that the causal relationship between vocabulary knowledge and reading comprehension is reciprocal—it goes in both directions. Having a big vocabulary does contribute to being a better reader. But being a good reader also contributes to having a bigger vocabulary. (p. 34)

This reciprocal relationship between wide reading and vocabulary growth is at the root of the continued disadvantage facing students with small vocabularies: students who enter school with smaller vocabularies find reading more difficult, and as a result, read less. Because they read less, they encounter fewer new words and are less able to use context clues to determine the meanings of the unknown words they do encounter. Therefore, their vocabularies grow at a slower rate. Stanovich (1986) explained:

> The very children who are reading well and who have good vocabularies will read more, learn more word meanings, and hence read even better. Children with inadequate vocabularies—who read slowly and without enjoyment—read less, and as a result have slower development of vocabulary knowledge, which inhibits further growth in reading ability. (p. 381)

In their work with students, Hart and Risley (2003) found that they could "easily increase the size of the children's vocabularies by teaching them new words," but "could not accelerate the rate of vocabulary growth so that it would continue beyond direct teaching" (p. 4).

These findings led Andrew Biemiller and Catherine Boote (2006) to conclude that "until schools are prepared to emphasize vocabulary acquisition, especially in the primary grades, less advantaged children will continue to be handicapped even if they master reading written words" (p. 44). Herein lies the key to helping all students—and especially certain subgroups—acquire the vocabulary they need to succeed in school and in life: direct vocabulary instruction as a regular part of school instruction. As Jennifer Berne and Camille Blachowicz (2008) stated, "the teaching of vocabulary is not a luxury; it is an equity issue" (p. 314).

The Need for Vocabulary Instruction

A number of studies have found that vocabulary instruction is effective at increasing students' vocabulary knowledge and reading comprehension (Beck & McKeown, 1991; Beck et al., 1982; Curtis & Longo, 2001; Davis, 1944, 1968; Graves, Juel, & Graves, 1998; Kame'enui, Carnine, & Freschi, 1982; Marulis & Neuman, 2010; McKeown et al., 1983; McKeown et al., 1985; McKeown & Curtis, 1987; Stahl, 1983, 1999; Stahl & Fairbanks, 1986). Here, we summarize the results of two meta-analyses regarding the effects of vocabulary instruction on language development (Marulis & Neuman, 2010) and reading comprehension (Stahl & Fairbanks, 1986).

A meta-analysis is a summary (or synthesis) of relevant research findings. In a meta-analysis, researchers use statistical techniques and processes to summarize a group of studies on a particular topic. Meta-analytical approaches are quite useful to educators because meta-analyses provide more and stronger support than a single study alone. Often researchers communicate the findings of a meta-analysis in terms of an average *effect size*. An effect size represents a student's expected improvement if he or she is exposed to a specific strategy, usually expressed in terms of standard deviations. Therefore, an effect size of 0.50 indicates that a student would be expected to improve five-tenths (or half) of a standard deviation as a result of being exposed to a specific strategy. Effect sizes can also be translated into percentile gains; an effect size of 0.50 translates into a gain of 19 percentile points. In other words, a student at the 50th percentile who was exposed to a strategy with an effect size of 0.50 could be expected to move up to the 69th percentile as a result of that instruction.

In their meta-analysis of the impact of vocabulary instruction on language development, Marulis and Neuman (2010) reviewed sixty-seven studies containing 216 effect sizes. They found that vocabulary instruction resulted in an overall effect size of 0.88 on students' language development, which translates into a percentile gain of 31 percentile points. That is, a student at the 50th percentile who is exposed to vocabulary instruction would be expected to move up to the 81st percentile. Regarding the effects of vocabulary instruction on reading comprehension, Steven Stahl and Marilyn Fairbanks (1986) found an average effect size of 0.97: "On the average, children at the 50th percentile of groups receiving vocabulary instruction scored as well as children at the 83rd percentile of the control groups" (p. 94). Their findings led them to conclude that "vocabulary instruction does appear to have an effect on comprehension" (p. 100). Table 1.1 presents additional meta-analytic findings regarding the effects of vocabulary instruction.

Table 1.1: Meta-Analyses on the Effects of Direct Vocabulary Instruction

Meta-Analysis	Focus	Effect Size	Percentile Gain
Elleman, Lindo, Morphy, & Compton, 2009[a]	Effects of vocabulary instruction on comprehension	0.50 for words taught directly	19
		0.10 for all words	4
Haystead & Marzano, 2009	Effects of building vocabulary on academic achievement	0.51	19
Klesius & Searls, 1990[b]	Vocabulary interventions	0.50	19
Marmolejo, 1990[b]	Vocabulary interventions	0.69	25
Marulis & Neuman, 2010	Effect of vocabulary training on word learning	0.88 overall	31
		0.85 for preK	30
		0.94 for kindergarten	33
Mol, Bus, & de Jong, 2009[a]	Effects of interactive book reading on oral language	0.28	11
	Effects of interactive book reading on print knowledge	0.25	10
Mol, Bus, de Jong, & Smeets, 2008[a]	Dialogic reading on oral language	0.50 for preK	19
		0.14 for kindergarten	6
National Early Literacy Panel, 2008[a]	Interactive book reading	0.75 for preK	27
		0.66 for kindergarten	25
Nye, Foster, & Seaman, 1987[b]	Language intervention	1.04	35
Poirier, 1989[b]	Language intervention	0.50	19
Stahl & Fairbanks, 1986[a]	Effects of vocabulary instruction on comprehension	0.97 for words taught directly	33
		0.30 for all words	12

[a] As reported in Marulis & Neuman, 2010.

[b] As reported in Hattie, 2009.

In light of these findings, it is reasonable to conclude that schools should give serious attention to vocabulary instruction. However, research has consistently found that vocabulary is underemphasized in schools.

In 2007, Isabel Beck and Margaret McKeown (citing Biemiller, 2001; Juel, Biancarosa, Coker, & Deffes, 2003; Scott et al., 2003; Watts, 1995) stated that "there is little emphasis on the acquisition of vocabulary in school curricula" (p. 252). Susan Neuman, Ellen Newman, and Julie Dwyer (2011) cited additional studies (Biemiller, 2006; Biemiller & Boote, 2006) and concurred: "Numerous studies have reported the paucity of vocabulary instruction in school curricula" (pp. 251–252). Susan Neuman and Kathleen Roskos (2005) examined early learning standards in the United States and found that they rarely included specific vocabulary guidelines. In a study of fifty-five kindergarten classrooms, Tanya Wright and Susan Neuman (2010) reported virtually no instances of explicit vocabulary instruction. Judith Scott, Dianne Jamieson-Noel, and Marlene Asselin (2003) studied a sample of twenty-three multicultural upper-elementary classrooms and found that "only 1.4% of the time spent in school is used to develop knowledge of academic, discipline-based vocabulary in social studies, science, math, or art" (p. 282). Furthermore, they observed that when vocabulary instruction does occur, "teachers do considerable mentioning and assigning and little actual teaching" (p. 282).

These data prompt the question, Why don't schools focus more time and instructional resources on vocabulary instruction? During the course of their research, Berne and Blachowicz (2008) made the following observation and hypothesis:

> Our informal conversations with classroom teachers suggest to us that they aren't confident about best practice in vocabulary instruction, and at times they don't know where to begin to form an instructional emphasis on word learning or to change one that they feel is ineffective. (p. 315)

In other words, teachers interviewed during the study wanted to implement best practices in vocabulary learning, but had not been given clear guidance about the elements of effective vocabulary instruction. We conclude this chapter by reviewing several characteristics of effective vocabulary instruction highlighted by the extant research.

Elements of Effective Vocabulary Instruction

The teachers in Berne and Blachowicz's (2008) study lacked confidence about best practices in vocabulary instruction; one reason for this lack of confidence might be that "the experimental research in vocabulary instruction involves many different variables and methodologies" (National Reading Panel, 2000, chapter 4, p. 3). However, several elements of effective vocabulary instruction emerge clearly from the available research. First, the National Reading Panel found that "a variety of direct and indirect methods of vocabulary instruction can be effective" (chapter 4, p. 27). In other words, vocabulary can be taught indirectly (for example, by reading aloud to students) or directly (for example, by explicitly identifying terms for instruction and focusing on those terms with students). While some studies have found indirect methods—such as reading aloud to students—to be somewhat effective, Beck and McKeown (2007) stated:

> The relation between reading aloud and learning vocabulary contained in the books is less straightforward than expected. . . . Researchers who examined the effects on vocabulary of just reading aloud reported findings that were from nonexistent to unimpressive (Biemiller & Boote, 2006; Elley, 1989; Nicholson & Whyte, 1992; Penno, Wilkinson, & Moore, 2002; Robbins & Ehri, 1994; Senechal, Thomas, & Monker, 1995). (p. 252)

Neuman and her colleagues (2011) observed that "although shared book reading represents a fertile ground for vocabulary development, it may not be intensive enough by itself to improve expressive and receptive language development for children at risk" (p. 250). In their meta-analysis, Marulis and Neuman (2010) found that the largest effect sizes were associated with vocabulary instruction that combined implicit (shared book reading) and explicit (introducing specific words and providing opportunities for meaningful practice and review) instruction. Essentially, shared book reading is a valuable practice and useful for increasing students' vocabulary knowledge. However, by itself it is not sufficient to create and sustain the level of vocabulary development necessary for all students, especially those subgroups whose low vocabulary knowledge leaves them at a disadvantage. Students also need direct vocabulary instruction.

Many have noted that there are several characteristics and elements that combine to make direct vocabulary instruction effective (Baumann & Kame'enui, 1991; Beck & McKeown, 1991; Blachowicz & Fisher, 2000; Blachowicz, Fisher, Ogle, & Watts-Taffe, 2006). Neuman and Dwyer (2009) noted that direct vocabulary instruction "must be more than merely identifying or labeling words. Rather, it should be about helping children to build word meaning and the ideas that these words represent" (p. 385). Indeed, research has shown that simply teaching students to recognize or recall definitions of terms is ineffective (McKeown et al., 1985; Mezynski, 1983; Stahl & Fairbanks, 1986):

> Methods that provided only definitional information about each to-be-learned word did not produce a reliable effect on comprehension, nor did methods that gave only one or two exposures of meaningful information about each word. Also, drill-and-practice methods, which involve multiple repetitions of the same type of information about a target word using only associative processing, did not appear to have reliable effects on comprehension. (Stahl & Fairbanks, 1986, p. 101)

Instead, research indicates that direct vocabulary instruction should incorporate these elements:

- **Presenting individual terms and their descriptions in rich contexts** (Graves, 2000; National Reading Panel, 2000; Stahl & Fairbanks, 1986)

- **Asking students to generate information about terms** (Anderson & Reder, 1979; Graves, 2000; Nagy, 2005; National Reading Panel, 2000; Scott et al., 2003; Stahl & Clark, 1987; Stahl & Fairbanks, 1986; Vogel, 2003)

- **Using multimedia methods (words, pictures, animations, and so on) to introduce and practice terms** (Mayer, 2001; Mayer & Moreno, 2002; National Reading Panel, 2000; Neuman et al., 2011; Sadoski & Paivio, 2001)

- **Asking students to relate new terms to words they already know** (Anderson & Reder, 1979; Booth, 2009; Chi & Koeske, 1983; Entwisle, 1966; Glaser, 1984; Levelt, Roelofs, & Meyer, 1999; Scott et al., 2003; Stahl & Murray, 1994; Stahl & Nagy, 2006; Tinkham, 1997)

- **Providing multiple exposures to new terms and opportunities to use those terms in the classroom** (Beck, McKeown, & Kucan, 2002; Beck et al. 1982; Bowman, Donovan, & Burns, 2000; Brophy & Good, 1986; Daniels, 1994, 1996; Dole, Sloan, & Trathen, 1995; Hoffman, 1991; Leung, 1992; McKeown et al., 1985; McKeown, Beck, & Sandora, 2012; National Reading Panel, 2000; Pressley, Allington, Wharton-McDonald, Block, & Morrow, 2001; Rosenshine, 1986; Scott et al., 2003; Sénéchal, 1997; Snow, Burns, & Griffin, 1998; Stahl & Fairbanks, 1986; Wharton-McDonald, Pressley, & Hampston, 1998)

Based on the research cited here, Robert Marzano (2004, 2010; Marzano & Pickering, 2005; Marzano & Simms, 2013) designed a six-step process that incorporates each element of effective vocabulary instruction. A unique body of research supports the effectiveness of this six-step process (Dunn, Bonner, & Huske, 2007; Gifford & Gore, 2008; Haystead & Marzano, 2009; Marzano, 2005, 2006). In the next chapter we detail each step of the process, elaborating on each of the previously listed characteristics of effective vocabulary instruction and explaining how each is accomplished during the process.

Chapter Summary

As shown here, vocabulary knowledge influences a student's ability to learn to read, comprehend what he or she is reading, and grow his or her vocabulary through wide reading. Research indicates that direct vocabulary instruction is effective for increasing students' vocabularies and reading comprehension, and that such instruction—while necessary for all students—is especially pivotal for low-income students and English learners. Elements of effective vocabulary instruction include presenting terms and descriptions in rich contexts, asking students to generate information about terms, using multimedia methods to introduce and practice terms, prompting students to relate new words to words they already know, and providing multiple exposures to new terms, as well as opportunities to use them. In the following chapter, we describe Marzano's six-step process for vocabulary instruction that incorporates each of these elements.

2

A Six-Step Process for Direct Vocabulary Instruction

Marzano's six-step process for vocabulary instruction (2004, 2010; Marzano & Pickering, 2005; Marzano & Simms, 2013) incorporates the research-based elements of effective vocabulary instruction outlined in the previous chapter. The six steps are as follows:

1. Provide a description, explanation, or example of the new term.

2. Ask students to restate the description, explanation, or example in their own words.

3. Ask students to construct a picture, symbol, or graphic representing the term or phrase.

4. Engage students periodically in activities that help them add to their knowledge of the terms in their vocabulary notebooks.

5. Periodically ask students to discuss the terms with one another.

6. Involve students periodically in games that allow them to play with terms.

In reference to the elements of effective vocabulary instruction outlined in chapter 1, step 1 involves presenting individual terms and their descriptions to students in rich contexts (using examples and student-friendly language). Step 2 asks students to generate information about terms; specifically, students use their own words to describe, explain, or give an example of the new term. Step 3 uses multimedia methods (words, pictures, animations, and so on) to introduce and practice terms as students are asked to construct a picture, symbol, or graph representing the new term or phrase. Both of the final characteristics of effective vocabulary instruction—asking students to relate new terms to words they already know and providing multiple exposures to new terms and opportunities to use those terms in the classroom—are embedded in each of the final three steps. During step 4, the teacher uses periodic activities that help students add to their knowledge of terms. Step 5 involves asking students to discuss new terms with each other on a regular basis, and step 6 engages students in games and activities that allow them to play with the terms. In this chapter, we review the six-step process and give explicit direction about how to implement each step in the classroom.

Step 1: Provide a Description, Explanation, or Example of the New Term

The first step of the process involves providing students with a description, explanation, or example of the new term. We recommend that teachers begin by stating the new term and asking students what they already know about it. For example, a teacher introducing the term *atmosphere* might ask students where they have heard that term before. Students might respond:

- "There's a song in Mary Poppins that goes, 'Up through the atmosphere, up where the air is clear, oh . . . let's . . . go . . . fly a kite!'"

- "My mom said the restaurant we ate at last week had good atmosphere."

- "My grandpa has an old barometer on his wall, and it has the word 'atmospheres' on it."

This exercise can be particularly useful if the term being introduced has multiple meanings. For example, terms like *work*, *speed*, *energy*, *force*, and *atmosphere* have common meanings with which students may already be familiar. In scientific contexts, however, many terms have precise meanings that are far more specialized than their common meanings.

Gina Cervetti, Elfrieda Hiebert, and P. David Pearson (2010) found that the everyday meanings of words in nonscience contexts can interfere with students' understanding of scientific meanings, especially if teachers assume that students who know a term's common meaning also know its scientific meaning. Hiebert and Cervetti (2012) pointed out that "for both students and teachers, the ordinary, everyday meanings of such a word may mean that knowledge of the word is assumed" (p. 337), and Bravo and Cervetti (2008) explained that "words that have one meaning in everyday language and a more specialized meaning in content area learning are especially vulnerable to misunderstanding and semantic 'interference'" (p. 133). They continued:

> Consider the shades of meaning in the terms *expression* in math, *current* in science, and *capital* in social studies. All of these terms have an everyday meaning familiar to students, along with a specialized meaning in their respective fields that is less likely to be known by students. Complicating the issue a bit more, the same multiple-meaning words can be found across content areas where within each domain a different specialized meaning is intended. The term *solution* in science, for example, can mean when one thing is dissolved in another. In mathematics, the term refers to the answer and steps taken to solve a problem; in social studies, the intended meaning can be the act of ending a dispute or the payment of a debt. As students move through instruction across content areas, an extra level of analysis is necessary to choose the intended meaning in the respective subject matter. Other terms that fall into this category include *property*, *add*, and *climate*. (p. 134)

In the previous example, the term *atmosphere* is commonly used to refer to how a place or situation feels, as in "The restaurant had great atmosphere." In contrast, the term is used in science for at least two specific purposes: (1) to refer to the layers of gas surrounding a planet's surface, and (2) as a measure of barometric pressure. Asking students what they already know about a term allows the teacher to identify various meanings he or she will need to address while describing, explaining, and exemplifying the term for students.

Provide a Description

Here we intentionally use the term *description* when referring to the meaning of a term, rather than the term *definition*. This is because dictionary definitions often do not provide the most useful or sufficient information when students are learning the meaning of a new term, due to the fact that dictionary definitions are usually written with one important consideration in mind: space in the dictionary. Because dictionaries include so many words, the definitions therein are designed to communicate meaning in as few words as possible. To achieve this, dictionaries typically rely on the Aristotelian view of meaning, which suggests that terms can be defined using a category (the group a term belongs to) and differentiation (how the term differs from other members of the group). For example, *Merriam-Webster's Collegiate Dictionary* (2012) defines *atmosphere* as the "mass of air [category] surrounding the earth [differentiation]" (p. 78). While this is an efficient way to save space, dictionary definitions do not provide the kind of rich, contextual information that students need to develop their understanding of a term (McKeown, 1991, 1993; Miller & Gildea, 1987; Scott & Nagy, 1997; Stahl & Fairbanks, 1986).

Instead of using definitions from the dictionary, teachers can provide students with descriptions. Descriptions explain and exemplify terms, often by using them in sentences or explaining contexts in which they are used. One excellent resource for descriptions is the *Collins COBUILD Illustrated Basic Dictionary* (Roehr & Carroll, 2010). The COBUILD dictionary seeks to provide students with descriptions of terms in student-friendly language and example sentences that contain each term. For *atmosphere*, the *COBUILD* dictionary entry says "*A planet's atmosphere is the layer of air or other gases around it. The shuttle Columbia will re-enter the Earth's atmosphere tomorrow morning*" (p. 28). This description provides more context for the term *atmosphere* and allows students to see it used in an example sentence. Table 2.1 shows a number of other science terms, their dictionary definitions, and their descriptions from the *COBUILD* dictionary for comparison.

Table 2.1: Definitions vs. Descriptions

	Definition in *Merriam-Webster's Collegiate Dictionary* (2012)	Description in *Collins COBUILD Illustrated Basic Dictionary* (Roehr & Carroll, 2010)
mass	The property of a body that is a measure of its inertia and that is commonly taken as a measure of the amount of material it contains and causes it to have weight in a gravitational field	**Mass** is the amount of physical matter that something contains. *Pluto and Triton have nearly the same size, mass, and density.*
molecule	The smallest particle of a substance that retains all the properties of the substance and is composed of one or more atoms	A **molecule** is the smallest amount of a chemical substance that can exist by itself. *When hydrogen and oxygen molecules combine, the reaction produces heat and water.*
organism	A complex structure of interdependent and subordinate elements whose relations and properties are largely determined by their function in the whole	An **organism** is a living thing. *We study very small organisms such as bacteria.*
ratio	The relationship in quantity, amount, or size between two or more things	A **ratio** is a relationship between two things when it is expressed in numbers or amounts. *The adult to child ratio is one to six.*

As shown in table 2.1, descriptions are often clearer and easier to understand than typical dictionary definitions.

Provide an Explanation

What constitutes an effective explanation of a word varies depending on what kind of word it is and how familiar students already are with it. Joseph Jenkins and Robert Dixon (1983) identified four possible relationships between a student and a new term, depending on the nature of the term:

1. The new term refers to a concept that can be described fairly easily (for example, *ice* is frozen water).

2. The new term has a simple synonym, but the student does not know the concept referred to by the synonym (for example, something that is *combustible* is flammable, but the student doesn't know the word *flammable*).

3. The new term does not have a simple synonym, but the student has experiences to draw on to understand it (for example, *population* means the people in a specific group, like the population of a city or school).

4. The new term does not have a simple synonym and the student does not have experiences to draw on (for example, the *cryosphere* [areas on Earth where water only occurs in its solid, frozen form] might be difficult to describe if a student has never seen pictures or video footage of polar regions).

If the new term fits into the first or third categories, explanation is fairly easy. However, if the term falls into the second or fourth categories, explanations will need to be more complex and will probably involve the introduction of new concepts (*combustible* refers to things that catch fire or burn easily) or exposures to new experiences (the student might watch a video about polar regions).

Explanations of new terms can also vary based on a term's part of speech (Stahl, 1999). The terms in parts II and III generally fall into three categories: nouns, verbs, and modifiers (adjectives and adverbs). Here we provide direction for explaining each of those parts of speech.

Explaining Nouns

Nouns are typically either concrete (*precipitation, pollen, oxygen*) or abstract (*interdependence, equilibrium, extinction*). Concrete nouns can generally be explained by helping students connect the new term to the item to which it refers:

- Precipitation is any sort of moisture that falls from the sky, such as rain, snow, sleet, or hail.

- Pollen is the yellow dust that is found inside flowers and blossoms on plants.

- Oxygen is a clear gas that humans need to breathe to survive.

Abstract nouns can be more difficult to describe and generally require many examples, nonexamples, and experiences to understand them properly. For example, explaining *interdependence* might require students to play a game in which students depend on their classmates' help to win the game. The teacher might also present examples of groups of animals that are interdependent, such as the gelada monkeys and Walia ibex in the Ethiopian Highlands, who work together to protect themselves from wolf predation.

Explaining Verbs

According to Stahl (1999), "verbs function differently from nouns and modifiers. . . . Each verb implies a frame that needs to be filled with nouns or noun phrases" (p. 20). In other words, verbs often require specific sets of nouns before or after them to make sense. Think of a verb like *absorb*. While explaining the term, the teacher might point out that students need to know what is doing the absorbing (subject) and what is being absorbed (object) and then provide example sentences to help students experience the verb in different contexts:

- The plant absorbed the sun's energy.

- The layer of sand absorbed the contamination.

In contrast, other verbs (such as *recycle*) might only require objects. For example:

- The waste products from the manufacturing process can be recycled.

- Glass, plastic, and paper can all be recycled.

Teachers can use sentence stems to reinforce the various "frames" that different verbs require. For example, "The _____ absorbed the _____" or "The _____ was recycled."

Explaining Modifiers (Adjectives and Adverbs)

When explaining adjectives and adverbs, it is often very useful to provide two kinds of explanations. The first simply describes the concept behind the term. For an adjective such as *magnetic*, the teacher might say:

- When something is magnetic, it attracts other objects.

Second, the teacher can give sentences that provide examples of the term, such as:

- There was a magnetic attraction between the magnet and the paper clip.

- The Earth has a magnetic field around it.

- Running an electric current through the coil produced a magnetic force.

To follow up, the teacher might ask students questions such as:

- What are some examples of magnetic objects in your life?

- How do you use magnetic forces in your life?

The same approach can be applied to adverbs, such as *collaboratively*, *immensely*, or *jointly*.

Provide Examples

As explained previously, many terms are best described by giving examples and nonexamples of the concept to which the term refers. Examples can occur in many forms:

- Experiences (field trips or guest speakers)

- Stories (personal experiences with the term)

- Images (videos, descriptions of mental pictures, or drawings)

- Drama (skits or pantomimes)

- Current events related to the term (news stories or magazine articles)

Depending on the amount of time available, these examples can be extensive or very brief. For instance, after describing and explaining a term such as *conduction* (when heat is transferred from one substance to another through direct contact), a teacher can give students examples of conduction, such as:

- Heating a pot on a stove

- Touching a metal spoon sitting in a pot of boiling water

- Lying under a heated blanket

- Picking up a mug of hot coffee

The teacher explains that heat transfer in all of these situations is occurring through conduction. The teacher might also present nonexamples of conduction, such as:

- The rising temperature of a greenhouse on a sunny day

- Warming one's hands over a fire

- Pasta noodles rising and falling in a pot of boiling water

- Getting tanned or sunburned while lying out in the sun

The teacher could explain that these are examples of different forms of heat transfer: *convection* (1 and 3) and *radiation* (2 and 4). These examples are rather simple and quick to use; a teacher with more time might use computer simulations, extended models, video segments, or guest speakers to further elucidate the concept for students.

To summarize, step 1 involves describing and explaining the important features of a term to students after determining what prior knowledge they have about the term. Descriptions and explanations should be accompanied by examples and nonexamples of the term, which can be abbreviated or more in-depth (as time allows).

Step 2: Ask Students to Restate the Description, Explanation, or Example in Their Own Words

During step 2, the teacher asks students to generate descriptions, explanations, and examples of a new term in their own words. This type of generative learning is particularly important for building vocabulary knowledge (Anderson & Reder, 1979; Bravo & Cervetti, 2008; Scott et al., 2003; Vogel, 2003). Stahl and Clark (1987) explained that "in generative models of learning, the process of generating a novel product is thought to lead to improved retention of information, because generation necessitates constructing more elaborate pathways between new information and already-known information" (p. 542). Therefore, it is important that students' descriptions, explanations, and examples are not simply copied from those presented by the teacher in step 1.

Instead, students should think about how they might describe the new term to a friend or use the new term in their own lives. For example, a student describing the term *atmosphere* in science might write, "When the space shuttle re-enters the atmosphere, the friction from the air creates heat, making the shuttle look like it is on fire." Another student might say, "When I ride in an airplane, I climb through different layers of the atmosphere." A third student might explain, "The atmosphere of Earth has oxygen in it so we can breathe, but the atmosphere on Venus is mostly carbon dioxide." Finally, a fourth student might describe *atmosphere* as "Earth's protective bubble of air." All of these are legitimate responses, even though some are detailed and others rudimentary. As long as major errors or misconceptions are avoided and the specific scientific meaning of the term (as opposed to its common meaning) is clear, it is completely acceptable for students' initial responses to be somewhat simplistic. Later in the process, students will return to these descriptions, explanations, and examples to revise and refine them (see step 4). To facilitate later revision, students should record their work in a vocabulary notebook.

Vocabulary Notebooks

Students can record and revise information about new vocabulary terms in vocabulary notebooks. Research has shown that the use of vocabulary notebooks positively affects student achievement (Dunn et al., 2007; Gifford & Gore, 2008; Marzano, 2005, 2006). Notebook entries for new terms can be organized in various ways, but we recommend the inclusion of:

- The new term

- The academic subject with which the term is associated, if applicable (for example, science or math)

- The category or measurement topic (discussed in chapter 3) the term is associated with (for example, Biogeology or Conservation of Matter)

- The student's current level of understanding of the term (for example, 4, 3, 2, or 1)

- The student's description, explanation, and example(s) of the term

- The student's visual depiction of the term (see step 3)

- Words related to the term, such as synonyms or antonyms

Figure 2.1 (page 22) shows an example vocabulary notebook page. Visit **marzanoresearch.com /reproducibles** for a reproducible version of this figure.

The level of understanding indicator shown in the upper-right corner of figure 2.1 is based on the following four-point scale (Marzano & Pickering, 2005, p. 32):

4 I understand even more about the term than I was taught.

3 I understand the term and I'm not confused about any part of what it means.

2 I'm a little uncertain about what the term means, but I have a general idea.

1 I'm very uncertain about the term. I really don't understand what it means.

Term:			
Subject:	Topic/Category:	Level of understanding: 1 2 3 4	
Description in words: _____ _____ _____ _____ _____		Synonyms:	
		Antonyms:	
Picture:			

Source: Adapted from Marzano & Simms, 2013.

Figure 2.1: Sample vocabulary notebook page.

As explained previously, students' initial familiarity with a word may prompt them to rate their initial understanding of a term below levels 3 or 4. This is to be expected during this step of the process since students have not yet had very many exposures to the term or many opportunities to practice using it in various contexts. As they engage in activities, discussions, and games during steps 4 through 6, students' understanding of the term should deepen and increase. Students should be encouraged to revise their initial self-ratings as they learn more about the term. (See chapter 4 for information about formal vocabulary assessment.)

Addressing Difficulties

In some cases, students may have difficulty generating their own description, explanation, or example of a new term. When this occurs, teachers can use prompts based on a word's features to help students hone in on a term's important characteristics. Table 2.2 lists sample prompts for eight different types of words.

Table 2.2: Questions About Key Features of Different Types of Words

Types	Questions About Key Features
People (for example, *scientist, engineer, Albert Einstein*)	What actions does this person perform? What is required to become this person? What physical or psychological characteristics does this person possess?
Objects (for example, *synthetic polymer, windbreak, pinhole box, superconductor, satellite*)	What is this object used for? How is this object created? What physical characteristics are associated with this object?
Places (for example, *hydrosphere, Milky Way, planet orbits, environment*)	Where is this place located? What physical characteristics are associated with this place? What events are associated with this place?
Events/Natural Phenomena (for example, *photosynthesis, erosion, ultraviolet radiation, endothermic reaction, volcanic eruption, earthquake*)	What process or actions are associated with this event? What causes and consequences are associated with this event? What location is associated with this event?
Intellectual, Artistic, or Cognitive Products (for example, *theory, Newton's law of gravitation, Avogadro's hypothesis, Coulomb's law, Bernoulli's principle*)	What purpose is associated with this product? What people are associated with this product? What process is associated with this product?
Mental Actions (for example, *urban planning, redesign process*)	What process is associated with this mental action? What purpose is associated with this mental action? What causes or consequences are associated with this action?
Shapes/Direction/Position (for example, *frame of reference, atomic arrangement, wave peaks*)	What uses are associated with this shape, direction, or position? What reference points are associated with this shape, direction, or position? What features are associated with this shape, direction, or position?
Quantities/Amounts/Measurements (for example, *nuclear mass, pressure, flexibility, hardness*)	What relationships are associated with this quantity, amount, or measurement? What reference points are associated with this quantity, amount, or measurement?

Source: Adapted from Marzano & Simms, 2013.

For example, if a term refers to an object (such as *synthetic polymer*) the teacher might ask students to include answers to the following questions in their descriptions, explanations, and examples:

- What are synthetic polymers used for?

- How are synthetic polymers created?

- What physical characteristics are associated with synthetic polymers?

These prompts can help students generate more detailed descriptions of terms and explain them in more depth.

Step 3: Ask Students to Construct a Picture, Symbol, or Graphic Representing the Term or Phrase

In 2001, Mark Sadoski and Allan Paivio posited a dual-coding theory of information storage in the brain. Essentially, they hypothesized that knowledge is stored in two types of packets: *logogens* (information stored as words) and *imagens* (information stored as pictures). They explained that information is better remembered when it is stored in both ways. During step 2, students generate linguistic (or word-based) descriptions, explanations, and examples for a new term, thus creating new logogens for that term. For step 3, students create imagens; that is, students construct pictures, symbols, or graphics that represent the new term and then record these images in their vocabulary notebooks.

As students create pictures—also referred to as *nonlinguistic representations*—for a term, it is important to keep in mind that different types of terms may lend themselves to different types of images. Table 2.3 shows five different methods for generating images for new terms.

Table 2.3: Methods for Nonlinguistic Representation

Method	Term	Picture
Sketch the actual object. If a term is concrete and easy to depict, simply sketch a picture of it.	Punnett square	
Sketch a symbol for the term. If a term is abstract, sketch a symbol that represents the term.	Fahrenheit	
Sketch an example of the term. If a term is abstract, sketch an example or examples of the term.	organism	

Sketch a cartoon or vignette with a character using the term. If a term is abstract, use speech bubbles to show how a character in a cartoon might use the term.	terrestrial	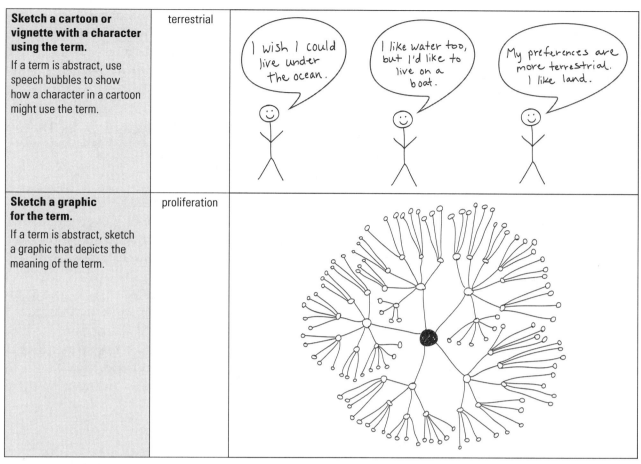
Sketch a graphic for the term. If a term is abstract, sketch a graphic that depicts the meaning of the term.	proliferation	

Source: Adapted from Marzano & Simms, 2013.

Even with these five methods, some students may still have trouble with this step, especially if they perceive that they are not good at drawing or art. Other students might invest too much time during this step, drawing overly detailed or elaborate pictures. Still others might argue that their linguistic description is adequate and a visual depiction of the term is unnecessary. To address these difficulties, teachers can model appropriate visual depictions of terms during step 1 when describing and defining the term. This will give students concrete guidance about the appropriate level of detail for sketches. Teachers might also incorporate multimedia graphics, videos, animations, or previous students' pictures into their explanations of terms to give students ideas of how to depict each new term visually. Allowing students to discuss their ideas for nonlinguistic representations in groups can help them generate ideas and talk through unclear aspects of a term. Finally, the teacher might allow students to select images for new terms from the Internet. This last alternative should be used with caution, however, and students should always be required to explain how the image they chose effectively illustrates the new term at hand.

At the end of step 3, the teacher might extend students' nonlinguistic representations by asking them to create mental pictures for each term. Mental pictures can be richer, more detailed, and include more elements of students' past experiences than the sketches they draw in their vocabulary notebooks. To guide this process, the teacher asks students to remember a time when they heard a new term used before. If students have not previously heard a new term, the teacher asks them to remember a time when they could have used the new term. For example, if the term being addressed is *thermal energy*, the teacher reminds students that thermal energy is energy stored in the form of heat. The teacher asks students to think of an object they encountered recently that contained thermal energy. One student thinks of his chicken nuggets at lunch, another student remembers the smell of asphalt on her walk home from school the day before, and another student thinks of the hot metal bench she sat on outside at recess. Associating the term *thermal energy* with these sensory experiences creates mental representations that help solidify the term in students' brains.

Step 4: Engage Students Periodically in Activities That Help Them Add to Their Knowledge of the Terms in Their Vocabulary Notebooks

Steps 1, 2, and 3 of the six-step process are designed to be executed in order, with the teacher introducing a term (step 1) and students representing it linguistically (step 2) and nonlinguistically (step 3). Steps 4, 5, and 6, however, do not need to be executed in order. That is, students add to and refine their knowledge of terms through multiple exposures in the form of activities (step 4), discussions (step 5), and games (step 6). Students might play games with new terms (step 6) before engaging in discussions (step 5) or activities (step 4) concerning those words. Additionally, teachers can incorporate steps 4, 5, and 6 into instruction as frequently or infrequently as they wish. Students might cycle through steps 1 through 3 several times, focusing on different new terms each time, and then engage in steps 4, 5, or 6 once a week using all the new terms introduced during that time. This is completely acceptable. As long as students continue to revise and refine their descriptions and nonlinguistic representations of words by adding to their vocabulary notebook entries during steps 4, 5, and 6, teachers should feel free to structure these steps in whatever way is most conducive to their classroom and schedule.

Incremental Development of Word Knowledge

As explained in chapter 1, one of the critical elements of direct vocabulary instruction is multiple encounters with and exposures to new terms. This is because "knowing a word is not an all-or-nothing phenomenon. Word learning happens incrementally; with each additional encounter with a word, depth of understanding accrues" (Stahl & Bravo, 2010, p. 567). Research has found that word knowledge is built incrementally over time in many steps, and involves much more than simply being able to recall a term's definition (Anderson & Pearson, 1984; Carey, 1978; Clark, 1993; Dale, 1965; Durso & Shore, 1991; Johnson & Pearson, 1984; Nagy & Scott, 2000; Paribakht & Wesche, 1996). Beck and McKeown (2007) noted that "vocabulary knowledge has long been acknowledged as a complex phenomenon that can be shallow or deep along a number of dimensions" (p. 254). Two of these dimensions are receptive vocabulary and productive vocabulary. *Receptive vocabulary* refers to the terms a person understands when he or she encounters them, but doesn't necessarily use. *Productive vocabulary* refers to the terms a person knows and uses. Receptive and productive vocabularies can be either oral or written, as shown in figure 2.2.

	Receptive Vocabulary	Productive Vocabulary
Oral Vocabulary	Words understood when heard	Words used in speech
Written Vocabulary	Words understood when read	Words used in writing

Figure 2.2: Relationship between receptive, productive, oral, and written vocabularies.

Dale (1965; as cited in Stahl & Bravo, 2010, p. 567) suggested an alternative conceptualization of word knowledge:

- *Stage 1*—Never having seen the term before

- *Stage 2*—Knowing there is such a word, but not knowing what it means

- *Stage 3*—Having context-bound and vague knowledge of the word's meaning

- *Stage 4*—Knowing the word well and remembering it

Bravo and Cervetti (2008) presented an example of how word knowledge of the term *adaptation* might gradually accumulate over time:

> In an initial encounter with the science term *adaptation* in the sentence "These plants and animals have many adaptations," students may understand that the term is in noun form and understand that it is something that a plant or animal possesses. In later encounters, as in the sentence "Those plants and animals adapted to their environment by way of certain behaviors and structures that develop over time," students gain access to additional information about the term, including the fact that the term can also be used in verb form and that the term refers to certain actions and body parts that plants and animals need in their environment and that it takes time to develop those behaviors and structures. (p. 138)

As seen here, each exposure to a new term allows students to learn a little more about the word. This learning might include information about the context in which the word was encountered, and how the term's meaning changes depending on the context. Stahl and Stahl (2012) pointed out that when students first learn a word, they tend to overgeneralize its meaning. Subsequent encounters serve to refine and narrow the meaning into a "more constrained and particular usage" that incorporates "the boundaries and nuances of that particular word" (pp. 73–74). The heart of step 4 is engaging students in activities that allow them to move toward this type of particular, specific, and refined understanding of a new term's meaning.

There are plenty of quick and simple activities that teachers can use to facilitate this deepening and refining process. For example, Robert Marzano and Julia Simms (2013) suggested that while students are standing in line or during the last few minutes before the end of class, the teacher might draw students' attention to one of the terms they have recently learned and ask them to brainstorm as many words as they can that relate to that term. Whether students do this as a whole class, or in small groups or pairs, the teacher allows the brainstorming to continue for a short period of time and then asks students to stop. If students were saying words aloud, the last student to say a word would then briefly explain how that word is related to the target word. If students were writing down their terms, students might trade lists and ask each other to explain any unfamiliar or unknown terms.

More extended activities for refining and deepening students' vocabulary knowledge could focus on identifying similarities and differences between terms or examining word roots and affixes. Here, we provide a number of activities for each.

Identifying Similarities and Differences

There are four specific strategies that can be used to identify similarities and differences. *Comparing and contrasting* involves identifying attributes that two or more items or concepts share or do not share. *Classifying* involves grouping like items or concepts into categories. *Creating metaphors* involves making connections between ideas or concepts that seem unconnected at the surface level. *Creating analogies* involves describing relationships by relating a pair of items to another pair. Teachers can use the following resources and templates for each of these strategies.

Comparing and Contrasting

One effective way to help students compare and contrast vocabulary terms is to present them with sentence stems, such as:

_____ and _____ are similar because they both:

- _____

- _____

_____ and _____ are different because:

- _____ is _____, while _____ is _____.

- _____ is _____, while _____ is _____.

These stems are designed to help students structure their thinking, make substantive comparisons, and compare terms logically. For example, a student comparing the terms *atom* and *molecule* might say:

Atoms and molecules are similar because they both:

- Are present in all objects and living things

- Are invisible to the naked eye

Atoms and molecules are different because:

- Atoms are the smallest particles that still have the properties of an element, while molecules are made up of two or more atoms.

Using the stems allows the student to identify and clearly express specific similarities and differences between atoms and molecules.

Another structure that can be used to help students organize their comparisons is a Venn diagram, where differences are written in an item or concept's individual circle and similarities in the area where the circles overlap. Figure 2.3 shows how a student might compare the terms *abiotic* and *biotic* using a Venn diagram.

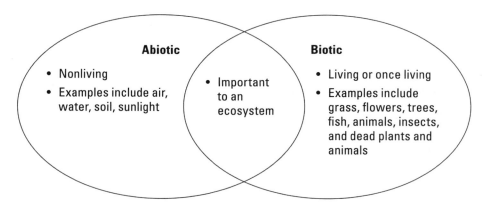

Figure 2.3: Venn diagram comparing *abiotic* and *biotic*.

Notice that in this Venn diagram, each characteristic under *abiotic* corresponds to a characteristic beneath *biotic*. Maintaining this sort of parallel organization is not required when creating a Venn diagram but can prompt students to think more rigorously and make more substantive comparisons.

A close relative of the Venn diagram is the double bubble diagram. Again, students compare two terms by identifying their shared and unique characteristics. In figure 2.4, a student has compared the terms *hydrogen* and *helium*.

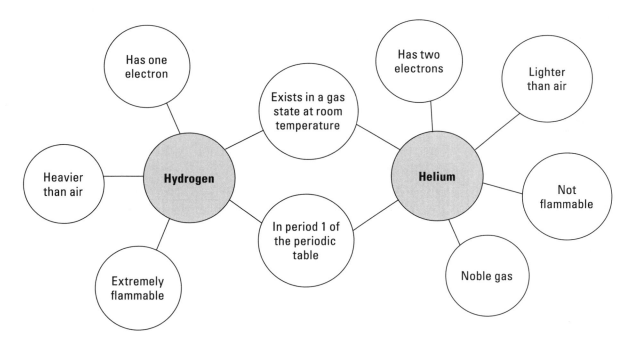

Figure 2.4: Double bubble diagram comparing *hydrogen* and *helium*.

Shared characteristics are written in bubbles that connect to both terms, while differentiating characteristics are written in bubbles that connect to only one of the terms.

Sentence stems, Venn diagrams, and double bubble diagrams are all very useful for making comparisons between two terms. However, when three or more terms are the subject of a comparison (such as *proton*, *neutron*, and *electron*), we recommend using a matrix (as shown in table 2.4).

Table 2.4: Comparison Matrix for *Proton, Neutron,* and *Electron*

	Proton	**Neutron**	**Electron**
Size	Smaller than an atom (subatomic), but larger than an electron; about the same size as a neutron	Smaller than an atom (subatomic), but larger than an electron; about the same size as a proton	Smaller than an atom (subatomic), a proton, and a neutron
Location	In the nucleus of an atom	In the nucleus of an atom	Outside the nucleus of an atom
Charge	Positively charged	Not charged	Negatively charged
Number	Determines the atomic number of the atom's element	Determines the isotope of an element	Determines how an atom forms ionic bonds with other atoms

Conclusions: Protons, neutrons, and electrons are all subatomic particles. Electrons are the smallest of the three, while protons and neutrons are about the same size. Protons and neutrons are both found in the nucleus of an atom, but electrons are outside the atom's nucleus. Protons and electrons are similar because they both carry charges but different because protons are positively charged and electrons are negatively charged. Neutrons are different from both protons and electrons because they do not carry a charge. The number of each type of subatomic particle in an atom determines its atomic number (protons), its isotope (neutrons), and how it forms ionic bonds with other atoms (electrons).

In this matrix, the terms being compared are written at the top of each column. The attributes being compared (size, location, charge, and number) are written at the left of each row. Then, students fill in information about those attributes for each term and summarize the similarities and differences they discovered in the conclusions cell at the bottom of the matrix. Teachers can provide the list of attributes they would like students to use, or for added rigor, ask students to generate the list of attributes for comparison. If teachers choose to have students do this, they will need to scaffold the process to ensure that students choose attributes that prompt them to make substantive comparisons.

Classifying

At a basic level, classifying simply involves grouping items or concepts into categories, and classroom activities that emphasize classifying can fall anywhere on a continuum from structured to open-ended. For the most structure, the teacher selects the vocabulary terms to be classified and the categories students will use to sort them. For example, a teacher might present students with the following list of terms and two categories: "Elements" and "Chemical Compounds".

hydrogen	helium	carbon
carbon dioxide	ammonium chloride	calcium chloride
chlorine	sodium	sodium hydroxide
oxygen	nitrogen	iron

Students sort each term into the appropriate category and explain their reasoning.

For a slightly more open-ended approach, the teacher presents students with a list of terms and asks them to select appropriate categories and sort the words accordingly. For example, if students were presented with the previously presented list of terms, but not given categories, they might select "Gases" and "Solids" for their categories and sort the terms accordingly. Again, students should be able to explain their rationale for each category and the logic behind their sorting scheme. Teachers can use prompts to help students refine their categories. For example, a teacher might ask a student who placed *hydrogen* in the "Gases" category, "What about liquid hydrogen?" This might prompt the student to refine his categories to include the qualifier "at room temperature."

Finally, the most open-ended form of classification tasks involves asking students to select both the terms and the categories into which they will sort them. To facilitate this type of task, a teacher might ask students to look back through their vocabulary notebooks to find all the terms previously studied that relate to chemistry and select ten that they consider to be the most important. Students would then create a categorization scheme for those terms and sort them accordingly. After students work individually, they might share their classifications with their peers, adding new terms or categories to further refine their work.

Creating Metaphors

When students create metaphors, they relate two terms to each other on an abstract or nonliteral level. For example, the expression "life is a roller coaster" does not literally refer to riding along a twisty track in a little car. Instead, it connects one aspect of being on a roller coaster—going up and down—with life's propensity to have high points and low points. A science teacher might ask students to create metaphors for a specific term, such as *DNA*. One student might say that "DNA is a barcode" because it contains a lot of information in a small space. Another student might say "DNA is a blueprint" because it contains instructions for synthesizing proteins. These two responses illustrate one of the most important aspects of asking students to create metaphors: explaining one's reasoning. Students should always include a "because" statement after their metaphors. One way to help students generate metaphors and explain their reasoning is to use a sentence stem, such as:

_____ is/are _____ because _____.

To create more complex metaphors, students can use a matrix such as the one in table 2.5.

Table 2.5: Metaphor Matrix

Term: *immune system*	General Descriptors	Term: *personal bodyguard*
Protects the body against damage	Prevents damage	Keeps you from getting hurt
Fights against microorganisms	Fights against outside invaders	Keeps strangers from hurting you
Fights against cancer	Fights against inside invaders	Keeps people who claim to be friends from hurting you
Doesn't attack our own cells	Knows who is a friend	Can sense who is a friend and who is an enemy
Responds to millions of different kinds of pathogens	Knows what to do in lots of different situations	Experienced
Remembers pathogens it has encountered before and deals with them more efficiently during subsequent infections (acquired immunity)	Has a good memory	Smart

As seen in table 2.5, the student chose (or was assigned) the term *immune system* as the first term in his metaphor. Therefore, he wrote *immune system* at the top of the left column. Then, he filled one characteristic of the immune system in each row of the left column, and filled in a more general description of each characteristic in the middle column. Finally, the student thought of another term (that may or may not be specific to science) that all the general descriptions would apply to—in this case, *personal bodyguard*— and filled in a corresponding characteristic of personal bodyguards in each cell of the right column. The student's final extended metaphor is "The immune system is a personal bodyguard because it prevents damage, fights against outside invaders, fights against inside invaders, knows who is a friend, and knows what to do in lots of different situations." Using a matrix like the one in table 2.5 allows students to create and explain more complex or sophisticated metaphors for science terms.

Creating Analogies

As explained previously, an analogy explains a relationship by relating one pair of items or concepts to another pair of items or concepts. For example, "Electrons are to the nucleus of an atom as planets are to the sun" indicates that the structure of an atom resembles the structure of the solar system. As with comparisons and metaphors, teachers can provide sentence stems to help students generate analogies. There are several different types of sentence stems a teacher might use:

- **Provide one pair of terms and ask students to generate the second pair**—Photosynthesis is to plant cells as _____ is to _____.

- **Provide the first term of each pair and ask students to generate a second term for each pair**—Photosynthesis is to _____ as eating is to _____.

- **Provide the second term of each pair and ask students to generate a first term for each pair**—_____ is to plant cells as _____ is to animal cells.

Alternatively, the teacher could use a visual analogy diagram such as the one in figure 2.5 to help students organize their analogies.

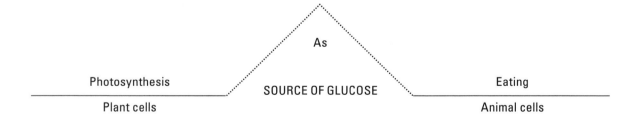

Figure 2.5: Visual analogy diagram.

Students fill in one pair of terms on the left side of the diagram and the corresponding pair of terms on the right side of the diagram. Students might also be asked to describe the relationship by writing a word or phrase under the peak in the middle of the diagram. In this example, the student has explained that the first term in each pair is a source of glucose for the second term in each pair.

Examining Word Roots and Affixes

William Nagy, Virginia Berninger, Robert Abbott, Katherine Vaughan, and Karin Vermeulen (2003) found that students' understanding of word parts and how words are constructed strongly correlated (0.83) with their vocabulary knowledge. As explained in chapter 1, correlations that are close to

1.00 indicate strong relationships between two variables. So as students' understanding of word parts and how words are constructed increases, so does their vocabulary knowledge. It is important to note that Marilyn Adams (1990) cautioned against teaching word parts to students who are still learning to read, because the segmentation of a word into syllables does not always match the segmentation of a word into word parts. For example, a student learning to read would probably try to segment the word *endothermic* into syllables (en-do-ther-mic) to decode it. However, its morphological segmentation is different (endo-therm-ic) and could be confusing to an immature reader. For confident readers who have reached a level of automaticity with decoding longer words, however, understanding word roots and affixes can help them remember words they have learned and figure out the meaning of unfamiliar terms. Stahl (2005) explained:

> A discussion of word parts should become an integral part of word-learning instruction. Discussions that include stories about word origins and derivations can stir interest in learning more about language—that is, build word consciousness. Stories that help children to see and understand how similarities in word spellings may show similarities in meaning, may solidify and expand their word knowledge. For example, the seemingly dissimilar words *loquacious*, *colloquium*, and *elocution* all come from the root word *loq*, meaning "to talk." Knowing this connection may make it easier for children to remember the words. (p. 111)

There are three distinct types of word parts: prefixes, suffixes, and root words. Prefixes, which come at the beginning of a word, typically add to or change the meaning of the root word to which they are attached. Suffixes, which come at the end of a word, typically affect the root word's part of speech. Collectively, prefixes and suffixes are referred to as affixes. Root words are often based on Greek or Latin and carry specific meanings.

Affixes

In 1989, Thomas White, Joanne Sowell, and Alice Yanagihara identified the most frequently used prefixes and suffixes in English. Interestingly, they discovered that 95–97 percent of words with affixes use a small set of prefixes and suffixes (shown in table 2.6).

Table 2.6: Frequently Occurring Prefixes and Suffixes

Prefix	% of All Prefixed Words	Suffix	% of All Suffixed Words
un-	26	-s, -es	31
re-	14	-ed	20
in-, im-, ir-, il- (meaning "not")	11	-ing	14
dis-	7	-ly	7
en-, em-	4	-er, -or (indicating agency)	4
non-	4	-ion, -tion, -ation, -ition	4
in-, im- (meaning "in" or "into")	4	-ible, -able	2
over- (meaning "too much")	3	-al, -ial	1
mis-	3	-y	1
sub-	3	-ness	1
pre-	3	-ity, -ty	1
inter-	3	-ment	1
fore-	3	-ic	1

continued →

Prefix	% of All Prefixed Words	Suffix	% of All Suffixed Words
de-	2	*-ous, -eous, -ious*	1
trans-	2	*-en*	1
super-	1	*-er* (indicating comparison)	1
semi-	1	*-ive, -ative, -itive*	1
anti-	1	*-ful*	1
mid-	1	*-less*	1
under- (meaning "too little")	1	*-est*	1

Source: Adapted from White et al., 1989, pp. 303–304.

Of the affixes shown in table 2.6, the top three prefixes are used in 51 percent of all prefixed words and the top three suffixes are used in 65 percent of all suffixed words. In light of their findings, White and his colleagues (1989) recommended that affix instruction should focus on those prefixes and affixes used most frequently and designed the series of lessons shown in table 2.7 to facilitate such instruction.

Table 2.7: White et al.'s (1989) Recommended Sequences for Teaching Affixes

Teaching Prefixes	Teaching Suffixes
Lesson 1: Present examples and nonexamples of words with prefixes (*unkind* and *refill* have prefixes [*un-* and *re-*]; *uncle* and *reason* do not have prefixes).	**Lesson 1:** Present examples and nonexamples of words with suffixes (*employee* and *natural* have suffixes [*-ee* and *-al*]; *bee* and *charcoal* do not).
Lesson 2: Explain and give examples of the negative meanings of *un-* and *dis-* ("not" as in *unlike* and *disagree*).	**Lesson 2:** Present words with suffixes whose spellings do not change when the suffix is added (such as *monkeys, foxes, walking, higher, jumped, softly, laughable, comical,* and *windy*).
Lesson 3: Explain and give examples of the negative meanings of *in-, im-,* and *non-* ("not" as in *incompetent, impossible,* and *nonconforming*).	**Lesson 3:** Illustrate each of the three major spelling changes that can occur with suffixes—
Lesson 4: Explain and give examples of both meanings of *re-* ("again" as in *rebuild* or *revise* and "back" as in *recover* or *relapse*).	• Consonant blending (*bigger, running, skipped, sunny*)
	• Change from *y* to *i* (*married, skies, happily, classifiable, filthiness*)
Lesson 5: Address the less common meanings of *un-* and *dis-* ("do the opposite" as in *unbutton* or *disown*) and *in-* and *im-* ("in" or "into" as in *inquire* or *implant*).	• Deleted silent *e* (*riding, gated, baker, advisable, natural, wheezy*)
Lesson 6: Explain and give examples of *en-* and *em-* ("in" or "into" as in *encircle* and *embrace*), *over-* ("above" or "beyond" as in *overreact*), and *mis-* ("bad" or "wrong" as in *mistrust* or *mistrial*).	**Lesson 4:** Provide examples of inflectional endings (*-s, -es, -ed, -ing*) and derivational suffixes (*-ly, -er, -ion, -able, -al, -y, -ness*).

Source: Adapted from White et al., 1989.

The left side of table 2.7 outlines lessons that focus on the most frequently used prefixes (*un-, re-, in-, im-, dis-, en-, em-, non-, over-,* and *mis-*) while the right side contains lessons that focus on the most frequent suffixes (*-s, -es, -ed, -ing, -ly, -er, -ion, -able, -al, -y,* and *-ness*) and how to add inflectional endings and derivational suffixes to words.

Root Words

Although many English words have Greek or Latin roots, there is a particular preponderance of such terms in the science domains. Knowing root words helps students discern the meaning of unknown words, but root words are extremely numerous and no rigorous studies have been done to identify which roots are most frequent or most useful for students. Several authors have compiled lists of common Greek and Latin roots (Fry, Kress, & Fountoukidis, 2000; Marzano, 2004; Padak, Newton, Rasinski, & Newton,

2008; Rasinski, Padak, Newton, & Newton, 2007; Stahl, 1999). We present a selection of word roots that are particularly applicable to science in table 2.8.

Table 2.8: Common Greek and Latin Roots

Root	Meaning	Origin	Examples
ambi/amphi	both, around	Latin	amphibian, ambidextrous
anthropo	man	Greek	anthropology, anthropogenic, philanthropist
ast	star	Greek	astronaut, astronomy, disaster, asterisk
bio	life	Greek	biology, biochemistry, biogeology, biopsy
cand	glow, white	Latin	incandescent, candle, candidate
centr	center	Latin	central, egocentric, eccentric
cide, cise	cut, kill	Latin	incision, scissors, insecticide
circ	around, circle	Latin	circulation, circumvent
corp	body	Latin	corpse, corpus, corporation
cosm	universe	Greek	cosmos, microcosm, cosmopolitan
cur	run	Latin	current, occur, excursion
duc	lead	Latin	conduct, conduction, duct, educate, induct
flect/flex	bend	Latin	reflect, reflex, flexible, reflection, deflect
fric	rub	Latin	friction, dentifrice
fug	flee	Latin	centrifugal, refuge, fugitive, refugee
geo	Earth	Greek	geography, geology, geometry
gram	letter, written	Greek	diagram, telegram, grammar
hab	hold	Latin	habitat, habit, rehabilitate
hydr	water	Greek	hydrogen, hydrate, hydrosphere, hydrant
ject	throw	Latin	inject, project
kine, cine	movement	Greek	kinetic, kinesthetic, cinema
lab	work	Latin	laboratory, labor, collaborate, elaborate
luc/lum	light	Latin	translucent, luminescent, luminous, illuminate, lucid, elucidate
luna	moon	Latin	lunar, lunatic
lys	break down	Greek	paralysis, catalyst, analysis
mar	sea	Latin	marine, submarine, maritime, mariner
merge/mers	dip	Latin	submerge, immerse, submerse, emerge, merge, merger
meter	measure	Greek	thermometer, centimeter, diameter
morph	shape	Greek	metamorphosis, amorphous, anthropomorphic
mot	move	Latin	motion, motor, promote, demote
mut	change, interchange	Latin	mutation, mutual, commute
ocu	eye	Latin	oculist, binocular
opt	eye	Greek	optic, optical, optician, optometrist
path	feeling, suffer	Greek	pathology, sympathy, empathy
pel	drive	Latin	propel, compel, expel, repel
pend	hang	Latin	suspend, pendulum, append, appendix
photo	light	Greek	photosynthesis, photograph, telephoto
phys	nature	Greek	physical, physique, physician
plex	fold	Latin	complex, duplex, plexiglass, perplex
pod	foot	Greek	podiatrist, podium, tripod

continued →

Root	Meaning	Origin	Examples
pop	people	Latin	population, popular, populace
port	carry	Latin	transport, portable, import
pos	place	Latin	deposit, position, compose, composite
put	think	Latin	computer, reputation, deputy, disrepute
quer/quir/ques	ask, seek	Latin	inquiry, query, question, request, quest
rad	ray, spoke	Latin	radio, radium, radius, radiology
rupt	break	Latin	erupt, interrupt, abrupt, rupture, bankrupt
sci	know	Latin	science, scientific, conscience, conscious
scop	see	Greek	microscope, telescope, periscope
sed	settle	Latin	sediment, sedative, sedentary, sedate
serv	save, keep	Latin	conservation, preservation, reservoir, reserve
sim	like	Latin	simulate, simultaneous, similar, simile
solv	loosen	Latin	dissolve, solve, solvent, resolve
spir	breathe	Latin	respiration, perspiration, inspire, spirit
stell	star	Latin	stellar, constellation
strict	draw tight	Latin	restrict, constrict, strict, stricture
struct	build	Latin	structure, construct, instruct, destruction
ten	stretch	Latin	tendon, tension, tendency, tent, tense
terr	land	Latin	terrestrial, territory, terrain, terrace
therm	heat	Greek	thermometer, thermal, thermostat, thermos
tract	pull, drag	Latin	traction, attract, tractor, subtract
turb	confusion	Latin	turbine, turbulent, disturb, perturb
ver	truth	Latin	verify, verdict, veracity
vid	see	Latin	video, evidence, provide
volv	roll	Latin	revolve, evolve, involve, revolution
vor	eat	Latin	carnivorous, herbivorous, voracious

The Internet also offers many resources for exploring word roots and affixes:

- **Online Etymology Dictionary** (www.etymonline.com)—Type in any part of a word (affix, root, or word) and see its origin, root words, and other words related to it.

- **English-Word Information** (wordinfo.info)—Type in a word and see information about its language of origin, what family of root words it belongs to, and how it is commonly used.

- **Merriam-Webster Online** (www.youtube.com/user/MerriamWebsterOnline)—These two-minute videos feature editors from Merriam-Webster discussing the etymology, roots, and correct usage of various English words (for example, *octopuses* vs. *octopi*, *healthy* vs. *healthful*, and many more).

Finally, Stahl (1999) cautioned that instruction about morphology (that is, how words are formed) should also make students aware of its weaknesses:

> The modern meanings of words (especially the most common derived words) often do not reflect the meanings of their historical roots, and . . . readers might be misled by a literal translation of root to meaning. For example, knowing -*mort* refers to "death" may help with *mortal* or *immortal*, but probably does not help a person guess the meaning of *mortgage* or *mortify*. (p. 47)

Therefore, it is important for teachers to help students identify examples and nonexamples of words whose meaning can be determined using root words, prefixes, and suffixes.

As students engage in activities like those described here, they should periodically return to their vocabulary notebooks to update and add to previous entries. This might include updating their linguistic or nonlinguistic descriptions of terms or adding additional examples or nonexamples of a term. Comparisons, classifications, metaphors, and analogies can be recorded in vocabulary notebooks, as can analyses of terms' word roots and affixes.

Step 5: Periodically Ask Students to Discuss the Terms With One Another

Step 5 focuses on extending students' vocabulary knowledge through peer discussions. Such discussions allow students to make semantic connections between new terms and previously learned terms and to use and hear terms in new contexts. Collaborating with their peers during these discussions gives students the benefit of a larger body of background knowledge, as observed by Stahl and Nagy (2006):

> Discussion adds an important dimension to vocabulary instruction. . . . Children benefit from the contributions of other children. . . . In open discussions, children are often able to construct a good idea of a word's meaning from the partial knowledge of the entire class. (p. 69)

Additionally, hands-on opportunities to further interact with new terms can be embedded within discussions. Hiebert and Cervetti (2012) observed that "in science, most words are conceptually complex and represent new concepts for many students. These concepts are not learned by rote but evolve from extensive discussions, demonstrations, and experiments" (p. 341). They emphasized that discussions can be sparked and enriched through the use of "demonstrations, illustrations, DVDs . . . experiments, and writing" (p. 338). These experiences and subsequent discussions are a critical element of effective vocabulary instruction and—as in step 4—they should be followed by time for students to review, revise, and augment existing entries in their vocabulary notebooks. Here, we address two types of strategies that teachers can use to cultivate effective discussions: (1) making semantic connections and (2) facilitating student engagement.

Making Semantic Connections

As observed by Hiebert and Cervetti (2012), "words are parts of a richly interconnected network" (p. 327). When students first learn a term, they typically use a process called *fast mapping* (Carey, 1988) to connect the new term with the item or concept to which it refers. This is a very efficient process, but unless the term is subsequently seen or used again, these initial mappings "can be notoriously fragile" (Neuman et al., 2011, p. 251; see also Gershkoff-Stowe & Hahn, 2007; Trueswell, Medina, Hafri, & Gleitman, 2013; Wilkinson, Ross, & Diamond, 2003). To solidify fast mappings, students need further exposure to a word, during which they solidify its meaning and make connections between it and other terms they know. These *semantic connections* are a fundamental element of knowing a word: "To know a word's meaning is to know what a word represents and to begin to understand the network of concepts that goes with it" (Neuman & Dwyer, 2009, p. 384). As Stahl and Nagy (2006) explained:

> In dictionaries, each word has a separate definition, and you might be tempted to think that words are stored in your memory in the same way—each word in its own separate little file drawer. However, that's not how human memory works. A somewhat more accurate picture is to think

> of word meanings as stored in semantic networks. Each word is connected to other words, and to other concepts, facts, and specific memories. When a word is recognized, the connections to other words in the network are also evoked. (p. 11)

As the network of semantic connections for a word grows, students acquire an increasingly refined understanding of its meaning; rather than understanding it in only one context (for example, *crystal* as a noun referring to a sparkly rock), students understand it in many contexts and forms (for example, something can *crystallize* [verb], forming a *crystal* [noun], that is typically a solid with a *crystalline* [adjective] structure). Hiebert and Cervetti (2012) highlighted a number of semantic relationships between terms, such as:

- Semantic classes (*eggs* are in the category of *food*)

- Words that commonly occur together (*dozen* is often paired with *eggs*)

- Superordination (*sedimentary* refers to a type of *rock*)

- Synonym (*glittering* and *sparkling* have roughly the same meaning)

- Part-whole (a *branch* is part of a *tree*)

- Instrumentality (a *broom* is used to sweep the *floor*)

- Theme (*hospital* and *nurse* are both medical-related terms)

According to Blachowicz and her collegues (2006), asking students to make semantic connections between words "and verbalizing or explaining those connections, supports learning the meanings of the targeted words" (p. 529). One excellent strategy to help students make semantic connections between words is semantic mapping and discussion.

Semantic Mapping

To begin the semantic mapping process, the teacher chooses a word to be the focus of the activity—for example, *endangered species*. This should be a previously introduced term students have described and depicted in their vocabulary notebooks, both linguistically and nonlinguistically. Next, students generate a list of words associated with the focus term. For *endangered species*, students might come up with the following list:

extinct	rhino	sea turtle
panda	bald eagle	poachers
hunting	ivory	blubber
whaling	whales	deforestation
climate change	habitat destruction	pollution
fur	invasive species	encroachment
disease	reproduction	natural selection
extant	zoos	legislation
Endangered Species Act	conservation	preservation

After generating such a list, students either work individually or in small groups to generate categories that the terms fit into and create a semantic map that shows how the terms relate to each other, as shown in figure 2.6.

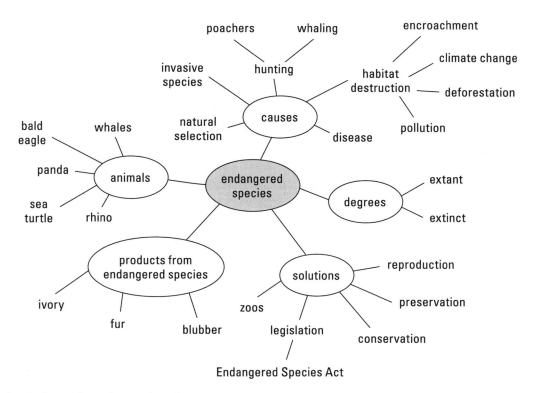

Figure 2.6: Semantic map for *endangered species*.

As seen in figure 2.6, students first created five categories for the terms they generated: *animals*, *causes*, *solutions*, *degrees*, and *products from endangered species*. Then they connected each term to the appropriate category. In some cases, a term was related to a category through another term; for example, *encroachment*, *climate change*, *deforestation*, and *pollution* are all types of *habitat destruction*, which is one cause of endangered species. The semantic map in figure 2.6 makes this indirect relationship clear. Finally, students explain their semantic maps. If they worked individually to create them, students might explain their maps to a partner. If they worked in groups, each group might pair with another group and take turns explaining their work to each other.

In brief, semantic mapping involves four steps:

1. Choose a focus term.

2. Ask students to generate a list of words associated with the focus term.

3. Have students work individually or in groups to create categories for the generated words and a semantic map that shows how the terms relate to each other and the focus term.

4. Prompt students to explain their semantic maps to their peers.

The final step of this process is critical. Steven Stahl and Sandra Vancil (1986) found that constructing semantic maps without discussing them was not effective. To facilitate discussions of semantic maps, or even individual terms, teachers can use a variety of strategies that actively engage students and allow them to practice and deepen their knowledge of new terms.

Facilitating Student Engagement

In 1987, Steven Stahl and Charles Clark found that students who anticipated being called on during vocabulary discussions learned just as much as students who were actually called on. Students who didn't expect to be called on learned less. In other words, students don't necessarily need to talk during a vocabulary discussion to learn. They just need to anticipate being called on. Stahl and Clark offered two possible explanations for this effect. First, they suggested that students who expected to be called on "were rehearsing covert answers during discussion" and "it may be that this rehearsal process produced more powerful effects on retention than passive listening" (p. 552). Alternatively, they hypothesized that students who expected to be called on "simply paid greater attention to the lesson. . . . If the students were generating responses and formulating cognitive links for the new material, they were paying attention to the discussion" (p. 552). An easy way to ensure that every student expects to be called on is to use a random names process.

Random Names Process

To use a random names process, first write each student's name on a piece of paper or popsicle stick. Then, randomly draw a name after asking a discussion question. Discussion questions need not be complex. In fact, Isabel Beck, Margaret McKeown, and Linda Kucan (2002) explained:

> They can be as simple as asking questions such as the following about newly introduced words:
>
> When might you . . . ?
>
> How might you . . . ?
>
> Why might you . . . ? (pp. 45–46)

The student whose name was drawn responds to the question. The teacher can then ask another question (after returning the first student's name to the pool), or might follow up with a response chain.

Response Chaining

To create a response chain, the teacher asks a question and calls on a student to answer. Once the first student answers, either that student or the teacher calls on a second student to respond to, add to, or correct the first student's response. The chain continues until the teacher is ready to ask a different question. Teachers might reinforce the chain and clarify the current speaker by having students pass or throw a small foam ball to the next person in the chain.

The random names process and response chaining are excellent strategies for engaging students in whole-group discussions. However, teachers should also facilitate small-group discussions, as they allow more students to contribute their knowledge and experiences. Here we present three strategies that can be used to structure paired or small-group vocabulary discussions: role cards, paired thinking, and inside-outside circle (Kagan & Kagan, 2009).

Role Cards

To use role cards, the teacher first identifies specific group roles that will help students deepen and extend their knowledge of a vocabulary term. For example, a teacher might create the following four roles:

1. **Etymology expert**—This student looks for facts about where a term came from, such as its language of origin and how it came to have its current meaning.

2. **Root researcher**—This student identifies roots and affixes of a word and finds examples of other words with similar roots or affixes.

3. **Synonym/antonym explorer**—This student finds synonyms and antonyms for a word.

4. **Discussion leader**—This student makes sure that everyone has a turn to talk and summarizes the group's discussion for the class.

The teacher writes each role on a separate card, creating enough sets of cards so that each group can have one. Next the teacher explains each role to students, divides the class into groups of four, and gives a set of role cards to each group. Alternatively, the teacher could pass out the role cards before the day of the discussion so that students have time to find information about new terms before sharing with their group. Roles should be rotated regularly so students have the opportunity to perform each role.

Paired Thinking

Paired thinking is an excellent way to quickly and informally ask students to share their thoughts and discuss new terms. One particularly popular version of paired thinking is called think-pair-share. There, students think about what they know regarding a vocabulary term, then pair up with a partner and share their thoughts.

Other variations can also be used. For example, after sharing their thoughts with a partner, groups of two can pair up to create groups of four, with each pair sharing their most important idea about a term. One student in the group of four might then share the group's best idea with the class.

Another variation is called give-one-get-one. Taking their vocabulary notebooks with them, students stand up and find a partner. Partners trade vocabulary notebooks (give one) and each student looks for one item of new information about a term (get one). To extend the activity, the teacher might ask students to look for any errors or misconceptions in their partner's notebook. To finish, each student retrieves his or her notebook and adds new information to it, at the same time correcting any errors or misconceptions identified by his or her partner.

Inside-Outside Circle (Kagan & Kagan, 2009)

Inside-outside circle was designed by Spencer Kagan and Miguel Kagan (2009) to allow students to have several conversations with different peers in a short amount of time. To set this up, the teacher divides the class into two equal groups and one group stands in a circle, facing outward. The other group forms an inward-facing circle around them, so that each student is facing another student. The teacher asks each student to have a quick conversation with his or her partner about a term or in response to a question. On the teacher's signal, students in the outside circle take one step to the left and have another quick conversation (on the same topic or a different one) with their new partner. As with other strategies, students should be given time after inside-outside circle to record new information in their vocabulary notebooks.

While using the strategies described here (random names process, response chaining, role cards, paired thinking, and inside-outside circle), the teacher can also facilitate and guide discussions by acknowledging the contributions of each student to the discussion, giving students positive feedback about correct parts of their responses, helping students correct incorrect parts of their responses by giving hints or cues or restating a question, and using techniques that allow students to rehearse their answers (such as asking students to share their answer with a partner before calling on someone to share his or her answer with the class). As in step 4, students should return to their vocabulary notebooks following a discussion to add to or revise previous entries for terms.

Step 6: Involve Students Periodically in Games That Allow Them to Play With Terms

The emphasis during step 6 is on word play—students engage in games that allow them to interact with new terms in a wide range of contexts. The benefits of word play are cited throughout the vocabulary literature. For example, Blachowicz and Fisher (2012, p. 190) stated:

- Word play is a motivating and important component of the word-rich classroom.

- Word play calls on students to reflect metacognitively on words, word parts, and context.

- Word play requires students to be active learners and capitalizes on possibilities for the social construction of meaning.

- Word play develops domains of word meaning and relatedness as it engages students in the practice and rehearsal of words.

In a survey of seventy-two educators concerning their vocabulary instructional practices, Berne and Blachowicz (2008) found that word play or word games was one of the top three most commonly cited effective practices for increasing students' vocabulary. Vocabulary games need not be complex or time-consuming. Blachowicz and Fisher (2012) pointed out that word play can be as simple as sharing puns or jokes, such as the following quips, with students:

- Never trust an atom; they make up everything.

- The other day I made a chemistry joke, but I got no reaction.

- I bet Earth makes fun of all the other planets for having no life.

- Two atoms were walking down the sidewalk and suddenly one slipped off the curb and said, "Oh no, I've lost my electron!" The other atom said, "Are you sure?" and the first atom replied, "Yes, I'm positive!"

- I would make a science joke, but all the good ones argon.

Not only are puns and jokes naturally engaging because of their humor, but they also activate students' cognitive and metacognitive systems, as explained by Blachowicz and Fisher (2012):

> Anyone who understands [a] pun has performed a metacognitive act. . . . The groan or laugh that results is our metacognitive check. We get the joke and we exhibit cognitive flexibility, the ability to look at the same thing in different ways. . . . Creating and sharing jokes, riddles, and puns can help develop this flexibility. (p. 192)

Other games can be extended to last for an entire unit, semester, or year. For example, conceptual word walls—where words are posted in categorical groupings as they are learned or discovered (as opposed to alphabetical word walls)—remind students and teachers to use new words in their speech and writing and allow students to infer meanings of unknown words by associating them with familiar terms and categories. For example, if the terms *conductor, current, electrical energy, charged object, charge repulsion,* and *electric force* were all listed under the category of "Electric and Magnetic Forces" on a word wall, a student who was unfamiliar with the term *conductor* could infer quite a bit of information about it from other, more familiar terms in the category. Isabel Beck, Charles Perfetti, and Margaret McKeown (1982) found that students whose teachers created and used word walls in their classrooms learned more incidental vocabulary than students who were exposed only to direct vocabulary instruction.

Occupying the middle ground between short, simple games (like sharing puns and jokes) and extended games (such as word walls) are structured games and activities that can be played within a class period or two. Here we describe a number of these, as created by various educators and researchers.

Alphabet Antonyms: Students write down a number of vocabulary words that all begin with the same letter. For example, for the letter *e*, a student might choose: *Earth, Earth materials, earthquake, ecosystem,* and *erosion.* Then he or she writes an antonym for each word:

- Earth—space
- Earth materials—living matter
- Earthquake—still tectonic plates
- Ecosystem—dysfunctional natural community
- Erosion—accretion

The student then presents only the antonyms to the class (that is, *space, living matter, still tectonic plates, dysfunctional natural community, accretion*). The class tries to guess the correct antonyms, all of which will start with the same letter—in this case *e* (for middle and high school students; Blachowicz & Fisher, 2008).

Classroom Feud: Modeled after *Family Feud,* this game has students work in teams to answer questions about vocabulary terms (for all grade levels; Carleton & Marzano, 2010).

Create a Category: Students work together to categorize a list of terms in a limited amount of time (for upper-elementary through high school students; Carleton & Marzano, 2010).

Definition, Shmefinition: Students try to identify the correct description of a vocabulary term out of a group of student-invented definitions (for upper-elementary through high school students; Carleton & Marzano, 2010).

Digital Vocabulary Field Trip: Using an online program like TrackStar (trackstar.4teachers.org), teachers collect and annotate a series of websites that pertains to a vocabulary term or group of terms. Students then explore the websites to answer a series of teacher-designed questions (for upper-elementary through high school students; Dalton & Grisham, 2011).

Draw Me: Modeled after Pictionary™, this game involves one student drawing pictures of terms in a predetermined category (for all grade levels; Marzano & Pickering, 2005).

Magic Letter, Magic Word: Students try to identify the vocabulary term (beginning or ending with the "magic letter") that is the correct response to a teacher-provided clue (for elementary and middle school students; Carleton & Marzano, 2010).

Motor Imaging: Students create gestures for vocabulary terms. For example, for the phrase *subduction zone*, students might hold their hands out in front of them—palms down, parallel to the floor—and then slowly move them toward each other. When the sides of their hands meet, they let one slide under the other to signify one tectonic plate sliding under another tectonic plate (for all grade levels; Casale, 1985).

Name It!: Students use vocabulary terms to express what they see in various photographs (for lower-elementary students; Carleton & Marzano, 2010).

Name That Category: The teacher provides a secret list of categories, and a designated student tries to help his teammates guess each category by naming vocabulary terms that fit in it. As soon as his team guesses one category, the clue-giver starts naming terms in the next category. The first team to name all the categories correctly wins (for upper-elementary through high school students; Marzano & Pickering, 2005).

Opposites Attract: Students work together to pair vocabulary terms with their antonyms (for elementary students; Carleton & Marzano, 2010).

Possible Sentences: The teacher selects six to eight words that students are not likely to know and four to six words that students are likely to know. Students create sentences (using that list), each of which must contain at least two words from the list. The teacher displays these sentences, and students discuss whether each one is correct, incorrect, or partially correct and modify them as needed so that they are all correct (for middle and high school students; Stahl, 2005).

Puzzle Stories: Students construct a puzzle and then use vocabulary terms to describe the scene depicted in the puzzle (for upper-elementary and middle school students; Carleton & Marzano, 2010).

Root Relay: From an array of prefixes, suffixes, and root words written on separate cards, students work in teams to construct words. One student from each team runs to the assortment of affixes and roots, selects one, and brings it back to his team. The next student does the same. The first team to form a complete word wins (for upper-elementary and middle school students; Scott, Miller, & Flinspach, 2012).

Secret Language: Two students try to communicate the meaning of a vocabulary term to the class by using it in context over the course of a day or class period. At the end of the designated time period, the class tries to guess what the secret word was and explain its meaning (for upper-elementary through high school students; Manzo & Manzo, 2008).

Sentence Stems: The teacher creates a sentence stem that requires students to explain the vocabulary term in order to complete it. For example, "*Percolation* is the stage of the water cycle when . . ." or "*Naturalistic observation* is different from *analog observation* because . . ." (for middle and high school students; Beck et al., 2002).

Silly Questions: Students answer questions created by combining two vocabulary terms, such as "Can a *backbone* be a *muscle?* Why or why not?" "Would a *proton* be in *equilibrium?* Why or why not?" and so on (for middle and high school students; McKeown et al., 1985).

Talk a Mile a Minute: The teacher prepares individual cards with a category at the top and a list of terms from that category beneath, as shown in figure 2.7.

```
┌─────────────────────────────┐
│                             │
│    Conservation of Matter   │
│                             │
│         product             │
│                             │
│         chemical            │
│                             │
│         properties          │
│                             │
│        phase change         │
│                             │
│         dissolve            │
│                             │
│         substance           │
│                             │
└─────────────────────────────┘
```

Figure 2.7: Sample card for Talk a Mile a Minute.

The teacher designates one member of each team the "talker" and passes a card to this student. The teacher starts a timer and, similar to the games Taboo™ and Catch Phrase™, the talker tries to get his or her teammates to say each word in the list without saying any of the other words on the card or in the heading (for upper-elementary through high school students; Marzano & Pickering, 2005).

Two of a Kind: Students match up synonyms, homonyms, or antonyms in this Memory-style game (for elementary school students; Carleton & Marzano, 2010).

Vocabulary Charades: Students try to guess which vocabulary term their teammate is acting out (for all grade levels; Marzano & Pickering, 2005).

Vocab Vids: Students create sixty-second videos that exemplify the meaning of a vocabulary term (for middle and high school students; Dalton & Grisham, 2011).

What Is the Question?: In this *Jeopardy!*-like game, students have to come up with questions that describe teacher-provided vocabulary terms (for upper-elementary through high school students; Carleton & Marzano, 2010).

Where Am I?: Students give clues to help a student guess his or her "secret location" (a vocabulary term referring to a specific place, such as *polar ice caps* or *wetland*) (for all grade levels; Carleton & Marzano, 2010).

Which One Doesn't Belong?: Students try to identify the vocabulary term that doesn't belong with the other three words in a group (for all grade levels; Carleton & Marzano, 2010).

Who Am I?: Students give clues to help a selected student guess his or her "secret identity" (a vocabulary term referring to a specific person, such as *Isaac Newton* or *Antoine Lavoisier*) (for upper-elementary through high school students; Carleton & Marzano, 2010).

Word Associations: After explaining several new vocabulary terms, the teacher selects words and phrases and asks students to figure out which vocabulary term goes with which word or phrase. For example, if students had already learned *chloroplast*, *magnification*, *organism*, and *chromosome*, the teacher might ask, "Which word goes with *photosynthesis?*" or "Which word goes with *DNA?*" Students should then explain the relationships behind their answers (for middle and high school students; Beck at al., 2002).

Word Harvest: Students "pick" words off of a construction paper tree or bush and sort them into baskets with different category labels (for lower-elementary school students; Carleton & Marzano, 2010).

Wordle: Teachers use this electronic tool (www.wordle.net) to help students create visual representations of various vocabulary terms. When a block of text is pasted into the tool, Wordle produces a "word cloud" with high-frequency words from the passage appearing larger and low-frequency words appearing smaller. Students can manipulate the way the cloud looks and which words are included using different colors and configurations (for upper-elementary through high school students; Dalton & Grisham, 2011).

Word Wizzle: Students make contrasting statements about words based on a rule. For example, for the rule "Properties of Light" a student might say:

- "I like *intensity* but not *mass.*"
- "I like *frequency* but not *density.*"
- "I like *wavelength* but not *melting point.*"
- "I like *speed* but not *boiling point.*"

The class tries to figure out the rule using the fewest clues possible (for middle and high school students; Scott et al., 2012).

These engaging games and activities and others like them give students opportunities to extend their knowledge about specific vocabulary terms. As in steps 4 and 5, students should return to their vocabulary notebooks after step 6 to record new knowledge and information about various terms.

Chapter Summary

The six-step process described here is designed to incorporate the five elements of effective vocabulary instruction outlined in chapter 1. Teachers introduce terms to students during step 1, ask students to represent terms linguistically (step 2) and nonlinguistically (step 3), and then students explore (step 4), discuss (step 5), and play (step 6) with new terms. In the next chapter, we narrow our focus and explain the process we used to identify, organize, and provide resources for specific vocabulary terms from the science standards.

3

Vocabulary Terms From the New Science Standards

One of the most critical components of effective vocabulary instruction is selecting appropriate terms for direct instruction. Margaret McKeown, Isabel Beck, and Cheryl Sandora (2012) obviated this need for critical selection of terms:

> There are too many words in the language to teach them all directly to students, so the goal is to select the most productive words to teach. That would be words that students are less likely to learn on their own and words that occur frequently enough in the types of texts students study to be of assistance to the comprehension process. That is, there is no need to teach easy words that students will hear and learn in conversation, and there is no need to teach words that are so rare that students may never encounter them. (p. 19)

To facilitate such selection, it is useful to have a classification system for different kinds of words. Beck and her colleagues (2002) suggested a system that classifies words into different tiers. Tier 1 terms are those that most native speakers learn in daily oral conversation, and therefore do not need to be taught (for example, *clock*, *happy*, *baby*, and so on). Tier 2 terms are those terms that are not domain specific (that is, they do not directly relate to mathematics, science, social studies, English language arts, or another content area) and are not used frequently enough in oral conversations or in texts for students to learn them from context (for example, *evaluate*, *observation*, *magnitude*, *sufficient*, and so on). Tier 3 terms are domain-specific terms that are usually encountered within particular disciplines (that is, they directly relate to a specific content area; for example, *biology*, *predation*, *exothermic reaction*, and so on).

As explained previously, most native English speakers will acquire Tier 1 terms from oral conversation; therefore, students whose first language is English do not typically require direct instruction for these terms. However, direct instruction in Tier 1 terms is crucial for school success for English learners (ELs). Marzano (2010) identified 2,845 Tier 1 terms and organized them in semantic categories to facilitate such instruction (visit **marzanoresearch.com/reproducibles** for an online list of Marzano's [2010] Tier 1 terms); those designing direct vocabulary instruction for ELs can consult that resource for further guidance.

Beck and her colleagues (2002) recommended that direct vocabulary instruction focus on Tier 2 terms, as they found a small but significant 12-percentile-point gain for such instruction:

Tier Two words are not only words that are important for students to know, they are also words that can be worked with in a variety of ways so that students have opportunities to build rich representations of them and of their connections to other words and concepts. (p. 20)

Others (Castek, Dalton, & Grisham, 2012; Kelley, Lesaux, Kieffer, & Faller, 2010; Zwiers, 2008) have concurred, noting that "learning to use academic language is one of the greatest challenges of schooling because this register tends to be abstract and distant from spoken vocabulary" (Castek et al., 2012, p. 305).

However, Stahl and Fairbanks (1986) found a larger gain (33 percentile points) for teaching Tier 3 words, and Beck and her colleagues (2002) acknowledged the importance of teaching Tier 3 terms; that is, "unfamiliar words that do not meet the criteria for Tier Two words but which nevertheless require some attention if students are to understand a selection" (p. 20). Therefore, the focus of this text is on direct instruction for Tier 2 and Tier 3 terms from the science standards.

While our analysis focused primarily on words in Tiers 2 and 3, the vocabulary terms in this book are not strictly organized by tier. In the interest of comprehensiveness and usefulness for teachers at all grade levels, we included particular Tier 1 terms that pertain directly to science. For example, we included terms from the clarification statements in the NGSS (such as *river* and *human*) in our analysis, even though they would ordinarily be classified in Tier 1, to give primary teachers the option of including them in direct science instruction. Additionally, we grouped Tier 2 terms that had a unique or specialized definition in the context of science (such as *atmosphere*, *magnitude*, and *environment*) in the same category as content-specific Tier 3 terms (such as *viscosity*, *cytoplasm*, and *germination*). Therefore, we organized the terms in this book into two broad categories: general academic words (predominantly Tier 2 terms; found in part II), and domain-specific words (predominantly Tier 3 terms; found in part III).

During our analysis, we identified 318 general academic terms and 1,690 domain-specific terms. We organized these terms into categories teachers can use to teach related words together. Research has shown that clustering words supports word learning and conceptual development as students learn key vocabulary (Booth, 2009; Chi & Koeske, 1983; Glaser, 1984; Hiebert & Cervetti, 2012; Neuman et al., 2011; Tinkham, 1997). For example, teaching a group of words associated with engineering (such as *engineer*, *material*, *cost*, *proposal*, *resource*, *criteria*, *limitation*, and *design task*) together allows students to more easily make connections between terms and build semantic networks between concepts. In this chapter, we explain how we identified the terms, how we organized them, and the resources we created to facilitate their use in direct vocabulary instruction.

General Academic Vocabulary

General academic terms are those words that are not specific to a particular content area but are necessary for success in school. Examples include *critique*, *proportion*, and *evidence*. Students need to know what these terms mean and how to use them to engage in learning in school, but they are not specific to any one subject. In the foundational document for the NGSS, *A Framework for K–12 Science Education*, the National Research Council (2012) explicitly highlighted the importance of teaching general academic vocabulary:

Not only must students learn technical terms [i.e., domain-specific terms] but also more general academic language, such as "analyze" or "correlation," which are not part of most students' everyday vocabulary and thus need specific elaboration if they are to make sense of scientific text. (pp. 76–77)

The examples given here, *correlation* and *analyze*, are two of the general academic words we identified and are examples of the two categories of general academic terms that we encountered during our analysis: (1) crosscutting practices and concepts and (2) cognitive verbs.

Crosscutting Practices and Concepts

The terms in the crosscutting practices and concepts category, which include nouns and modifiers, were taken from two overarching organizational dimensions of the NGSS. The first dimension, called crosscutting concepts, identified ideas that "bridge disciplinary boundaries, having explanatory value throughout much of science and engineering" (National Research Council, 2012, p. 83). The second dimension, which contained scientific practices, specified the "behaviors that scientists engage in as they investigate and build models and theories about the natural world" (Achieve, 2014). In other words, terms in the crosscutting practices and concepts category pertain to overarching ideas and skills that apply to every domain of science. The National Research Council (2012) pointed out:

> Although crosscutting concepts are fundamental to an understanding of science and engineering, students have often been expected to build such knowledge without any explicit instructional support. . . . Explicit reference to the concepts, as well as their emergence in multiple disciplinary contexts, can help students develop a cumulative, coherent, and usable understanding of science and engineering. (p. 83)

We suggest that an excellent way to provide "explicit instructional support . . . in multiple disciplinary contexts" (National Research Council, 2012, p. 83) is to provide direct vocabulary instruction in terms related to these crosscutting concepts and scientific practices.

We identified 158 terms that represented crosscutting concepts and scientific practices in the standards. As explained previously, teaching terms in categories is an effective way to help students develop rich, contextual understanding of their meanings and use. Therefore, we sought an organizational scheme for the terms we identified. The most natural organizational structure seemed to be the categories used in the NGSS for the concepts and practices. The nine crosscutting concept categories outlined by the NGSS Lead States (2013) are as follows:

1. Cause and effect

2. Energy and matter

3. Influence of engineering, technology, and science on society and the natural world

4. Interdependence of science, engineering, and technology

5. Patterns

6. Stability and change

7. Structure and function

8. Scale, proportion, and quantity

9. Systems and system models

The eight scientific practice categories outlined by the NGSS Lead States (2013) are as follows:

1. Engaging in argument from evidence

2. Analyzing and interpreting data

3. Constructing explanations and designing solutions

4. Obtaining, evaluating, and communicating information

5. Planning and carrying out investigations

6. Using mathematics and computational thinking

7. Developing and using models

8. Asking questions and defining problems

Together, there are seventeen crosscutting concept and scientific practice categories. We sorted the terms into these seventeen categories and, to facilitate direct instruction, generated a description and examples for each term. For example, the entry in part II for the term *function* is as follows:

> The **function** of something is its purpose or what it does to be useful.
>
> Examples: The different body parts of a plant or animal serve different functions. For instance, the function of a porcupine's quills is to protect the porcupine from predators. The function of a beaver's long, sharp teeth is to allow the beaver to chew down trees and branches to build its home.

We provided descriptions and examples for these terms because many of the crosscutting practices and concepts refer to concepts that can be abstract and difficult to describe. For example, consider a term such as *relevant*. Throughout the NGSS, students need to understand what *relevant* means in order to meet the expectations of the standards. While most adults understand the concept of relevance, describing the word clearly and concretely can be more challenging. Therefore, we provided descriptions that teachers can use as a jumping-off point to further explain the features of the word. Most examples are drawn directly from the NGSS and are meant to give teachers ideas about further experiences, stories, images, and examples that could be used to elucidate the term for students. As stated previously, terms from the crosscutting practices and concepts are important in all content areas. However, some terms have slightly or completely different definitions in the context of science. For example, the words *theory* and *experiment*, while also used in other disciplines, mean something very specific in science. In this case, because the terms were identified from the NGSS, we chose to only include examples of the term's use within the context of science content.

Cognitive Verbs

Most of the verbs used in the NGSS referred to cognitive processes and actions that students need to understand and perform to meet the expectations of the standards. In order to analyze and interpret data from fossils, for example, a student must know how to *analyze* and *interpret*. Many of these cognitive verbs were identical or similar to the verbs identified by Marzano and Simms (2013) in their analysis of the Tier 2 terms in the Common Core State Standards (CCSS). This is to be expected, as Tier 2 terms (by definition) are those that cut across content areas and are useful to students as they engage in the cognitive work required by rigorous curricula. Therefore, we recommend that cognitive verbs also be the subject of direct vocabulary instruction.

We identified 160 verbs that represented cognitive processes and actions from the NGSS. Because many of the verbs from the science standards matched those in Marzano and Simms's (2013) list of cognitive verbs from the CCSS, we decided to adapt their organizational scheme for use in categorizing the verbs. They classified the verbs into twenty-four basic categories of cognitive processes which were based on previous research on critical thinking, reasoning skills, and cognitive processing (Marzano, 2007; Marzano et al., 1988). Because the standards did not contain verbs that fit into two of the categories, we used the remaining twenty-two categories to organize the cognitive verbs from the NGSS. The twenty-two organizational categories for cognitive verbs are:

1. Add To
2. Arrange
3. Compare/Contrast
4. Collaborate
5. Create
6. Decide
7. Define
8. Evaluate
9. Execute
10. Explain
11. Hypothesize
12. Infer
13. Measure
14. Prove/Argue
15. Problem Solve
16. Pull Apart
17. Redo
18. See the Big Picture
19. Seek Information
20. Symbolize
21. Think Metacognitively
22. Transform

To illustrate the idea of a basic cognitive process, consider the Symbolize category. There are eight verbs in this category (see page 98 in part II): *demonstrate*, *display*, *graph*, *illustrate*, *map*, *model*, *represent*, and *visualize*. Although each term has a different meaning, they all describe cognitive processes and actions associated with representing concepts using symbols. Thus, we classified them together in the Symbolize cognitive category.

As with the crosscutting practices and concepts, we generated descriptions and examples for each cognitive verb. For example, the entry in part II for the term *classify* is as follows:

> If you **classify** things, you organize them into groups based on their traits.
>
> Examples: Make observations of a substance and use them to classify it as a gas, liquid, or solid. Classify an animal as an amphibian if it has a backbone and uses both gills and lungs at different points in its life cycle. Classify an animal as an insect if it has a segmented body with six jointed legs but does not have a backbone.

Readers should note that for verbs that also appeared in Marzano and Simms's (2013) list of cognitive verbs from the CCSS, we used the same description of the term but generated unique examples in the context of science. To ensure that readers could easily locate terms, we also deemed it important in several cases to include both the noun and verb forms of a term (for example, *observation* and *observe*) in part II. When this was the case, we used parallel entries for the two forms of the term. That is, the description and examples for the noun form are consistent with the description and examples for the verb form. When teaching terms, teachers can choose to introduce one form of the term, but explain and give examples of the term in both of its forms.

Again, the descriptions are meant as jumping-off points for teachers to further explain the terms to students and the examples are taken from the standards. As with the crosscutting concepts, we provide examples from science because our analysis was focused on the science standards. However, the cognitive verbs are applicable and useful in all content areas. (For cognitive verb examples for ELA and mathematics, please see *Vocabulary for the Common Core* [Marzano & Simms, 2013].)

Domain-Specific Vocabulary

Unlike general academic terms, domain-specific terms correspond to a particular content area—in this case, science. Bravo and Cervetti (2008) highlighted several characteristics of domain-specific terms:

- They are typically numerous.

- They are often abstract.

- They frequently carry more than one meaning.

- They are likely to be new labels for unknown ideas even when their form is recognizable.

Essentially, as students learn new Tier 3 terms, they are usually simultaneously learning new and often challenging concepts.

In our analysis of the science standards we identified 1,690 domain-specific terms. To identify these terms, we began by compiling a list of terms from the NGSS document. We then compared that list with the list of science terms presented in *Building Background Knowledge for Academic Achievement* (Marzano, 2004), which lists terms derived from an analysis of national standards documents in eleven subject areas.

Many of the terms from the Marzano (2004) list and the NGSS list overlapped. When this was the case, we included those terms. However, there were a number of terms that did not overlap. For example, the term *igneous rock* appears only in *Building Background Knowledge for Academic Achievement* but is an important term for science studies. Therefore, it is included in the list of domain-specific terms in part III. As previously mentioned, all of the terms in part III pertain directly to science, but some of the terms are not Tier 3 words. To make the lists as useful as possible for all teachers, we included Tier 1 terms that might be taught directly as a part of science instruction at primary grade levels (such as *color, earthquake,* and *birth*).

As with the general academic terms in part II, we also sought an organization scheme for the domain-specific terms in part III. Unlike the terms in part II, the terms in part III refer to very specific scientific concepts in the four disciplinary core ideas (Physical Science, Life Science, Earth and Space Science, and Engineering), and as Stahl and Bravo (2010) observed, teaching such terms "requires situating the word within a system of ideas to be developed" (p. 566). To situate each term firmly within its specific system of ideas, we settled on an organizational scheme used by researchers at Marzano Research to develop proficiency scales in various content areas: measurement topics. *Measurement topics* are categories of knowledge and skill found in a specific content area that extend across a range of grade levels. Measurement topics are designed to facilitate the process of organizing content in a way that makes the progression of learning from one grade level to subsequent grade levels more obvious and efficient.

To identify science measurement topics in the NGSS, we organized the standards themselves into learning progressions. That is, we sought to identify natural progressions of knowledge and skill that extended across multiple grade levels. As a result of this analysis, we identified forty-seven science measurement topics: fifteen in Physical Science, fifteen in Life Science, fourteen in Earth and Space Science, and three in Engineering. Table 3.1 lists the measurement topics for each disciplinary core idea (DCI).

Table 3.1: Measurement Topics in Each Disciplinary Core Idea

DCI	Measurement Topics
Physical Science	Forces and Interactions; Electric and Magnetic Forces; Gravity; Energy and Forces; Energy Definitions; Energy Conservation and Energy Transfer; Waves; Electromagnetic Radiation; Information Technologies; States of Matter; Structure and Properties of Matter; Conservation of Matter; Chemical Reactions; Bonds; Nuclear Processes
Life Science	Growth and Development of Organisms; Matter and Energy in Organisms; Ecosystem Dynamics; Interdependent Relationships in Ecosystems; Matter and Energy in Ecosystems; Humans, Biodiversity, and Ecosystems; Structure and Function; Information Processing; Cell Theory; Inheritance of Traits; Variation of Traits; Adaptation; Natural Selection; Fossils; Evidence of Common Ancestry
Earth and Space Science	The Solar System; The Universe and Stars; Weather and Climate; Natural Hazards; Weathering and Erosion; Water and Earth's Surface; Earth's History; Plate Tectonics; Earth Systems; Humans and Earth Systems; Biogeology; Natural Resources; Global Climate Change; Carbon Cycle
Engineering	Defining Problems; Designing Solutions; Evaluating and Testing Solutions

Based on the standards within each measurement topic, we sorted the vocabulary terms in part III into their corresponding measurement topics. The measurement topics serve as semantic categories; they allow teachers to teach related groups of terms together and allow students to make connections between new terms and terms they already know. This makes it more likely that students will retain and use newly learned scientific vocabulary. If a term that appeared in part II was an important element of a certain measurement topic in part III, we also included it there. For example, we included the term *cost* in part II because it is a general academic word, but we also included it in part III because it is important to measurement topics in Engineering (namely, Defining Problems and Evaluating and Testing Solutions).

Readers will notice that instead of providing descriptions and examples for each term in part III, we instead identified the grade levels at which each term is especially appropriate to teach. We did this for two reasons. First, there are over five times as many terms in part III as there are in part II. Therefore, providing descriptions and examples for each term was outside the scope of this work. Second, unlike the terms in part II (which can apply to many different grade levels depending on the context in which they are taught), the terms in part III can be fitted into specific grade-level ranges. These grade-level ranges are indicated with X marks.

We acknowledge that determining grade-level ranges for terms is an inexact science, and we encourage teachers to adjust the grade levels (and measurement topics) according to students' needs and the details of their curricula. For example, a second-grade teacher might decide to include the term *force* as part of her unit on gravity, even though we designate it as a third-grade term. A middle school teacher might determine that his students need additional practice and review with the term *biodiversity* even though we designated it as an upper-elementary term. For a unit on weathering and erosion, a teacher might decide to include the term *canyon* even though we include it in the measurement topic Earth's History. Adjustments like these are completely appropriate.

To make our grade-level designations, we used a combination of common sense and data from the NGSS. For example, consider the term *environment*. This word appears in the NGSS starting in kindergarten and continues to be used all the way up to the high school level. However, most students are expected to understand and use this term during elementary school. Therefore, we designated this term as appropriate to teach in kindergarten through second grade. In contrast, there were other cases in which a simple term—such as *coral reef*—first appeared at the high school level. However, since many students learn about coral reefs in elementary school or middle school, we designated a lower grade level for that term. Finally, there were a number of fairly complex or sophisticated terms that appeared in lower-grade-level standards. For example, consider the following first-grade standard:

> 1-PS4-3. Plan and conduct an investigation to determine the effect of placing objects made with different materials in the path of a beam of light. [Clarification Statement: Examples of materials could include those that are transparent (such as clear plastic), translucent (such as wax paper), opaque (such as cardboard), and reflective (such as a mirror).]

In this case, we interpreted the standard to imply that first graders need to be able to test different kinds of materials—such as a clear piece of plastic—and determine whether light could shine through them, but not necessarily know the more sophisticated labels—such as *transparent*—for the types of materials. However, the NGSS's inclusion of the terms *transparent*, *translucent*, and *opaque* in the clarification statement indicates that they are important terms, so we included them in the list but designated that they be taught at the middle school or high school level.

Because we opted to use grade-level ranges rather than assigning each term to one specific level, many terms appear at two or three consecutive grade levels. For example, the term *species* is designated for grades 2, 3, and 4. This feature of the lists in part III highlights a critical feature of selecting vocabulary terms to teach: it is best done in collaboration with other grade levels. In the case of *species*, second-grade teachers might introduce it to students, third-grade teachers might help students master the term, and fourth-grade teachers might review the term. Essentially, teachers at each grade level can introduce new terms that appear at their grade level for the first time, help students master terms that have been introduced at previous grade levels, and review terms that have been mastered at the previous grade level.

Chapter Summary

The lists of terms in parts II and III were identified from the NGSS and organized in categories to facilitate teachers' introduction of related terms in semantic clusters. As additional resources, we generated descriptions and examples for all of the terms in part II and designated appropriate grade-level ranges for the terms in part III. Teachers interested to know which standard each term came from should consult the online source list at **marzanoresearch.com/reproducibles**. In the final chapter, we discuss how schools and districts can use the lists in parts II and III to design comprehensive programs of direct vocabulary instruction that span multiple grade levels. We also address the issue of vocabulary assessment, offering several options for assessing and reporting students' vocabulary knowledge.

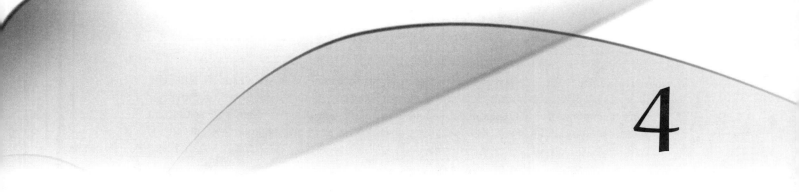

Building a Vocabulary Program

As explained in chapter 1, vocabulary instruction has historically been underemphasized in schools despite its critical role in students' language and conceptual development. This is perhaps because teachers with limited time deem other instructional emphases more critical to students' success. Beck and McKeown (2007) raised this question in the course of their research: "Given that direct instruction in vocabulary requires teacher planning and teacher and student time and results in less than complete learning, should direct instruction be viewed as an overly time-consuming way to build vocabulary?" (p. 265). Their answer is particularly illuminating:

> Consider what is required for purely incidental learning of word meanings. . . . [Hart and Risley (1995)] estimated that higher-SES [socioeconomic status] children were exposed to over 30 million words of spoken language by the time they were 3 years old and on average had a vocabulary of about 1,100 words. Children from working-class homes were exposed to over 20 million words and had vocabularies of about 700 words, and children from lower-SES homes heard about 10 million words and knew about 500. The message here is that learning word meanings is not particularly efficient, no matter how it is done. When it happens incidentally—outside of instruction—people are not aware of the enormous number of words and encounters that come their way in order for learning to take place. (p. 265)

Their salient point can be summarized as follows: learning word meanings is a time-consuming process, and although direct vocabulary instruction takes time, it is ultimately more efficient than waiting for students to learn terms from context or oral conversation. Given the importance of vocabulary knowledge to academic success, direct vocabulary instruction is arguably one of the most productive activities in which teachers and students can engage.

It is also important to keep in mind that lack of time may not be the most significant inhibitor of direct vocabulary instruction in schools. Indeed, Marulis and Neuman (2010) found that "longer, more intensive, and more frequent [vocabulary] interventions did not yield larger effect sizes than smaller dosages. In fact, even brief doses of vocabulary intervention (e.g., Whitehurst et al., 1988) were associated with large effect sizes" (p. 325). Rather, it may be that teachers are not comfortable implementing direct vocabulary instruction by themselves. Teachers may instead seek systemwide programs of coordinated vocabulary instruction, which ensure that students' vocabulary knowledge is built and supported across grade levels in a logical way that supports conceptual development in all content areas. In their study of teacher attitudes toward vocabulary instruction, Berne and Blachowicz (2008) found that this was indeed the case:

When we [looked] . . . at the surveys, we fully expected time to be the biggest concern. Although teachers did cite that as an area they worried about when considering vocabulary instruction, far more teachers expressed their concern about a lack of district- or building-wide consistency in vocabulary practices and the assumptions and shared vocabulary that underpin these practices. (p. 319)

As Biemiller and Slonim (2001) expressed, "although vocabulary development is crucial for school success, it has not received the attention and interest that work on identifying printed words and spelling have received. . . . [There is] the need to create a more systematic approach to facilitating vocabulary development in the schools" (p. 511). Addressing that need is the focus of this chapter. We give concrete guidance to teachers and school or district leaders who are interested in designing a systemwide program of vocabulary instruction. Typically, such a system involves two components, both of which are addressed here: (1) selecting terms to teach and (2) assessing and reporting students' vocabulary knowledge and growth.

Selecting Terms to Teach

As explained in chapter 3, the terms in parts II and III are designed to be a menu from which educators select the terms they consider to be most critical to the content being taught. Teachers should not attempt to teach all of the terms presented in this book. Doing so would not only be impossible but also counterproductive, as trying to teach such a large number of terms would not allow students enough time with each term to develop a useful, working knowledge of its meaning and contextual nuances. Instead, the lists in parts II and III represent a starting point from which teachers should exercise professional judgment in selecting appropriate terms for instruction.

The next logical question is, therefore, How many terms should be taught? This is a difficult question to answer, as each classroom and school are subject to a wide range of variables that make recommending a specific number difficult. However, the research does provide a measure of guidance. In his review of the literature, Biemiller (2012) concluded that extant vocabulary studies suggested "children can acquire an average of 10 words per week, assuming that around 25 words per week are taught. . . . Vocabulary work over 40 weeks could add 300 root words to children's vocabularies" (p. 47). Citing Beck and McKeown (2007) and his own previous work (Biemiller & Boote, 2006), he further observed that "teaching *more* meanings per week *in less depth* (20–25 meanings) appears to result in the acquisition of more meanings than teaching *fewer* meanings *in greater depth* (5–10 meanings)" (p. 43). We acknowledge that various educational researchers differ about exactly how many terms it is possible to teach and exactly how many terms of those taught will be retained by students. However, based on our analysis of the research, we believe that planning to teach ten to twenty terms per week is a reasonable rough estimate from which to begin the selection process, always keeping in mind that individual teachers may find it profitable to teach more or fewer terms (depending on their individual circumstances and students' unique needs). It is also important to keep in mind that this estimate refers to *all* vocabulary terms taught in a week; estimates for individual subjects (such as science) will be lower since they make up only a part of the total. For example, a middle school grade-level team might decide to focus on five terms from each content area (ELA, mathematics, science, and social studies) per week, thus teaching a total of twenty terms each week.

Another pertinent question is, Who should select the terms to teach? This question has a more definitive answer than the previous one: teachers, and in some cases, students. Research has shown that teachers are skilled at identifying appropriate vocabulary terms (Beck et al., 2002; Beyersdorfer, 1991; Breland,

Jones, & Jenkins, 1994; Calderón, Hertz-Lazarowitz, & Slavin, 1998; Carlo et al., 2004; Marzano, 2002; Shapiro, 1969). Blachowicz and her colleagues (2006) observed that "content area teachers produced word-study lists with a high degree of overlap across teachers" (p. 531).

Regarding student selection of terms, research has found considerable evidence that allowing students to select some of the terms they will study increases their motivation and retention (Blachowicz, Fisher, Costa, & Pozzi, 1993; Dole et al., 1995; Fisher, Blachowicz, & Smith, 1991; Fisher & Danielsen, 1998; Haggard, 1982, 1985; Harmon, Hedrick, Wood, & Gress, 2005; Jimenez, 1997). In light of these findings, we recommend that when designing a program of vocabulary instruction, teachers and teacher teams select the words that will be directly taught throughout the year, but leave room in the schedule for students to also study self-selected terms in each content area. For example, if a teacher decided to teach ten terms a week during a school year, he or she might select eight to nine terms for each week, leaving one or two open spots to be filled with terms selected by students.

In this section, we first address how individual teachers, in the absence of a schoolwide or districtwide program of vocabulary instruction, could select terms to teach in their classrooms. Next, we address how teams of teachers within the context of a schoolwide or districtwide program of vocabulary instruction could create sets of terms to be taught in each content area at each grade level, thus building a logical learning progression of vocabulary development for students. Finally, we address how teachers can help students self-select and study vocabulary terms of interest to them.

Selection of Terms by Individual Teachers

An individual teacher would begin selecting terms by estimating how many terms it is feasible to teach during a school year. For example, a middle school science teacher might decide that he can teach five terms each week for thirty-two weeks, resulting in a total of 160 terms. An elementary school teacher (who teaches all content areas herself) might decide that she can focus on three terms from each content area (ELA, mathematics, science, and social studies) per week, for a total of twelve terms per week and roughly 380 terms per year.

Once a teacher has decided how many terms from each content area to teach in a year, he or she then examines lists of terms in the appropriate content areas, asking whether or not each term is critical to the content that he or she will be teaching that year. Semantic categories (such as the crosscutting practices and concepts categories and cognitive verb categories in part II and the measurement topics in part III) can be extremely useful to this end. Although the focus of this book is terms derived from the science standards, standards-based lists are also available for other content areas (for ELA and mathematics terms organized into semantic categories, see Marzano & Simms, 2013; for social studies, health, physical education, the arts, and technology terms, see Marzano, 2004).

As an example of how semantic categories facilitate the selection process, consider a high school biology teacher planning a unit of instruction. The teacher might decide that two measurement topics from the Life Sciences DCI are particularly important to the unit: (1) Matter and Energy in Ecosystems and (2) Matter and Energy in Organisms. Additionally, he might decide that one crosscutting practices and concepts category and one cognitive verb category are also important to the unit: Developing and Using Models (crosscutting practices and concepts category) and See the Big Picture (cognitive verb category). Table 4.1 (page 58) shows the high school terms in each category.

Table 4.1: High School Terms in Selected Semantic Categories

Matter and Energy in Ecosystems	Matter and Energy in Organisms	Developing and Using Models (Crosscutting practices and concepts category)	Create (Cognitive verb category)
biological	carbon	abstract	build
carbon	carbon dioxide	description	construct
chemical process	chemical process	diagram	create
interdependent	chemical reaction	model	develop
molecule	interdependent	representation	engineer
oxygen	molecule	simulation	formulate
photosynthesis	nutrient	sketch	generate
biomass	oxygen	type	produce
carbon cycle	photosynthesis		record
cellular respiration	protein		
durable	amino acid		
energy requirements of living systems	amino acid sequence		
hydrogen	biological molecule		
inefficient	bond		
nitrogen	cellular respiration		
respiration	chemical equation		
solar energy	compound		
stable	DNA		
trophic level	flow of matter		
	germ theory		
	hydrocarbon		
	hydrogen		
	living system		
	net transfer		
	photosynthesizing organism		
	transfer system		

The teacher might begin by putting a checkmark next to every term he deems critical to the content that will be taught during the unit. Then he counts how many terms have checks next to them, counting any duplicate terms across lists (such as *carbon*) only once, and compares the number of terms with checkmarks to the number of terms he deems feasible to teach during the unit. If he is planning a three-week unit of instruction and believes he can effectively teach five terms per week, he can select fifteen terms. If there are more than fifteen terms with checks next to them, he will have to either:

- Re-examine the terms with checks to determine which fifteen are the most critical

- Re-examine his estimate of how many terms he can teach each week, if he deems all the terms with checks to be critical

If there are fewer than fifteen terms with checks next to them, he can either select more terms or reserve the extra spots for student-selected terms.

Selection of Terms by School or District Teams

Although individual teachers can use the process just described to select sets of vocabulary terms for their classrooms, school- or districtwide vocabulary programs can be even more powerful. Marzano and Pickering (2005) recommended a five-phase process similar to the process used by individual teachers that schools and districts can use to create comprehensive, cohesive sets of vocabulary terms across grade levels and content areas:

1. Decide the target number of words to be taught at each grade level and across each grade-level interval (K–2, 3–5, 6–8, or 9–12) or multi-grade span (such as K–6 or K–12).

2. For each subject area, create a rank-ordered list of critical words by selecting words from appropriate lists and adding words that reflect local standards and curriculum materials.

3. Based on the number of words identified, determine how many terms should be taught in each subject area.

4. Generate a final list of terms for each subject area by adding or deleting terms, or by otherwise altering the lists.

5. Assign terms in each subject area list to specific grades.

Teacher teams or groups working to select terms for a school or district should include teachers from all grade levels involved. During the first phase, the group estimates how many terms can be addressed each year in each subject at each grade level, similar to the first step for individual teachers described in the previous section. During phase 2, the group selects words for instruction. For science terms, the lists in parts II and III can be used for this phase; as mentioned previously, standards-based lists are also available for other content areas (for ELA and mathematics terms organized into semantic categories, see Marzano & Simms, 2013; for social studies, health, physical education, the arts, and technology terms, see Marzano, 2004).

To ease the selection process, teachers might use a simple rating system to rate the level of importance of a term to the content that will be taught, as shown in table 4.2.

Table 4.2: Rating Scale for Potential Vocabulary Terms

4	This word should definitely be included.
3	This word should probably be included.
2	This word should probably not be included.
1	This word should definitely not be included.

Teachers in each group individually rate terms, and then compare their ratings to make determinations about which words should definitely be included or excluded and which words may require further discussion. In all cases, a group working to select words should remain aware that their initial selections are not set in stone. Revisions, additions, and deletions will almost certainly be necessary as schools and districts implement vocabulary programs and receive feedback from teachers and students.

During the third phase, the group counts the number of terms identified and compares that number to the original estimate of how many words can be taught at each grade level. Phase 4 involves revising the list by adding or deleting terms so that the number of terms in each list matches the total identified during phase 1. Finally, the group assigns terms to specific grade levels during phase 5.

Selection of Terms by Students

To facilitate student selection of terms, the teacher might present a list of options to students and ask them to pick one or two that are especially interesting. Teachers might also ask students to be on the lookout each week for new terms they encounter in texts, media, or daily life that are unfamiliar and relate to the topic of study at hand. Student-selected terms can be taught in the same way as teacher-selected terms, with students adding them to their vocabulary notebooks and practicing and deepening their knowledge of them through activities, discussions, and games.

To increase rigor, teachers might ask students to share their descriptions, explanations, and examples of self-selected terms with the class during a designated time at the end of each week, thus increasing whole-class exposure to new terms and giving students an opportunity to share their new vocabulary knowledge with their peers.

Assessing Vocabulary Knowledge

The final component of building a comprehensive vocabulary program is to determine how students' vocabulary knowledge will be measured and reported. Vocabulary can be assessed both informally and formally. Informal assessments are often unobtrusive; that is, instruction does not stop when they are occurring. As explained in chapter 2, there are a number of dimensions to vocabulary knowledge: productive vocabulary versus receptive vocabulary and oral vocabulary versus written vocabulary (see figure 2.2, page 26). Additionally, student self-reports can be a useful way to measure vocabulary knowledge. Here, we present strategies to collect assessment information about each of these dimensions of vocabulary knowledge.

Productive Vocabulary

Informal, unobtrusive assessments are excellent ways to assess students' written and oral productive vocabulary. The teacher simply looks at a student's writing or listens to a student's conversation in class and notes when the student uses vocabulary terms that have been taught and whether or not they were used correctly. Teachers might also periodically look through students' vocabulary notebooks to identify areas of confusion or uncertainty about the meaning of a term. Correct use of a new term in context typically indicates that a student has a firm grasp of its meaning. Incorrect use of a new term typically indicates that while the term has entered the student's internal lexicon, it has been learned with misconceptions or errors. In these situations, a short conversation can be very useful to clarify misconceptions or round out a term's meaning for a student.

Receptive Vocabulary

Assessing students' receptive vocabularies usually requires more obtrusive assessment techniques, where instruction stops to allow assessment to occur. Because receptive vocabulary, by definition, involves presenting students with terms, vocabulary assessment items must usually be designed. These can be written items or orally administered items. John Read (2000) offered a useful system to use when thinking about designing vocabulary assessments. He suggested that assessments vary along three continua:

- **Discrete vs. embedded**—To assess discrete vocabulary knowledge, terms are presented by themselves and students are asked to give their meaning. To assess embedded vocabulary knowledge, terms are presented within a passage and students are asked to give their meaning.

- **Selective vs. comprehensive**—A selective vocabulary assessment seeks to find out if students know a particular set of terms (such as those taught directly). A comprehensive vocabulary assessment seeks to find out if students are familiar with a larger body of terms, many of which may not have been taught directly.

- **Context dependent vs. context independent**—As explained in chapter 1, many content area terms have common meanings and specialized meanings within specific content areas (for example, *atmosphere*, *work*, *speed*, and so on). If an assessment seeks to measure students' understanding of terms' specialized meanings within a specific content area (or *context*), it is context dependent. If an assessment seeks to measure students' understanding of terms' common meanings (or to find out if they can attach any meaning to a term), it is context independent.

For example, if a teacher had completed a unit on engineering (in which twenty specific terms had been taught) and wanted to assess students' understanding of the terms when they encounter them in texts, he might design a vocabulary assessment with embedded items (terms presented within a text). Such an assessment would likely be selective, since the teacher is seeking to assess a particular set of terms (those engineering-related terms that were taught directly). Since the terms were taught within the context of engineering, the teacher would be assessing students' understanding of their specialized engineering meanings, so the assessment would be context dependent.

One additional issue that must be considered when designing obtrusive assessment items for receptive vocabulary is how student responses will be evaluated. Although the most intuitive approach might be to create multiple-choice or yes-no questions, Marzano and Pickering (2005) warned teachers to use these types of items with caution:

> The six-step teaching process we have described allows for great variation in the ways students describe and represent terms. Consequently, a multiple-choice or matching test might not be a valid assessment, especially if words within the test items are unfamiliar to the student. We recommend constructing tests with open-ended questions that allow the students to show what they understand about the terms. (pp. 33–34)

They recommended that teachers ask students to explain a term in their own words, draw a picture or other graphic representation of a term, or write a short dialogue between two characters in which the term is used and which makes the term's meaning clear. Stahl and Bravo (2010) offered other examples of open-ended vocabulary assessments. For example, table 4.3 shows an assessment for terms related to Humans and Earth Systems.

Table 4.3: Open-Ended Assessment for Terms Related to Humans and Earth Systems

Term	Causes	Consequences	Human Responses
flood			
earthquake			
hurricane			
volcanic eruption			
severe weather			
drought			
tsunami			

Alternatively, an assessment such as the one in table 4.4 might be used.

Table 4.4: Open-Ended Assessment for Terms Related to How Humans Interact With Water-Related Natural Disasters

In the list of words below, put a circle around those that have something to do with **how humans interact with water-related natural disasters**. For each word you circled, write a short explanation of how it is related to the topic.			
flood	ocean	drought	river delta
severe weather	dam	tsunami	aquifer
precipitation	river	levee	economic
earthquake	stream	wetland	water usage
erosion	fresh water	biosphere	urban development
hurricane	crops	groundwater	sea level

An assessment such as the one in table 4.5 could also be used.

Table 4.5: Open-Ended Assessment for Terms Related to Humans and Earth Systems

Terms that describe different types of natural disasters:	Terms that describe human responses to natural disasters:
Terms that describe how ecosystems are affected by natural disasters:	Terms that describe human actions that contribute to natural disasters:

The focus of each assessment in tables 4.3, 4.4, and 4.5 is slightly different. However, each one allows students to flexibly demonstrate their current level of understanding of various terms.

If teachers do want to use multiple-choice items to assess vocabulary knowledge, they must be designed with care. For example, Beck and McKeown (2007) recommended designing items that require students to "make sense of a context in which the word was being used" (p. 265). Beck and her colleagues (2002) presented strong and weak examples of multiple-choice items, as shown in table 4.6.

Table 4.6: Weak and Strong Multiple-Choice Vocabulary Items

Weak	Strong
Diligent means:	*Diligent* means:
a. fast	a. making a lot of money
b. hardworking	b. working at an interesting job
c. lost	c. always trying one's best
d. punished	d. remembering everything

Source: Beck et al., 2002, p. 96.

As another example of a strong multiple-choice item, Beck and McKeown (2007) presented students with pictures of different scenes and asked them which picture best matched a given term:

> For example, a first-grade item for *dignified* asked, "Which picture shows people being dignified?" The four pictures showed (1) a couple dressed in elegant clothes standing together, (2) people in ghost and witch Halloween costumes, (3) two men leaning toward each other and looking around as if hiding from someone, and (4) two children pulling at different arms of a teddy bear. (p. 265)

Here, students must interpret the term *dignified* and identify an example of its appropriate use. In this instance, option 1 would be the correct answer.

Self-Reported Vocabulary Knowledge and Tracking Student Progress

As explained in chapter 2, asking students to assess their own knowledge of a vocabulary term is an excellent way to help them become more aware of how well they understand a term. Students' self-evaluation scores on the four-point scale in their vocabulary notebooks (presented on page 21) should be revised as their knowledge of a term improves. For example, a student might initially rate her knowledge of a term as a 2, meaning that she has a general idea of the term's meaning but is still uncertain about it. Several days later, after she has had the chance to discuss the term with other students and make some revisions to her description and picture for the term, she might change her rating to a 3, indicating that she understands the term and is not confused about it. Several weeks later, the student might encounter the term online in a new context that expands her understanding of its component word parts and contextual uses. Based on her new learning, she might make revisions to the term's entry in her vocabulary notebook and change her self-rating to a 4: *I understand even more about the term than I was taught.*

An excellent way to help students track their overall vocabulary knowledge and growth is with a chart like the one in table 4.7, which allows students to visually summarize their current level of knowledge for the terms in their vocabulary notebooks.

Table 4.7: Tracking Chart for Vocabulary Knowledge

Number of Terms	Level 1	Level 2	Level 3	Level 4
10				
9		X		
8		X		
7		X	X	
6		X	X	X
5		X	X	X
4		X	X	X
3		X	X	X
2	X	X	X	X
1	X	X	X	X

As shown in table 4.7, the student puts an X in the appropriate column for each term in his or her vocabulary notebook, depending on his or her current self-rating for the term. The student whose ratings are shown in table 4.7 has rated herself at level 1 for two terms, at level 2 for nine terms, at level 3 for seven terms, and at level 4 for six terms. Teachers might ask students to fill out a chart like the one in table 4.7 weekly, monthly, or at the end of each unit. If the chart is filled out in pencil or electronically, students can easily move the Xs around to reflect changes in their vocabulary knowledge.

Chapter Summary

Building a comprehensive program of direct vocabulary instruction requires careful selection of terms and effective assessment and tracking systems so students have a clear picture of what they already know and what they need to work on relative to target terms. Blachowicz and her colleagues (2006) described such a program as *integrated* and *comprehensive:*

> By *integrated*, we mean that vocabulary is a core consideration in all grades across the school and in all subject areas across the school day. . . . By *comprehensive*, we mean that vocabulary instruction encompasses much more than a list of words to teach at the beginning of the week. Rather, it involves a common philosophy and shared practices among teachers in a school or district based on a solid understanding of the knowledge base on vocabulary development and word learning. (pp. 526–527)

Based on the research supporting the efficacy of direct vocabulary instruction, we recommend that direct vocabulary instruction utilize a six-step process for teaching target terms in the classroom. Such terms can be selected from the menus of terms in parts II and III of this book. Ideally, educators will collaborate to build comprehensive programs of vocabulary development for their classrooms, schools, and districts.

PART II

General Academic Vocabulary Terms

Part II contains general academic terms from the science standards, many of which could be categorized as Tier 2 words. As explained in chapter 3, the general academic terms in part II include (1) crosscutting practices and concepts and (2) cognitive verbs. Recall from chapter 3 that the crosscutting practices and concepts section includes terms from two dimensions of the NGSS: crosscutting concepts (overarching ideas that apply to every domain of science) and scientific practices (skills that students use to carry out scientific tasks).

The words in part II are organized into categories that allow teachers to introduce sets of related words together. The crosscutting practices and concepts are organized into seventeen categories. The NGSS Lead States (2013) devised nine categories of crosscutting concepts and eight categories of scientific practices. Therefore, we found it suitable to use the same seventeen categories here. The seventeen crosscutting practices and concepts categories and the initials used to designate each one in the appendix are:

1. Engaging in argument from evidence (ARG)

2. Cause and effect (C/E)

3. Analyzing and interpreting data (DATA)

4. Energy and matter (E/M)

5. Constructing explanations and designing solutions (E/S)

6. Influence of engineering, technology, and science on society and the natural world (INFL)

7. Obtaining, evaluating, and communicating information (INFO)

8. Interdependence of science, engineering, and technology (INT)

9. Planning and carrying out investigations (INV)

10. Using mathematics and computational thinking (MCT)

11. Developing and using models (MOD)

12. Patterns (PAT)

13. Asking questions and defining problems (Q/P)

14. Stability and change (S/C)

15. Structure and function (S/F)

16. Scale, proportion, and quantity (SPQ)

17. Systems and system models (SYS)

The cognitive verbs are organized into twenty-two categories. Because many of the verbs were identical or similar to the cognitive verbs identified by Marzano and Simms (2013) in their analysis of the Common Core State Standards (CCSS), we adapted that organizational scheme for use in categorizing the verbs from the NGSS. Our adapted list of cognitive verb categories and the initials we used to designate each one in the appendix are as follows:

1. Add To (ADD)

2. Arrange (ARR)

3. Compare/Contrast (C/C)

4. Collaborate (COLL)

5. Create (CRE)

6. Decide (DEC)

7. Define (DEF)

8. Evaluate (EVAL)

9. Execute (EXEC)

10. Explain (EXP)

11. Hypothesize (HYP)

12. Infer (INF)

13. Measure (MEAS)

14. Prove/Argue (P/A)

15. Problem Solve (PS)

16. Pull Apart (PULL)

17. Redo (REDO)

18. See the Big Picture (SBP)

19. Seek Information (SI)

20. Symbolize (SYM)

21. Think Metacognitively (TM)

22. Transform (TRANS)

An alphabetical master list of all the words in parts II and III and their category (for part II words) or measurement topic (for part III words) is included in the appendix (page 179). For a complete alphabetical listing of the terms in this section and the source of each term, please consult the online resource at **marzanoresearch.com/reproducibles.**

Each word in part II is accompanied by a description of the word and examples of how that word might be used in science, drawn from the term's use in the NGSS. These descriptions and examples are meant to be starting points for student exploration of each term. If a teacher feels that the examples given are too advanced or too simple for her class, she can revise them to apply more directly to the content being taught.

Crosscutting Practices and Concepts

Engaging in Argument From Evidence (ARG)

argument

When you make an **argument** for or against something, you try to convince someone that it is right or wrong using reasons and evidence.

Examples: When you make an argument, provide evidence to support your perspective. If your argument is that plants and animals alter their environments to suit their needs, you might provide examples of organisms changing the environment—such as a prairie dog burrowing underground—to support your claim.

bias

A **bias** is a preference for one thing, outcome, person, or group over another.

Examples: If you are doing an experiment, you might have a bias toward a particular result or outcome. To avoid bias, use objective data sources and set criteria and procedures ahead of time.

empirical

Something that is **empirical** is based on evidence that you can physically see or show.

Examples: When you make a scientific claim, especially about a causal relationship, it is important to use empirical evidence to back it up. When you are defining a design question, make sure it can be tested in an empirical way.

evidence

Evidence is information you can gather to back up or support a statement.

Examples: The fossil record can be used to provide evidence for the occurrence of a variety of different events. For instance, you can use the distribution of fossils and rocks to show evidence of the motions of tectonic plates.

logical

Something is **logical** when it makes sense and is reasonable.

Examples: In science, it is important to develop logical arguments about the natural world. In a logical argument, the evidence relates clearly to the claim and contains no errors in reasoning.

reasoning

When you use **reasoning**, you think about a situation and use what you know to make sensible choices and judgments.

Examples: When you explain the ideas and evidence you used to construct an argument, you are explaining your reasoning. If you explain that a reaction occurs faster when particles are heated because higher temperatures mean particles are moving faster, you are explaining your reasoning.

sufficient

Something that is **sufficient** is adequate or enough.

Examples: When you make a claim, make sure that you have sufficient evidence to defend it. Create a model of your solution with sufficient precision to be sure it will work in the real world. A plant will die if it does not get sufficient water.

valid

Something that is **valid** is reliable, reasonable, and logical.

Examples: Use valid evidence to construct explanations and support arguments. Valid solutions to design problems take into account all of the limitations and requirements of the design task.

Cause and Effect (C/E)

causality When there is **causality**, it means that one thing triggered something else to happen.

Example: If you want to argue that one thing led to something else, you would need evidence to show causality.

causation If there is **causation** between two events, it means that one event happened because of the other.

Example: There is a causation relationship between pushing a ball and it rolling forward.

correlation If there is **correlation** between two events, it means they are related in some way but not necessarily that one event caused the other to happen.

Example: The trend of murder rates rising at the same time as ice cream sales is a just a correlation relationship; although the events correlate, that does not mean ice cream causes murder or that murder causes people to eat ice cream.

effect An **effect** is a change that happens as a result of something else.

Examples: A change in the structure of a gene, also called a mutation, can have positive or negative effects on the way an organism functions. You can lessen the effect of a natural hazard by using weather forecasting to prepare for it in advance.

result A **result** is something that happens or exists because something else occurred.

Examples: The result of a chemical reaction is a new compound. Analyze the result of your experiment to see if your prediction is accurate.

Analyzing and Interpreting Data (DATA)

accurate Something that is **accurate** is correct.

Examples: If a theory correctly predicts the results of an experiment, it is likely to be accurate. Genetic mutations occur when DNA replication is not accurate.

analysis When you do an **analysis** of something, you look closely at each of its parts and see if they fit together in a way that makes sense.

Examples: Do an analysis of maps to describe patterns in the formation of the Earth's landforms. After an analysis of a topographic map, for instance, you might determine that volcanoes and mountain ranges often form along the edges of tectonic plates or that earthquakes occur at tectonic boundaries.

assumption When you make an **assumption**, you guess that something is probably true based on what you already know, even though you do not know for certain.

Examples: When thinking about the physical laws of the universe, you can make the assumption that they are unchanging. You can state your assumption that Newton's laws of motion function today exactly as they always have and always will.

bar graph A **bar graph** is a visual representation of data that uses rectangles of different heights to express larger or smaller values.

Examples: You could use a bar graph to show the average outdoor temperature, wind direction, or precipitation during various months. Bar graphs can make it easier to see patterns in data.

chart A **chart** is a table, graph, or diagram that shows information about something.

Examples: You can use a chart to display data and make them easier to understand. For instance, you might make a chart showing that Seattle gets more rain on average than Denver by writing each city's name on the x-axis, marking how much rain each city gets on the y-axis, and creating bars that show the different totals.

comparison

If you make a **comparison** between two or more things, you identify ways that they are the same or different.

Examples: You can create a comparison of the diversity of life in multiple habitats by showing how living things function differently based on their environments. For instance, you might make a comparison between the types of plants found in the desert and the types of plants found in the rainforest. In your comparison, point out the different structures and components each plant uses to gather the right amount of water, avoid predators, and reproduce.

data

Data are pieces of information in the form of facts, numbers, or statistics.

Examples: Collect data to show that pushing a ball causes it to roll by pushing a ball and recording an observation of its rolling. Graph weather data—such as average temperatures, precipitation, and wind directions—to show what kind of weather is typical during a certain season.

finding

A **finding** is a piece of information you discover during an investigation or experiment.

Examples: Stay informed about the findings of new scientific investigations and experiments. You can use scientific findings to help make decisions in your life; for instance, the finding that aerobic exercise is good for your heart might inspire you to start running or biking.

formula

A **formula** is a process, relationship, or rule that is usually expressed using mathematical symbols or equations.

Examples: Use a formula to determine an object's velocity or acceleration. There are formulas associated with Newton's laws of motion.

graph

A **graph** is an image that shows how a set of numbers or measurements relate to each other.

Example: If your science findings are mostly numbers, you can display them in a graph to make them easier to read and interpret.

histogram

A **histogram** is a visual representation of data that uses rectangles to group and express data points in ranges.

Examples: Use a histogram to show the distribution of different age groups within a population. Use a histogram to show the range of heights for different specimens of the same species of tree.

inference

An **inference** is a conclusion based on observations and reasoning.

Example: If data follow a consistent pattern, you can make an inference about what further data might show.

interpretation

When you make an **interpretation**, you figure out what you think something means.

Examples: Make an interpretation of data from an investigation and draw conclusions about what you found. It can be easier to make interpretations if you organize data into a graph, chart, or table.

linear

Something that is **linear** is in a straight (or nearly straight) line.

Examples: If you can draw a straight line through most of your data points, there is a linear relationship within the data. If two variables increase or decrease at the same rate, they have a linear relationship.

nonlinear

Something that is **nonlinear** is not in a straight (or nearly straight) line.

Examples: If your data points are scattered and cannot be connected by a straight (or nearly straight) line, the relationship between the data points is nonlinear. If two variables increase or decrease at different rates, they have a nonlinear relationship.

pictograph

A **pictograph** is a visual representation that uses pictures to represent data.

Example: Use a pictograph to show the type of weather expected during a particular season.

pie chart

A **pie chart** is a visual representation that shows data as a percentage of the whole.

Examples: Use a pie chart to show how many trees in a group are diseased. Use a pie chart to show patterns and relationships within data.

qualitative	Data that are **qualitative** contain descriptions and sensory observations.
	Examples: If you observed a marble rolling down a ramp, you might make the qualitative observation that it rolled faster as it moved farther down the ramp. If you made a qualitative observation about how many people on your block recycled every week, you might say that all of the recycling bins were half full one week and almost completely full the next week.
quantitative	Data that are **quantitative** use numbers and measurements.
	Examples: If you measured the time it took for a marble to roll four inches at the top of a ramp (after it had just been released) and the time it took for a marble to roll four inches at the bottom of a ramp (after it had rolled down the whole ramp), your observations would be quantitative. If you weighed the material recycled by everyone on your block over the course of a week, your observations would be quantitative.
technique	A **technique** is a special strategy that you use to do a particular thing.
	Examples: You can use statistical techniques to analyze your data. Different techniques can tell you different things about your data, such as your margin of error or how strongly your variables relate to each other.

Energy and Matter (E/M)

energy	**Energy** is power from the sun, electricity, food, or other sources that people use to move, create light or heat, and create fuel for machines.
	Examples: Energy is involved whenever an object moves or produces sound, light, or heat. Where kinetic energy is concerned, the faster an object moves the more energy it has.
material	**Material** refers to the components something is made of. **Materials** are the tools you need for a specific activity.
	Examples: Your genetic material is stored in your cells in the form of DNA molecules. During the process of mitosis, genetic material is distributed evenly from both parent cells to the daughter cell. You can use the materials your teacher gives you to design and build a solution to an engineering problem.
matter	**Matter** is any physical substance that takes up space.
	Examples: The three main states of matter are solid, liquid, and gas. When liquid matter changes to solid matter (such as when water freezes and becomes ice), solid matter becomes liquid (such as when ice melts), or liquid matter becomes gas (such as when water evaporates into steam), it is called a phase change.
motion	Something is in **motion** when it is moving.
	Examples: Kicking a ball will change the speed and direction of its motion. You can use information about the motion of distant galaxies—such as a red shift of light—to show that the universe is expanding.
object	An **object** is a nonliving thing that can be seen and touched.
	Examples: Rocks, chairs, rollerblades, and spoons are all objects. Objects cannot be seen unless they are illuminated by a light source (such as the sun or a flashlight). You can make an object move by enacting a force on it, such as a push or pull.
physical	Something is **physical** when it exists outside the mind and can be seen and touched.
	Examples: You can create a physical model of something by building it out of materials (like clay or paper). When you are just discussing a design, it is not physical, but when you build the design in the real world, it becomes physical.

Constructing Explanations and Designing Solutions (E/S)

basis　　　　　　The **basis** of something is what it was built on or developed from.

Examples: When you collect data during an experiment, you can use it as the basis for evidence to support a claim. If your experiment was modeled after information from another scientist, you can say that the other scientist's work is the basis for your work.

benefit　　　　　The **benefit** of something is the good, helpful, or useful thing you get from it.

Examples: Improve something by giving it more benefits. For instance, a prosthetics engineer might redesign an artificial leg so that it gives more benefits to its user. The benefits of biodiversity include pollination, pest control, genetic diversity, and disease prevention and control.

design　　　　　When you create a **design** for something, you create a plan for it.

Examples: Sketch out a design for a structure that causes a marble to speed up, slow down, or turn. Share your design with classmates, and ask them what you can do to make it better.

design solution　　A **design solution** is a way to deal with or respond to a design problem.

Examples: Create multiple design solutions that respond to the problem in different ways. You can test your design solutions to determine which one best meets your criteria.

designed [by humans; human-made]　　Something that is **designed** is made by humans instead of occurring naturally.

Example: An example of a natural structure that provides shelter is a tree with thick, leafy branches that protect from the rain, whereas an example of a designed structure might be a concrete building with a shingled roof.

explanation　　　When you provide an **explanation** of something, you make it easier to understand by saying information about it or giving reasons for it.

Examples: You can give an explanation for why something happens in nature using scientific theories. When you talk about your methods, you give an explanation of the way you did an investigation. To give an explanation about why scientific research is important, you might start by saying that science affects all humans.

idea　　　　　　An **idea** is a thought, plan, or suggestion.

Examples: In order for an idea to be scientific, it needs to be backed up with evidence, such as data from an experiment or investigation. You can use a variety of different formats to express your ideas, including oral, graphical, textual, and mathematical ones.

merit　　　　　　Something has **merit** if it has good or high-quality characteristics.

Examples: Decide whether an argument has merit by evaluating the quality of its evidence and reasoning. You can also determine whether a design solution has merit by seeing how well it fits your criteria for success.

reliable　　　　　Something that is **reliable** is something you can trust to do a good job.

Examples: The more scientific findings confirm an explanation of the natural world, the more reliable the explanation is. If evidence is the same across multiple sources, it is more reliable than evidence that only has one source to back it up.

solution　　　　A **solution** is a way to fix a problem or answer a question.

Examples: There are often many different, possible solutions to the same problem. In order to decide which solution is best, consider all of the different effects each solution will have and weigh the pros and cons of each.

theory　　　　　A **theory** is an idea or a set of ideas, supported by evidence, that tries to explain some part of the world.

Examples: If new evidence arises, modify your theory to be consistent with the available data. If a theory doesn't make sense, ask questions to find out more information about it. The theory of plate tectonics is often used to explain past and current movements of the Earth's crust.

Influence of Engineering, Technology, and Science on Society and the Natural World (INFL)

influence

You have an **influence** on something when you change it in some way.

Examples: Influence the field of science research by replicating others' experiments and conducting new ones. Have an influence on the development of new technologies by using your science knowledge. You can also have an influence on the cultivation of new science knowledge by making observations and doing experiments.

interaction

When you have an **interaction** with someone or something, your actions affect each other.

Examples: You can have a positive interaction with the Earth by doing your part to reduce your carbon footprint. If you contribute to environmental problems such as drought, food shortages, or rising sea levels, then you have a negative interaction with the Earth.

natural

Something is **natural** if it occurs in nature and is not made by humans.

Examples: Glaciers, rainstorms, and erosion are all natural because they would still occur if humans did not exist. Drilling for oil and mining for coal are not natural because they are things humans do to the environment.

natural world

The **natural world** is made up of everything that exists in nature that is not made by humans.

Example: Science helps us answer questions, develop laws, and test theories about the natural world.

risk

Something is a **risk** when there is a possibility that it could have a bad effect.

Examples: One important job of an engineer is to develop tools that help decrease the risk of activities that can be dangerous. Seat belts, for instance, were designed to reduce the risk of injury in case of a car accident. Life preservers were designed to lessen the risk of drowning.

scientist

A **scientist** is a person who studies the physical and natural worlds through observation and experiments.

Examples: Scientists help people understand the world by explaining how events and processes happen in nature. Scientists often spend time reading and learning about other scientists' research and discoveries so that they can use that knowledge to help them in their own work.

society

A **society** is a group of people that live in the same general area and follow a number of spoken or unspoken rules.

Examples: Advances in science and engineering have helped society in different ways. New synthetic materials such as medicines, foods, and fuels are constantly being designed to benefit everyone in society. Still, it is important to keep in mind that new technologies can have unintended consequences for individuals and for society as a whole.

standard

If something is **standard**, it is common or normal.

Examples: Sometimes what is standard in the world of science is not the same as what is standard in a society. For instance, in the United States the standard unit for measuring weight is pounds. In science, however, the standard unit for measuring weight is grams.

Obtaining, Evaluating, and Communicating Information (INFO)

appropriate

Something that is **appropriate** is right for a particular situation.

Examples: Gather evidence from appropriate sources to support your claim or argument. Once you have collected initial observations of a phenomenon, it is probably appropriate to frame a hypothesis about it.

computer

A **computer** is an electronic machine that stores and uses information.

Examples: You can use a computer to simulate interactions between the ocean, the atmosphere, and the biosphere. A computer can also be used to receive and decode information that humans have transmitted over a long distance.

cost

The **cost** of something is what you have to give up in order to have it.

Examples: If you are designing a prototype, try to reduce cost while maintaining benefits. Use what you know about engineering to reduce the cost of innovations. When gathering data, try to get accurate measurements for the lowest cost possible.

criteria

Criteria are the standards by which something is judged.

Examples: When designing a solution to a design problem, make sure the solution meets all the criteria. When selecting the best materials for a model, choose the ones that meet the most criteria (strength, flexibility, cost, and so on).

decision

When you make a **decision**, you think about several choices and then choose one of them.

Examples: When planning an investigation, make a decision about how much data you will need to collect in order to produce reliable measurements and draw reasonable conclusions. You should make a decision about which type of data—qualitative or quantitative—best suits your research question.

digital

Something that is **digital** uses thousands of small signals to record or send information.

Examples: Computers are digital tools that can be used to access information on the Internet. You can create digital representations of data using software programs like Excel. Waves are used to send digital information.

feedback

Feedback is the type of response you get after you do something.

Examples: When you put your hand on a hot stove, your nerves and brain give you negative feedback (pain) that tells you to move your hand. When you eat good food, your body gives you positive feedback to encourage you to get more of the fuel you need. Give feedback to a classmate about a design solution to help improve it.

information

Information is a set of facts about something.

Examples: Humans use technology tools—such as the Internet—to share information with millions of people over long distances. All animals process information in their brains using their senses. Different sense receptors pick up different kinds of information which are then processed by the brain. For instance, when the sense receptors in your nose pick up the scent of smoke, your brain processes this information and tells you there might be a fire nearby.

knowledge

You gain **knowledge** about something when you understand and learn facts about it.

Examples: Scientific knowledge can be used to create solutions to problems, defend claims about the natural world, or help you understand new concepts in science. For instance, you might use your knowledge of what plants need to survive to understand that certain environmental conditions—such as drought—keep plants from growing.

media

Media are different forms of communication, including books, newspapers, television, and the Internet.

Examples: You can use media to help you understand different science concepts. For instance, you might use newspaper reports from different years, a time-lapse video from a space satellite, or other media to help you understand the gradual effects of climate change.

objectivity

Objectivity is when your thinking is not influenced by personal feelings or prejudices.

Examples: When you evaluate the results of your experiment, try to maintain objectivity. Objectivity will help you base your arguments on facts rather than opinions.

oral

Something that is **oral** is spoken rather than written down.

Examples: If you present an oral argument, you explain your claim and evidence aloud. It is important to be able to communicate information in both oral and written forms.

peer review

A **peer review** is an evaluation of your work by others who are studying the same topics you are studying.

Examples: When you construct an explanation, incorporate information from simulations, models, experiments, theories, and peer reviews. If you want feedback about your work, send it to others for a peer review.

relevant

Something that is **relevant** to an idea is appropriate for or connected to it.

Examples: Scientific evidence is not useful in an argument unless it is relevant to your claim. For instance, Newton's third law of motion is relevant to the subject of car collisions because it tells us that a car with a greater mass will suffer less damage in an accident than a car with a smaller mass, even if the two vehicles have the same acceleration. Fossil evidence, on the other hand, would not be relevant in this case.

research

When you collect **research** on something, you study it and try to learn as much as you can about it.

Examples: Do research on the role of cells in body systems by reading several different articles and looking at diagrams about cells. Use your research to explain what cells do to support the life functions of organisms. Use existing scientific research to find out what scientists still don't know and what new research needs to be done.

source

The **source** of something is where it came from in the first place.

Examples: When presented with a piece of information about science, make sure it came from a reliable source, such as an academic textbook, a scientific journal, or an encyclopedia. Double-check the source of any information before being too sure about what it says.

value

The **value** of something is how much it is worth. Your **values** are the things you believe in and care about.

Examples: Scientists can choose not to do an experiment or investigation because of their values, even if the research might help them understand new information about the natural world. Because protecting and bettering lives is an important value in science, scientists usually do not do research that would physically hurt people. Some scientists also refuse to do research that might hurt animals because they believe the value of an animal's life is greater than the value of the knowledge they might gain.

Interdependence of Science, Engineering, and Technology (INT)

connection

A **connection** is a link or relationship between two or more things, people, or ideas.

Examples: Make a connection between science and engineering by explaining the link between them. For instance, one connection between space science and engineering is that technology, which has been engineered, has allowed humans to observe, explore, and travel to different places in the solar system.

engineering

Engineering is the process of using scientific knowledge to design and build solutions to problems.

Examples: Progress in engineering has led to important discoveries in many different fields of science. Medical engineering products (such as the X-ray or the heart monitor) have benefited the field of medicine, and environmental engineering feats (such as the solar panel) have furthered the field of environmental science. Similarly, scientific discoveries have advanced the development of engineering industries.

relationship

A **relationship** is the connection between two or more people, things, or ideas.

Examples: A physicist understands the relationships between energy and forces. In an ecosystem, plants and animals have interdependent relationships, which means they depend on one another to meet their needs for survival.

research and development [R&D]

Research and development [R&D] is a process that scientists and engineers use to design, produce, and test new systems and technologies.

Examples: The process of research and development (R&D) works in a cycle. The first step in the R&D cycle involves scientists and engineers working together to think of a solution to a problem. Next, they design, develop, and test the solution. Then they implement and improve the solution. Finally, they begin again at the first step in the R&D cycle by rethinking the solution.

science

Science is the study of the physical and natural worlds through observation and experiments.

Examples: People rely on science to help them understand the world by explaining how events and processes happen in nature. Keep up to date with scientific research and discoveries throughout your life in order to use science knowledge to make important decisions.

technology

A piece of **technology** is a tool someone uses to accomplish a goal more quickly, efficiently, or successfully.

Examples: Engineers develop different technology tools to help humans accomplish goals. For instance, a microscope is a piece of technology that helps people see objects too small to be visible to the naked eye.

Planning and Carrying Out Investigations (INV)

discovery

When you make a **discovery**, you learn something that you didn't know before.

Examples: Sometimes a single discovery (such as penicillin) leads to the development of entire scientific fields or industries. The discovery of new genetic technologies changed the way humans influence the inheritance of desired traits in plants and animals.

experiment

An **experiment** is a scientific test you do to discover new information or confirm old information.

Examples: If you want to find out about the relationships between energy transfer and mass, you can do an experiment. This experiment might involve melting different masses of ice in samples of water with the same volume and temperature and then comparing the different final temperatures of the water.

factor

A **factor** is something that helps make a certain result happen.

Examples: One factor that affects the number of organisms that can live in an ecosystem, called carrying capacity, is the amount of resources (such as food and water) available in that ecosystem. Other factors that affect carrying capacity are climate, boundaries, and competition.

firsthand

When you see or experience something **firsthand**, it means you were personally there when it happened.

Examples: You can make firsthand observations about sunlight's effect on Earth's surface by touching the sand in a sandbox in the morning before the sun shines and touching it again in the afternoon. If you make observations of dolphin behavior in a video, your observation is not firsthand. If you observe the behavior of a live dolphin at an aquarium, your observation is firsthand.

hypothesis

A **hypothesis** is an explanation based on available evidence that forms the starting point for an extended investigation.

Examples: A good way to form a hypothesis is to ask a scientific question and try to answer it using what you already know. When you make a hypothesis, you should also keep scientific principles in mind.

investigation

When you conduct an **investigation**, you study or examine something closely.

Examples: Conduct an investigation of an animal's characteristics to classify it as a mammal, fish, insect, amphibian, bird, or reptile. You can also perform an investigation of a plant's characteristics to figure out whether it is a tree, shrub, grass, or flower. After an investigation of the characteristics of a material, you can classify it as wood, rock, glass, metal, plastic, or something else.

method

A **method** is a particular way of doing something.

Examples: You can study different impacts of humans on the environment to help you create a method for reducing them. When you are reading about a scientific experiment, pay close attention to the scientist's methods to determine how reliable the findings will be.

observable

Something that is **observable** is something you can see and learn about by watching it.

Examples: Although sunlight looks white, it is actually made up of many different colors that are usually not observable to humans. If sunlight passes through a prism, the light bends and the other colors become observable.

observation

When you make an **observation**, you see something happen or look carefully at something to find out what will happen.

Examples: When space phenomena are too large or far away to see with the naked eye, you can make observations using a telescope or a small-scale model. Similarly, you can make observations of cell functions and other tiny phenomena using a microscope or a large-scale model.

prediction   When you make a **prediction**, you say what you think will happen.

Examples: If you observe or measure the way certain objects move, you can make a prediction about how they will move again in the future. A logical prediction when watching someone move back and forth on a swing is that after the person moves backward on the swing, he or she will move forward again. A logical prediction when watching two children on a see-saw is that whenever one child moves down, the other child will move up.

scientific method   The **scientific method** is an investigation process that uses experiments and observations to draw conclusions.

Examples: Begin using the scientific method by asking a question. Then, do research and form a hypothesis about what you think the result of an experiment might be. Last, conduct the experiment, make observations, and analyze your data to draw a conclusion.

test   If you run a **test** on something, you try it out to see how well it works.

Examples: Run a test on an engineering solution to figure out which elements of the design still need improvement. After your test, make any necessary changes and run the test again.

variable   A **variable** is a part or element of something that is likely to change. In science, a **variable** is a factor in an experiment that can be controlled, measured, or changed.

Examples: If you want to investigate the different effects of water erosion, you might test variables such as the slope of the water's downhill movement or the volume of water involved. If you want to investigate the different effects of wind erosion, you might test a variable such as the speed of the wind.

Using Mathematics and Computational Thinking (MCT)

algebraic   Something that is **algebraic** is expressed using numbers, letters, and symbols.

Example: Algebraic thinking can be used to predict how changes in variables will affect the results of an experiment.

computational   Something that is **computational** is related to a mathematical operation or to a computer.

Examples: You might use computational thinking to find averages in a set of data. You could use a computer to make a computational model of an experiment that you are not able to conduct in real life.

concept   A **concept** is an idea.

Examples: It is important to understand science concepts if you are going to engineer a solution to a design problem. For instance, if you are designing a device that flies, you must understand the scientific concept of gravity.

exponential   Something that is **exponential** is increasing or decreasing at an increasingly rapid rate.

Examples: Sometimes the relationship between two variables is exponential; as one increases, the other's rate of change increases, meaning that the second variable gets bigger faster than the first variable. Atmospheric pressure decreases exponentially as you move to higher altitudes.

logarithm   A **logarithm** is how many times one number needs to be multiplied by itself to get a specific product.

Examples: Use a logarithm to express the relationship between the magnitude of an earthquake and the energy released by it. Use a logarithm to describe the relationship between time and population size. The logarithm of 8 with a base of 2 is 3 because $2 \times 2 \times 2 = 8$.

mathematical   Something that is **mathematical** has to do with numbers and operations in mathematics.

Examples: You can use mathematical models to explain how different things happen in the natural world. For instance, you can use the mathematical concepts of probability and proportional reasoning to explain how, over time, natural selection leads to changes in specific traits in species.

statistical	Something that is **statistical** is related to statistics and is usually used to collect, analyze, interpret, explain, or present data.
	Examples: Use statistical processes to analyze your data. Use statistical information to calculate the size of features on other planets. Use a computer to perform complex statistical analyses.
trigonometric	Something that is **trigonometric** is related to relationships between the side lengths and angles of triangles.
	Example: A trigonometric function relates the angles of a triangle to the lengths of its sides.

Developing and Using Models (MOD)

abstract	Something that is **abstract** is based on thoughts or ideas, rather than physical things.
	Examples: Use a model to express an abstract idea. If you draw a picture to explain an abstract idea, it can make the idea easier to understand.
description	When you give a **description** of something, you explain what it is like.
	Examples: Write a description of the movements of the sun, moon, and stars in the night sky. Use this description to predict patterns in the way these objects move.
diagram	A **diagram** is a visual representation that shows the parts of something or how something works, often using lines, labels, or both.
	Examples: Use a diagram to plan what your model will look like before you build it. To show how the energy in animals' food originally comes from the sun, you could draw a diagram of a food web.
model	A **model** is a structure or system that illustrates something.
	Example: You can create a model of the relationship between an animal's needs and its environment by drawing, labeling, and annotating diagrams of different animals in different environments.
representation	When you make a **representation** of something, you create a sign or symbol that reminds people of what it is like.
	Example: You could make a representation of the Earth and the sun to explain patterns in the way shadows change in length and direction throughout the day.
simulation	A **simulation** is something made to look and behave like something else in order to help you learn about it.
	Examples: You can use computer simulations to create animations of processes that you can't physically re-create in the real world. For instance, you might use a computer simulation to show how Earth's continents broke apart, shifted, and collided throughout the planet's history.
sketch	A **sketch** is a quick drawing that does not include very many details.
	Examples: Create a sketch of your design to help you explain it to others. Draw a sketch to show how a specific object's properties make it a good resource for solving a problem.
type	A **type** of something is a specific kind of that thing.
	Examples: Reptiles and birds are two different types of animals. Different types of physical interactions include gravitational, electric, and magnetic interactions.

Patterns (PAT)

consistent

Something that is **consistent** always happens the same way.

Examples: You can sometimes predict consistent patterns of interactions in ecosystems. One consistent pattern in any ecosystem is competition among organisms with similar requirements for food, water, and other resources. These species consistently compete with each other for limited resources, and this pattern puts limits on the amount that each species can grow.

difference

A **difference** between two things is a way in which they are not the same.

Examples: Understand the similarities and differences in the life cycles of different types of animals. For instance, a difference between a mammal and a fish is that a mammal uses lungs to breathe, whereas a fish uses gills.

pattern

A **pattern** is something that happens in a repeated way.

Examples: In physics, a wave is just a repeating pattern of a certain wavelength, frequency, and amplitude. In chemistry, you can use electron patterns on the periodic table to predict the reactivity of metals.

range

A **range** is a set of different things that all belong to a particular category.

Examples: A range of events has shaped the Earth's formation, from ancient events to relatively recent ones. Because scientists can choose from a range of different methods when doing investigations, they can pick the ones that work best with their subject matter.

routinely

You do something **routinely** if you do it regularly or in a predictable pattern.

Examples: Scientists routinely identify cause-and-effect relationships in the natural world and then use these relationships to explain changes. The Earth routinely travels around the sun.

similarity

A **similarity** is something that two things have in common.

Examples: You can find similarities between the appearance of modern organisms and fossil organisms. Use these similarities to make inferences about the evolutionary relationships between the organisms.

Asking Questions and Defining Problems (Q/P)

constraint

A **constraint** is a rule or situation that puts a limit on something.

Examples: When you are designing a solution to an engineering problem, you need to consider the constraints of your solutions. If you are trying to solve the problem of limited clean, drinkable water on Earth, you should keep certain constraints in mind (such as the amount of money people can reasonably spend for your solution).

design problem

A **design problem** is a difficulty that can be fixed by engineering an object, tool, process, or system.

Examples: A well-defined design problem includes criteria for success in solving the problem and any constraints that accompany it. For instance, a design problem might be, "Without taking longer than five minutes and without purchasing new materials, increase the speed of a marble as it travels down this ramp." You can define this design problem more clearly by adding specific criteria for success, such as by specifying how much faster the marble must move; should it move as quickly as possible or simply faster than it had traveled previously?

desire

A **desire** is a strong want.

Examples: Engineers often develop technology tools to respond to human desires. For instance, artificial selection technology allows humans to influence a new baby's genes and produce the traits they desire in a child.

feasible Something that is **feasible** is possible to do fairly easily.

Examples: When you don't have the time, money, or resources to carry out your solution, it is probably not feasible (even if it fits all other criteria). If you want to reduce toxic emissions from cars, for instance, it is not feasible to ban driving outright. If all people had useful alternatives to cars—such as access to high-quality public transportation or bicycle lanes on major roadways—this solution might be more feasible.

principle A **principle** is a rule or idea about how something is supposed to work.

Examples: The practice of science is governed by many different principles. For instance, the principle of entropy says that a glass of chilled lemonade will gradually become warm as the liquid adjusts to room temperature. The Bernoulli principle says that the pressure of a fluid (liquid or gas) decreases as its speed increases. You can use scientific principles to help you solve engineering design problems.

problem A **problem** is a situation that is difficult to fix. A problem can also be a question that is difficult to answer.

Examples: Engineers use science knowledge to solve real-world problems, such as the problem of producing energy that does not involve fossil fuels, a type of nonrenewable resource. Before you try to fix a problem, always make sure you clearly understand what the problem is.

research question A **research question** is a focused issue or topic that forms the basis for an investigation.

Example: If you want to investigate how much water a plant needs to grow best, your research question might be, "Does a tomato plant grow tallest when it receives a quarter of a liter of water per day, half a liter of water per day, or a liter of water per day?"

specific Something that is **specific** has a clear and exact definition.

Examples: Be specific when you identify constraints and criteria for a design problem. When defining a constraint about cost, for instance, a statement such as "Design materials cannot cost more than twenty dollars" is much more specific than a statement like, "It shouldn't cost too much money."

Stability and Change (S/C)

condition The **condition** of something is the state that it is in.

Examples: If you want to thoroughly test an engineering solution, see how well it performs in a range of different conditions. If you are designing solar panels to put on your roof, for instance, you should first test how well the panels respond to different weather conditions. You might observe that the panels work well in calm conditions but are not very durable in wind or a thunderstorm.

episode An **episode** is one occurrence in a sequence of events.

Example: Tell the story of a specific episode in scientific history to support your claim or theory.

event An **event** is something that happens.

Examples: A variety of natural events occur on Earth. Weather forecasting technology gives humans time to prepare for dangerous events that happen quickly, such as hurricanes, tornadoes, and floods.

historical Something that is **historical** relates to things that happened in the past.

Examples: Compare a current data set with a historical data set to find out how a population has changed over time. Use historical data as evidence to support your argument or claim.

rate The **rate** of an event is how fast it happens.

Examples: Earth's processes and events occur at different rates. An earthquake is an example of an event that can occur at a very quick rate. On the other hand, erosion occurs at a very slow rate.

stability If something has **stability**, it is steady and unlikely to change.

Examples: The roots of a plant have many functions, but one of these is to help the plant maintain stability as it grows larger and is buffeted by wind and rain. In a healthy, balanced ecosystem, various species meet each other's needs, but a newly introduced species can change this stability.

Structure and Function (S/F)

basic

Something that is **basic** is very simple.

Examples: If you have a basic understanding of what a cell is, you might know that all living things are made up of tiny units called cells, but you may not know the specific names for the different parts of cells. Basic skills in mathematics are addition, subtraction, multiplication, and division.

complex

Something that is **complex** is complicated or hard to understand because it has many different parts.

Examples: If an organism becomes more complex as it evolves, it has more and more connected parts that must work together in order for the organism to survive. The patterns in the way water moves through the atmosphere are complex, which means there are many factors involved in how they affect the weather.

composition

The **composition** of something is what it is made of or how it is put together.

Examples: According to scientific observations, the composition of ordinary matter in the universe is three-quarters hydrogen and one-quarter helium. The land composition of the planet Venus is similar to Earth's in that it has a rocky core and an iron mantle. However, the atmospheric composition of Venus is very different from Earth's; the atmosphere of Venus is mostly comprised of carbon dioxide and nitrogen.

function

The **function** of something is its purpose or what it does to be useful.

Examples: The different body parts of a plant or animal serve different functions. For instance, the function of a porcupine's quills is to protect the porcupine from predators. The function of a beaver's long, sharp teeth is to allow the beaver to chew down trees and branches to build its home.

individual

Something that is **individual** is one thing on its own.

Examples: Although all of the animals in a species have the same general characteristics, each individual animal in the species has slight variations in its traits. For instance, all saguaro cactuses have spiky thorns, but one individual saguaro might have slightly longer thorns than another. All cheetahs have spots, but each individual cheetah has its own unique pattern.

mechanism

A **mechanism** is a part of a machine. A **mechanism** is also one part of a system.

Examples: Producing sweat is a mechanism your body uses to cool you down. In a human cell, the lysosome is the digestive mechanism—it breaks up molecules using digestive enzymes. The ribosomes contain the mechanism for protein synthesis, which is the process of translating RNA into protein.

need

A **need** is something a living thing cannot survive without.

Examples: Basic human needs include food, water, and shelter. Basic plant needs include water, sunlight, and nutrients from the soil.

structure

The **structure** of something is how it is made, set up, or put together.

Examples: Humans often build structures that lessen the impact of heat energy from the sun. Human-made structures that reduce the warming effect of the sun include umbrellas and tents.

Scale, Proportion, and Quantity (SPQ)

amount

An **amount** of something is how much of it there is.

Examples: You can measure a specific amount of water using a graduated cylinder. Depending on the time of year, each day has a different amount of daylight. Your circulatory system keeps the right amount of blood moving to your heart and other organs.

distance

The **distance** between two things is how far apart they are.

Examples: The brightness of a star is determined by its distance from Earth. You can use information technologies like computers and cell phones to communicate over a long distance.

magnitude	The **magnitude** of something is how big or extensive it is.
	Examples: Use orders of magnitude to scale a model up to life-size. The magnitude of human impact on the global climate is larger than ever before.
measurement	If you take a **measurement** of something, you describe its size using units.
	Examples: A graduated cylinder allows you to take measurements of a liquid's volume using units such as milliliters or liters. A ruler or tape measure allows you to take measurements of length using units such as centimeters or meters. A balance allows you to take measurements of mass using units such as grams and kilograms.
multiple	There are **multiple** items in a group when there are two or more items.
	Examples: You can find similarities in the body parts of multiple species and use these similarities to find patterns in the way they develop. Find evidence from multiple sources to make sure your facts match up with scientific principles and theories.
proportion	A **proportion** relates part of something to the whole thing.
	Example: Use mathematics to communicate the different proportions of masses of atoms in a chemical reaction.
quantity	A **quantity** of something is a specific amount of it.
	Examples: Different units of measurement describe different quantities. You might use milliliters to measure a very small quantity of liquid, but kiloliters to describe a very large quantity of liquid.
scale	The **scale** of something is the size of it.
	Examples: You can use different scales to study phenomena that are too large or too small to see, such as space and energy phenomena. For instance, you might study the solar system at a much smaller scale than the scale at which it actually exists.
size	**Size** is how big or small something is.
	Examples: The size of an atom is very small. The size of the universe is very large.
time	**Time** is the passing of moments in minutes, hours, days, and years.
	Examples: Earth has changed very much over a long period of time. Living things also change as time passes, often in response to the way the environment has changed.
total	A **total** is a complete group of something put together. Something happens in **total** when it happens completely.
	Examples: In a chemical reaction, the total number of each type of atom is conserved. Because the total number of atoms does not change, mass does not change and mass is conserved.
various	There are **various** things when there are many different kinds.
	Examples: Life on Earth would be very different for humans without technology because we use it in various ways. The various technologies humans depend on include communication tools (such as the telephone) and transportation tools (such as the automobile).

Systems and System Models (SYS)

activity	An **activity** is something you do for some amount of time. *Activity* can also mean something that is happening.
	Examples: An eruption is one type of volcanic activity. Other types of volcanic activity include bursts of gas or ash. Burning fossil fuels, making cement, and growing crops are examples of human activities.

boundary   A **boundary** is the line where one thing ends and something else begins.

Examples: The boundary between North America and South America on a map is between Panama and Colombia. In a cell, the cell membrane is a boundary that controls what comes into the cell and what leaves.

component   A **component** of something is a part or piece of it.

Examples: Photosynthesis is an important component of the carbon cycle, which describes the way carbon is transferred between different Earth systems. In physics, you can figure out a change in energy of one component of a system if you know the changes in energy in all of the other components.

input   An **input** is something that is put into and worked on by a process or system.

Examples: Plants and animals have specific parts that allow them to respond to inputs from the outside world. For instance, a fox's ears are large and pointed, which allow it to capture sound inputs and process them in its brain.

output   **Output** is something that a person, process, or system produces.

Examples: You can design and build a device that takes one form of energy and produces an energy output of a different form. In a wind turbine, for instance, the input of motion energy can produce an output of electrical energy.

phenomenon   A **phenomenon** is an event that is unique, interesting, and sometimes hard to explain.

Examples: A scientist might use a combination of observation and measurement to explain a natural phenomenon such as an earthquake or a tsunami. You may need to use a small-scale model to show what is happening in a large-scale space phenomenon, such as a black hole.

process   A **process** is a series of changes that happen in nature. A **process** is also a series of steps you take to reach a certain goal.

Examples: You can use what you know about geoscience processes—such as subduction zone activity and deposition of rock—to explain why energy and mineral resources are not distributed evenly on Earth. If you notice you are making a lot of errors when you are carrying out an experiment, adjust your process to make it more precise.

system   A **system** is a set of connected parts or people that work together to do something.

Examples: When an energy system is not controlled, it tends to become more stable as the energy is distributed more equally. This is why a hot cup of soup cools down at room temperature; the uncontrolled system of energy is stabilizing.

Cognitive Verbs

Add To (ADD)

accumulate	If you **accumulate** something, you slowly gather more and more of it.
	Examples: Accumulate raindrops in a graduated cylinder to measure the amount of rainfall during a storm. Take many different measurements of rainfall and average them together to accumulate data on precipitation in a particular area.
assemble	If you **assemble** something, you put its pieces together to make it complete.
	Examples: Assemble toothpicks and marshmallows to create models of different types of molecules. Assemble reasons and evidence for a claim to form an argument.
combine	If you **combine** things, you put them together.
	Examples: If you combine baking soda and vinegar, they bubble and form carbon dioxide. When writing a report on weather patterns in different times and areas, combine information from multiple reliable sources (such as books, encyclopedias, and scientific websites).
enhance	If you **enhance** something, you improve it or make it better.
	Examples: Enhance your solution to a physics problem by using a computer or a calculator to check your work. Enhance your understanding of the world by learning about scientific theories (such as the germ theory of disease or Darwin's theory of evolution).
expand	If you **expand** something, you make it larger.
	Example: Expand your knowledge of chemistry by learning to use information on the periodic table to identify properties of elements.
extend	If you **extend** something, you make it longer.
	Example: To weaken the attraction of two magnets, extend the distance between them.
improve	If you **improve** something, you make it better.
	Example: After conducting an experiment, make adjustments to improve your process.
include	If you **include** something, you make it part of a larger whole.
	Examples: Include different types of data (such as qualitative and quantitative) to support a scientific argument. When you are working on a group project, include your group members by asking for their input.
incorporate	If you **incorporate** something, you add it or include it.
	Example: When you test a design for the first time, take notes on how it works and incorporate changes to make it better.

integrate   If you **integrate** something, you combine it with other things to form a complete whole.

Example: When writing a report about endangered species, integrate information from many different sources (such as notes from class, observations from videos, and information from books, websites, or articles).

introduce   If you **introduce** something, you present it for the first time.

Examples: If you introduce a new species into a habitat, you might disrupt the balance of the ecosystem. You can introduce a speech about Marie Curie, who famously discovered radium, by giving her date of birth or pointing out an interesting fact about radium (such as its use in treating cancer patients).

link   If you **link** things together, you connect them.

Examples: Link the feeding connections of different living things using a food web, explaining that there are fewer organisms at the top of the chain because the amount of energy available from a food item gets smaller as it is passed up the chain. Link your opinions to reasons and evidence to make them stronger and more scientifically sound.

mix   If you **mix** things, you put them together to make a material or group.

Examples: When you mix two substances together, they may or may not make a new substance. If you mix two substances together and they make a new substance, a chemical reaction took place. Mix zinc with hydrogen chloride to produce heat and hydrogen gas.

Arrange (ARR)

arrange   If you **arrange** items, you place each one in a particular place, order, or location.

Example: When you arrange the three time periods in the Mesozoic Era from oldest to most recent, they appear in this order: Triassic, Jurassic, Cretaceous.

classify   If you **classify** things, you organize them into groups based on their traits.

Examples: Make observations of a substance and use them to classify it as a gas, liquid, or solid. Classify an animal as an amphibian if it has a backbone and uses both gills and lungs at different points in its life cycle. Classify an animal as an insect if it has a segmented body with six jointed legs but does not have a backbone.

distribute   If you **distribute** something, you give out portions or shares of it.

Examples: If you could distribute natural resources as equally as possible, you would give all humans a more equal chance to survive. When testing how quickly ice melts at different water temperatures, you should distribute the same amount of ice into each sample of water to get accurate results.

organize   If you **organize** things, you arrange them in a certain order or plan them in a certain way.

Examples: Use analyses of the fossil record to organize Earth's history into different geologic time periods. After you collect data, organize it into a table or graph to make it easier to analyze.

sort   If you **sort** items, you put them into different groups based on what they are like.

Examples: Sort pictures of creatures into one of five basic animal groups—amphibians, birds, insects, mammals, or reptiles—by looking at traits such as gills, fur, feathers, scales, backbones, and phases of growth. Sort rocks into igneous, metamorphic, and sedimentary categories based on how they were formed.

Compare/Contrast (C/C)

compare   If you **compare** things, you identify ways that they are the same or different.

Examples: You can compare the different kinds of living things in different habitats to show how plants and animals function differently depending on where they live. For instance, you might compare the types of plants found in the desert to the types of plants found in the rainforest, pointing out the different structures each plant uses to gather the right amount of water, avoid predators, and reproduce.

differentiate   If you **differentiate** between two things, you show how they are not alike.

Examples: Differentiate between evidence that shows a cause and evidence that shows a correlation when you make claims about the relationship between two variables. Differentiate a push from a pull by comparing the effects of pushing a ball and pulling a toy car on a string.

distinguish   If you **distinguish** something, you recognize it for a specific reason.

Examples: When you think about how certain behaviors help a species survive, distinguish group behaviors (such as herding, migrating, and swarming) from individual behaviors. Distinguish between living and nonliving things when explaining that all living things are made up of cells.

relate   If you **relate** things, you find connections between them.

Examples: Relate the characteristics of certain plants or animals (such as poisonous berries or fish scales) to their roles in protecting the plant or animal from harm. When you are trying to design an object to protect humans, you can relate your design to a specific plant or animal part to help come up with an idea. For instance, you might relate the protection you get from a barbed wire fence to the protection a plant gets from the thorns on its branches.

vary   If you **vary** something, you make it more diverse.

Examples: Vary the types of animals you represent in a diorama of biomes to show that different types of animals live in different types of habitats. When creating models to describe different atomic structures, you can vary the complexity of the molecules you create by making some simple and others more intricate.

Collaborate (COLL)

collaborate   If you **collaborate**, you work together with other people.

Examples: Collaborate with classmates to plan and conduct investigations and collect data. You can use data when collaborating to answer a question or solve a problem.

contribute   If you **contribute**, you give or add something to a situation.

Examples: When you contribute to changes in the natural environment, you also contribute to changes in the organisms that live there. For instance, if you remove trees from a rainforest area, you might contribute to the decline or extinction of species that depended on the trees to survive. Contribute to a scientific discussion by saying what you think and expressing your ideas.

depend   If you **depend** on something, you need it to help you accomplish a task. If you **depend** on someone, you need that person to give you help or support.

Examples: You depend on your safety goggles to protect your eyes during a chemistry lab. When a teacher requires that your lab report be typed, you depend on technology to help you complete the work. If your report is a group project, you must depend on the classmates in your lab group to put in an equal level of effort.

engage   If you **engage** in something, you participate in it. If you **engage** someone, you keep him or her interested in something.

Examples: Engage in global movements related to science, technology, society, and the environment by reading scientific journals and newspaper articles. Engage other students in creating environmental solutions by screening a climate change documentary in your school's auditorium or by spearheading a schoolwide recycling initiative.

interact   If you **interact** with something, your actions affect each other.

Examples: Interact with the Earth in a positive way by doing your part to reduce your carbon footprint. If you are not mindful of the way you interact with the Earth (for instance, if you throw something away that you could recycle instead), your actions contribute to some of the adverse effects of climate change (such as drought, food shortage, and rising sea levels).

involve   If you **involve** someone, you bring that person into an activity or situation.

Example: When testing a solution to a problem, involve others to help you observe how well your solution works in a range of possible conditions.

lead
If you **lead** someone, you set an example for that person to follow.

Examples: When presented with a difficult engineering problem, lead a team of classmates to help develop a solution. Lead your group members through an iterative process by working with them to test the most promising solutions and change the design based on the results.

manage
If you **manage** something, you are in charge of making sure it works.

Examples: When you make a plan to manage humans' use of natural resources, you must consider the cost of resource mining, waste management, per-capita consumption, and the potential for new technologies. Manage your time during a big assignment by planning out and budgeting time for each step of the project.

provide
If you **provide** something, you give or offer it.

Examples: Provide data about overpopulation, habitat demolition, pollution, invasive species, and climate change to support the claim that human activity has negative consequences for biodiversity. When explaining how a population adapts through natural selection, provide data about ranges of seasonal temperature, acidity, light, or evolution of other living things to show how these factors gradually cause changes in gene frequency.

rely
If you **rely** on something, you count on it to help you when you need it.

Examples: When making decisions about the natural and material world, rely on social and cultural information in addition to scientific information. You can rely on science to determine the possibilities of what *can* happen, but you should also rely on ethics, social responsibility, and cultural awareness to help you figure out what *should* happen.

share
If you **share** information, you let others know about it.

Examples: When describing how weather patterns differ from winter to spring, you might share observations from the months of January, March, and May. Share new research and constructive criticism with your classmates to help them develop their ideas.

suggest
If you **suggest** something, you recommend it or present it for people to think about.

Examples: Use data about individual relationships in a natural system to suggest bigger cause-and-effect relationships in the larger system. When trying to solve a design problem, you can use tests to figure out difficulties with your design solution, and then suggest elements of the solution that could be improved.

Create (CRE)

build
If you **build** something, you join separate items or concepts together to create something new.

Examples: When you read and learn about a topic, you build knowledge about it. Build background knowledge about energy conversion by examining designs for wind turbines, solar ovens, generators, or Rube Goldberg devices. When designing a solution to the problem of fossil fuel reduction, you might decide to build a device that converts one form of energy into another.

construct
If you **construct** something, you build it by putting separate parts together.

Examples: Construct an explanation about how certain plants and animals depend on other animals in order to reproduce (such as plants that depend on animals to pollinate them). To construct a body of evidence for your explanation, you can use observations of plants depending on animals (such as a carpenter bee moving a tulip's pollen from one part of the tulip to another to help fertilize it).

create
If you **create** something, you make it.

Examples: Create a new substance by combining two substances that produce a chemical reaction. For instance, combine sodium and chlorine to create table salt, or combine oxygen and iron to create rust.

develop
If you **develop** something, you work on it over a period of time, during which it grows or changes.

Examples: Develop a model that shows how Earth's systems interact with each other. For instance, you might draw a series of diagrams that represent the ocean's effect on the shape of a landform to show how the geosphere and hydrosphere interact. Develop a solution to an engineering problem by repeatedly testing and revising it.

engineer   If you **engineer** something, you design and build it.

Examples: Use a paper cup and string to engineer a device that helps you communicate over a distance. Engineer a solution to a problem by brainstorming solutions and then testing them.

formulate   If you **formulate** an idea, you carefully create it.

Examples: Formulate an answer to the question, What happens when objects vibrate? by plucking a stretched string and observing that the vibration makes a sound. By learning about what happens at the atomic and molecular scales, you can formulate conclusions about the properties of matter.

generate   If you **generate** something, you bring it into being or existence.

Examples: Using your background knowledge of natural disasters (such as floods, earthquakes, tsunamis, and volcanic eruptions), you can generate ideas for lessening their effects on humans. For instance, you might generate designs for earthquake- and flood-resistant buildings or for a structure that deflects tsunami waves.

produce   If you **produce** something, you make it.

Example: Produce data by conducting an experiment and recording the results.

record   If you **record** something, you create a written, audio, or video version of it that can be looked at or listened to in the future.

Examples: Record day-to-day observations of the weather and use them to describe patterns in the weather over time. For instance, if you record the weather each day for six months and find instances of rain on fifteen days in March and nineteen days in April but only on six and four days in July and August respectively, you might conclude that spring is a rainier season than summer.

Decide (DEC)

accept   If you **accept** something, you decide to take it or agree to it.

Examples: You should only accept a scientific theory once it has been supported with a large body of evidence by experts in the scientific community. Be slow to accept claims that do not have sound evidence and reasoning to back them up.

decide   When you **decide** something, you think about several choices and then choose one of them.

Examples: When planning an investigation, decide how much data you will need to collect in order to produce reliable measurements and draw reasonable conclusions. Decide which type of data—qualitative or quantitative—best suits your research question.

intend   If you **intend** to do something, you have made the decision to do it.

Examples: If you intend to change the speed of an object, you might design a solution that uses a ramp to speed up or slow down a ball. When you test the solution, collect data that shows whether it works as you intended.

prescribe   If you **prescribe** something, you suggest that someone use it to fix a problem.

Examples: You can prescribe recommendations for policymakers and citizens based on scientific knowledge. For instance, you might prescribe a plan of action to conservationists for preserving biodiversity in an area. Keep in mind that people do not necessarily do what scientists prescribe.

Define (DEF)

define   If you **define** something, you explain what it means very clearly and specifically.

Examples: When you define a design problem, think carefully about what the problem is supposed to address and put your thoughts into words. Define your standards for success before you begin in order to make your design as effective as you can.

delimit   If you **delimit** something, you determine its boundaries or limitations.

Examples: Delimit the goals of a design problem as precisely as possible to set yourself up for success. Clearly delimit the line between success and failure by writing down specific criteria before you begin the design process.

determine   If you **determine** something, you discover it or decide on it.

Examples: Determine the type of reaction that occurred by observing properties of the substances involved before and after the reaction. For instance, you might heat a bar of chocolate and determine that although it has melted into a liquid, its properties show that it is still chocolate. Therefore, you can determine that the chocolate has not undergone a chemical reaction.

identify   If you **identify** something, you say what it is.

Examples: You can identify a substance by observing its properties. Identify metals, minerals, and liquids using properties such as color, hardness, reflectivity, electrical conductivity, thermal conductivity, response to magnetic forces, and solubility.

locate   If you **locate** something, you find it or figure out where it is.

Example: Use a map to locate different landforms and bodies of water on Earth.

Evaluate (EVAL)

assess   If you **assess** something, you estimate its value or quantity.

Examples: When reading a scientific text, assess how well the data support any claims the author is making. Assess the effectiveness of a design solution by coming up with clear criteria for success and deciding whether the solution meets your criteria.

critique   If you **critique** something, you look at it carefully to find things that could be improved.

Examples: After creating a plan for an investigation, critique elements of the procedure that seem incomplete, faulty, or overly difficult to carry out. Critique your own theories and conclusions to make them stronger.

evaluate   If you **evaluate** something, you decide if it is good or bad or right or wrong.

Examples: Evaluate a design solution for water purification by considering things like cost, time, environmental sustainability, social justice, and so on. Evaluate a scientific argument by carefully thinking about whether the claim seems reasonable and well-supported with evidence.

interpret   If you **interpret** something, you figure out what you think it means.

Examples: Interpret data from an investigation and draw conclusions about what you found. You can sometimes interpret data more easily if you organize them in a graph, chart, or table.

prioritize   If you **prioritize** something, you think of it as more important than other things.

Examples: Prioritize certain design criteria over other design criteria when thinking about a design solution. For instance, if a design is too heavy to function properly but lightweight materials are more expensive, you might prioritize your need for lightweight materials over your desire to save money.

Execute (EXEC)

achieve   If you **achieve** something, you succeed at it.

Examples: Achieve a change in motion by exerting a net force on an object that does not equal zero. When coming up with a solution to an engineering problem, achieve the best possible design through testing and revising a proposal.

begin   If you **begin** something, you start it.

Examples: Begin every scientific experiment or investigation with a research question. If you want to investigate the forces involved in falling, you might begin by asking, If dropped from the same distance, will a feather hit the ground before, after, or at the same time as a hammer?

calculate   If you **calculate** something, you think very carefully about all of its details and create a plan to make it happen. If you **calculate** something in math, you figure out a solution using numbers and mathematical operations.

Examples: Calculate the likelihood that a trait will be inherited using a Punnett square. In physics, you can calculate the change in energy of one component in a system based on the change in energy of all other components in the system.

carry out   If you **carry out** something, you continue to work on it until it is finished.

Example: Carry out an investigation to find out whether sound can cause materials to vibrate by holding a piece of paper near a speaker playing music.

conduct   If you **conduct** something, you plan and do it.

Examples: You can conduct scientific investigations to find answers to your questions or help fill in gaps in your science knowledge. For instance, you might conduct an investigation to figure out what happens when different types of objects (such as a transparent material like plastic, a translucent material like wax paper, an opaque material like cardboard, or a reflective material like a mirror) are placed in the way of a beam of light.

continue   If you **continue**, you keep going.

Examples: Continue to develop your understanding of science concepts as you learn new information. You can also continue to learn new theories, data, and information about science for the rest of your life.

coordinate   If you **coordinate** something, you organize it.

Example: Coordinate new patterns in scientific evidence with current conversations in scientific theory to see how they fit together.

implement   If you **implement** something, you carry it out or put it into action.

Example: Create a plan for your experiment and implement it carefully to avoid errors.

maintain   If you **maintain** something, you keep it the same.

Example: Maintain biodiversity in an ecosystem by learning and avoiding human activities that harm, destroy, or pollute animals' habitats.

protect   If you **protect** something, you keep it safe and unharmed.

Examples: Protect Earth's resources and natural environment by changing the way you interact with agriculture and industry. Protect humans in new ways by studying how other animals protect themselves; for instance, you might create a better bike helmet by studying turtle shells, acorn shells, or armadillo scales.

undertake   If you **undertake** something, you start doing it.

Examples: Make a careful plan before you undertake a large project. Undertake an engineering project by constructing, testing, and modifying a device that serves a certain purpose, such as releasing or absorbing energy.

Explain (EXP)

account   If you **account** for something, you recognize it or make sense of it.

Examples: When you evaluate the effectiveness of a design solution, account for a variety of functional issues (such as cost, safety, and dependability). Account for the greater social or environmental impacts of your decision when you choose where to purchase your food or clothing.

answer   If you **answer** someone or something, you respond with information you think is correct or true.

Examples: Answer the question, Why is the sun brighter than all other stars? by explaining that the brightness of a star depends on its distance from Earth, and the sun appears brightest because it is closer to Earth than any other star. Answer design questions by generating and testing different solutions until you find one that works.

clarify   If you **clarify** something, you explain it in a way that makes it easier to understand.

Examples: To make a complicated set of data easier to understand, clarify it using a visual graph, chart, or image. Clarify a complex scientific relationship (such as the relationship between chromosomes and inheritance of traits) using a diagram, model, or step-by-step explanation.

communicate   When you **communicate**, you share information with others, usually through speaking or writing.

Examples: Communicate your views about global climate change by presenting evidence of its impacts. Communicate information and evidence that support your explanation of the ways human activities influence changes in weather and climate.

convey   If you **convey** something, you communicate it.

Example: Convey your design solution to an engineering problem through sketches, drawings, physical models, or computer simulations.

describe   If you **describe** something, you explain what it is like.

Example: Describe movements of the sun, moon, and stars in the night sky. Take measurements of rain, snow, and temperature to describe the weather on a given day.

explain   If you **explain** something, you give information about it or reasons for it that make it easier to understand.

Examples: Use science to explain why something happens in nature. Explain the way you did an investigation by talking about your methods. Explain why scientific research is important by describing how it affects all humans.

guide   If you **guide** someone, you help that person understand steps to being successful.

Examples: Guide someone through your design or investigation process by talking about each step in detail. Learn the principles of academic honesty, open-mindedness, patience, and skepticism and use them to guide your own science and engineering practices.

indicate   If you **indicate** something, you point it out.

Examples: Indicate relationships between weather conditions and seasons by displaying data such as average temperature, precipitation, and wind direction in a bar graph or pictograph. Study the location of certain fossil types, which can indicate the order in which rock layers were formed.

present   If you **present** something, you show or give it to someone.

Examples: Present the claim that gravitational interactions depend on the masses of interacting objects by saying it to someone or by writing it down. Present evidence such as a chart showing a relationship between mass, strength of interactions, distances from the sun, and orbital periods.

report   If you **report** something, you tell someone about it.

Example: After conducting an investigation, report your findings in an ethical way by being honest about what your data show.

respond   If you **respond** to something, you react to it.

Example: Be prepared to respond to severe weather by paying attention to weather forecasting, patterns, and variations.

synthesize   If you **synthesize** information, you combine it in a logical way.

Examples: You can synthesize information from a variety of sources to fully explain a scientific theory or phenomenon. In an essay on artificial selection, for instance, you might synthesize information from sources such as genetics textbooks, medical reports on genetic modification, journal articles on gene therapy, and credible websites about animal husbandry.

Hypothesize (HYP)

anticipate   If you **anticipate** something, you predict that something will happen and prepare for it.

Example: When engineering a new solution to a design problem, anticipate the unintended consequences of your solution on the user, as well as on society and the environment.

consider   If you **consider** something, you think carefully about it.

Examples: Before beginning to design a solution to an engineering problem, consider all criteria you may want the solution to meet (such as function, sustainability, aesthetics, and so on). Additionally, consider any constraints on time, cost, or resources. Only consider a design solution successful if it meets these pre-established criteria for success.

predict   If you **predict** something, you say that you think it will happen.

Examples: You can observe or measure the way certain objects move to predict how they will move again in the future. When watching someone move back and forth on a swing, you might predict that after the person moves backward on the swing, he or she will move forward again. When watching two children in a see-saw, you might predict that whenever one child moves down, the other child will move up.

test   If you **test** something, you try it out to see how well it works.

Examples: Test an engineering solution to figure out which elements of the design still need improvement. After you test your design, make any necessary changes and then test it again.

Infer (INF)

assume   If you **assume** something, you guess that it is probably true based on what you already know (even though you do not know for certain).

Examples: When thinking about the physical laws of the universe, you can assume that they are unchanging. For instance, assume that Newton's laws of motion function today exactly as they always have and always will. Do not assume that your theory is correct before confirming it with research, experiments, and observations.

infer   If you **infer** something, you decide it is true after gathering and considering information about it.

Examples: You can use fossil data to infer what the environment was like long ago. If Arctic fossils appear to be of tropical plants, you might infer that the Arctic climate was once very warm. When you identify evidence of sea creatures in fossils found on dry land, you might infer that the environment there was once covered in water.

Measure (MEAS)

control   When you **control** for something, you work around a factor that could confuse your results.

Examples: In an experiment, control for the effect of any variable you are not testing. When you control for a variable you do not want to test, it helps you be sure that the cause-and-effect relationships in your findings are accurate. When investigating how much water a seed needs to grow, for instance, you might give two seeds different amounts of water but control for other variables by giving each seed the same amount of soil, sunlight, and so on.

measure   If you **measure** something, you describe its size using units.

Example: A graduated cylinder allows you to measure a liquid's volume using units such as milliliters or liters. A ruler or tape measure allows you to measure length using units such as centimeters or meters. A balance allows you to measure mass using units such as grams and kilograms.

quantify   If you **quantify** something, you say how much of it there is.

Examples: When you quantify scientific data, it can help you be more precise. Quantify your observations about the decrease in daylight from summer to winter by recording the exact number of minutes of daylight over several days in each season and then calculating and comparing averages for each.

Prove/Argue (P/A)

allow
If you **allow** something, you let it happen.

Example: Allow new research from the scientific community to change the way you think about scientific concepts and theories.

argue
If you **argue** for or against something, you try to convince someone who disagrees with you that it is right or wrong using reasons and evidence.

Examples: When you argue for or against a claim, provide evidence to support your perspective. If you argue that plants and animals alter their environments to suit their needs, you might provide examples of organisms changing the environment—such as a tree breaking concrete with its roots or a prairie dog burrowing underground—to support your claim.

challenge
If you **challenge** something, you question or dispute it.

Examples: Challenge a scientific argument by presenting evidence that contradicts the evidence already presented. For instance, you might challenge the claim that human activity does not influence climate change by showing evidence of the link between fossil fuel consumption and the production of greenhouse gases.

claim
If you **claim** something, you say it is true.

Examples: Using mathematical reasoning as evidence, you can claim that mass is conserved during a chemical reaction. In life science, you might claim that matter and energy are conserved during their cycle and flow through ecosystems.

confirm
If you **confirm** something, you make sure it is true.

Examples: Confirm scientific data by replicating the experiments that yielded them. Confirm the results of a scientific investigation by finding other investigations that produced the same results.

defend
If you **defend** something, you say why you think it is true.

Examples: Defend scientific claims with various types of evidence to make your argument stronger. For instance, you might use a combination of mathematical representations and computer simulations to defend the claim that the wavelength and frequency of waves are related to each other by the speed of the wave.

propose
If you **propose** something, you bring it up as a possible idea.

Examples: Propose design solutions to your classmates; then ask them to tell you what they think about your reasoning. Whenever you propose a scientific explanation or solution, use data and evidence to back up your thinking. You can also propose your ideas using a model to help explain what you mean.

refute
If you **refute** something, you give evidence that proves why it is wrong.

Examples: Refute the claim that animal behaviors cannot affect plant reproduction by pointing out examples of animal behaviors that do affect plant reproduction, such as pollination by bees. You can also refute a claim by pointing out flaws in its reasoning or problems with its evidence.

specify
If you **specify** something, you describe or explain it clearly and in detail.

Examples: Specify a cause-and-effect relationship between an electrically charged balloon and human hair by showing or telling what happens when the two objects get closer together. When you design an experiment, specify which variable you want to test and which variables you need to control.

substantiate
If you **substantiate** something, you give evidence that supports it.

Examples: Substantiate a scientific explanation by providing facts, evidence, and multiple studies that show the same supportive findings. When the scientific community substantiates an explanation of some part of the natural world with a large body of evidence, the explanation becomes a scientific theory.

support
If you **support** something, you help it succeed or explain why it is right.

Examples: Support an argument with evidence, data, or a model. To support the claim that landscapes change over time, you might explain patterns in rock formations and show how various fossils are embedded in specific layers.

validate   If you **validate** something, you show how it is fair, true, or reasonable.

Examples: Validate a hypothesis by carrying out an experiment and finding results that support it. Validate a scientific theory by locating evidence to support it.

verify   If you **verify** something, you make sure it is true.

Examples: When someone presents scientific findings to defend an argument, verify their data as much as possible. When you use mathematics to solve a chemistry problem, use a calculator to verify your result.

Problem Solve (PS)

address   If you **address** something, you deal with it or talk about it.

Examples: Use scientific data to address questions about the natural world. For instance, address questions about the distribution of fresh water on Earth by graphing percentages of fresh water in various oceans, lakes, rivers, glaciers, groundwater, and polar ice caps.

limit   If you **limit** something, you do not let it grow beyond a specific amount.

Examples: Limit the negative effects humans have on the environment. For instance, you can limit your future impact on a personal level by reducing, reusing, and recycling. Humans can also limit future impact on a larger scale through geoengineering the atmosphere or ocean to alter global temperatures.

mitigate   If you **mitigate** a problem, you make it less hurtful or severe.

Examples: You can mitigate the effects of natural hazards by using technology to forecast, monitor, or protect against their occurrence. Mitigate the effects of hurricanes or forest fires by using global satellite systems to spot and track them. Mitigate the effects of tornadoes and droughts by building basements and reservoirs, respectively.

prevent   If you **prevent** something, you stop it from happening later.

Examples: Prevent water and wind from changing the shape of the land by building dikes and windbreaks, respectively. Prevent or minimize landslides by planting shrubs, grasses, and trees on slopes.

resolve   If you **resolve** a problem, contradiction, or issue, you find a solution for it.

Examples: Resolve the issues caused by climate change in various contexts. Resolve issues of unclean energy and resource mismanagement from an engineering perspective, but resolve the issue of human overconsumption by supporting a cultural shift.

solve   If you **solve** a problem, you find an answer or a solution for it.

Examples: You can use magnets to solve engineering problems. For instance, you might solve the problem of keeping a door shut by constructing a magnetic latch.

Pull Apart (PULL)

analyze   If you **analyze** something, you look closely at each of its parts and see if they fit together in a way that makes sense.

Examples: You can analyze maps to describe patterns in the formation of the Earth's landforms. After you analyze a topographic map, for instance, you might determine that volcanoes and mountain ranges often form along the edges of tectonic plates or that earthquakes occur at tectonic boundaries.

disassemble   If you **disassemble** something, you take it apart.

Example: To show that a variety of objects can be created from the same set of pieces, disassemble a set of building blocks and put them back together to make something new.

examine	If you **examine** something, you look at it closely.
	Examples: Examine models of the solar system to understand how eclipses, tides, and seasons happen in cycles. Examine geoscience data to learn about processes and events in Earth's history.
investigate	If you **investigate** something, you study or examine it closely.
	Examples: Investigate a scientific question to find an answer. Investigate the characteristics of a plant to figure out whether it is a tree, shrub, grass, or flower. Investigate the characteristics of a material to classify it as wood, rock, glass, metal, plastic, or something else.

Redo (REDO)

reinterpret	If you **reinterpret** something, you think about it again in a different way.
	Examples: When you come upon new evidence that does not fit with your previous theories, reinterpret your ideas. Reinterpret existing scientific evidence when contradictory evidence is presented.
repeat	If you **repeat** something, you do it again.
	Example: Repeat a scientific investigation to see if you get the same findings as the original investigator.
reverse	If you **reverse** something, you put it back the way it was before.
	Examples: You can reverse certain changes caused by heating or cooling, but not all changes. For instance, you can reverse the freezing of water by heating ice and causing it to melt. Once you have cooked an egg, however, you cannot reverse it back to its uncooked form.

See the Big Picture (SBP)

frame	When you **frame** something, you think about it in a specific way.
	Examples: Frame a theory or hypothesis based on your observations or research rather than on your emotions or intuitions. Frame a design problem in its social or cultural context.
maximize	If you **maximize** something, you make it as large or effective as you can.
	Example: Maximize the amount of thermal energy you absorb from the sun by wearing dark or black-colored clothing instead of light or white-colored clothing.
optimize	If you **optimize** something, you use it in the best possible way.
	Examples: Optimize a design solution by making trade-offs between competing criteria. For instance, you might optimize a solution by sacrificing one criterion (such as the way your design looks) in favor of a different, more important criterion (such as decreasing the amount of money your design would cost to build).
understand	If you **understand** something, you know what it means, how it occurs, why it happens, or why it is important.
	Examples: Understand a design problem before you try to create a solution. Understand why it is important to address negative human impacts on the environment.

Seek Information (SI)

acquire   If you **acquire** something, you gain it.

Examples: Acquire an understanding of the different ways the environment affects the traits of organisms. Before starting a chemistry lab, be sure to acquire all of the required safety materials.

ask   If you **ask** a question, you are trying to find an answer or get some information.

Examples: If someone makes a scientific claim, always ask to hear the supporting evidence. When learning about climate change, ask questions about factors that may have contributed to a rise in global temperatures (such as fossil fuel combustion and agricultural industry).

collect   If you **collect** things, you bring together many similar items.

Example: Collect data from weather maps, diagrams, and laboratory experiments to show how air masses interact and change the weather.

encounter   If you **encounter** something, you experience it.

Example: When you encounter questions about the natural world, take observations and measurements to help you answer the questions.

gather   If you **gather** things, you collect them together in a group.

Examples: Gather evidence to support your ideas about cause-and-effect relationships. Gather information about the structure and function of cells to explain how the different parts of a cell relate to one another.

observe   If you **observe** something, you see it happen or you look carefully to find out what will happen.

Examples: When space phenomena are too large or far away to observe with the naked eye, you can observe them using a telescope or a small-scale model of the solar system. Similarly, you can observe phenomena that are too small to see (such as cell functions) using a microscope or a large-scale model.

obtain   If you **obtain** something, you acquire it.

Examples: You can obtain information by asking questions or doing research. Obtain information about what different living things need to survive by looking up the organisms in a scientific encyclopedia.

receive   If you **receive** something, another person gives it to you.

Examples: You can receive information over a long distance by using a communication device such as a cell phone or computer. If you receive criticism about your design solution, use it to improve your plan instead of becoming defensive.

search   If you **search** for something, you look for it.

Examples: Search for cause-and-effect relationships to figure out how things happen in the natural world. Search for evidence that Earth events can occur quickly by reading about volcanic eruptions and earthquakes. Search for evidence that Earth events can occur slowly by reading about erosion.

study   If you **study** something, you work to learn about it.

Examples: You can study one specific part of something to help you learn about another part. For instance, you might study the brightness and light spectra of a star to figure out information about its makeup, movements, and distance from Earth.

trace   If you **trace** something, you follow it closely.

Examples: You can trace the food that almost any animal eats back to plants because most animals either eat plants directly or eat animals that eat plants. When you trace the path of a beam of light as it travels in a vacuum, you will trace a straight line. However, when you trace a beam of light through the surface of a body of water or a plate of glass, the light path bends.

track   If you **track** something, you watch or monitor what it is doing.

Examples: You can track energy as it is transferred through a natural system, such as when food energy moves through a food web. You can also track energy as it is transferred through a designed system, such as in a solar cooker.

Symbolize (SYM)

demonstrate   If you **demonstrate** something, you show how to do it.

Examples: You can demonstrate your understanding of a science concept by using a model. For instance, inflate a soccer ball or dissolve salt in water to demonstrate that matter is made of particles that are too small for humans to see.

display   If you **display** something, you put it in a place where people can easily see it.

Example: Display data in a spreadsheet, table, graph, or computer simulation to make them easy to interpret and understand.

graph   If you **graph** something, you create a picture that represents it using a grid or horizontal and vertical lines.

Example: Graph quantities of a substance before and after it has undergone a phase change (such as liquid water and frozen water or hardened chocolate and melted chocolate) to show that the total weight of the matter stays the same no matter what state it is in.

illustrate   If you **illustrate** something, you use images to explain it.

Examples: Illustrate the concepts of wavelength and amplitude using drawings or physical models made of wire. Use molecular-level diagrams to illustrate the idea that a chemical reaction releases or absorbs energy depending on the changes in total bond energy.

map   If you **map** something, you create a diagram or picture that shows what it looks like.

Examples: Map different types of landforms to show where they tend to occur on Earth. Map land and water patterns over time to show how tectonic plates have moved and collided.

model   If you **model** something, you create a structure or system that illustrates it.

Example: Model the relationship between a plant or animal's needs and the environment in which it lives by creating a diorama, diagram, or drawing showing different types of animals in different types of environments.

represent   If you **represent** something, you create a sign or symbol that reminds people of the original idea or object.

Example: Represent data about the position and motion of Earth and the sun in a graph that shows patterns in the way shadows change in length and direction throughout the day.

visualize   If you **visualize** something, you create a picture of it in your head.

Example: Visualize a diagram of a cell when thinking about how different parts of a cell function together as a whole.

Think Metacognitively (TM)

approach   If you **approach** something, you think about or encounter it for the first time or in a certain way.

Examples: Approach a situation that people want to change as an engineering problem. Approach an engineering problem in a way that allows for several possible solutions. Approach each solution as an idea that can still be improved.

design   If you **design** something, you create a plan for it.

Examples: Design a structure that causes a marble to speed up, slow down, or turn by sketching out a plan on a piece of paper. When you design something new, share it with classmates and ask them what you can do to make your design better.

learn   When you **learn** something, you know or understand it for the first time.

Examples: It is important to learn about science throughout your life, even if you are not planning to have a job that directly relates to science, engineering, or technology. Learn about science issues that affect everyone in society, such as treating disease, producing enough food and water, and generating clean energy.

monitor	If you **monitor** something, you check its progress over a period of time.
	Examples: You can monitor natural weather hazards to help inform people about what they can do to be safe. For instance, you might use a satellite system to monitor the trajectory of a hurricane or the spread of a forest fire.
plan	If you **plan** to do something, you decide in advance what you are going to do.
	Examples: Plan a scientific investigation by deciding how you will record data, what data you will record, and what you will identify as the dependent and independent variables. When you plan an engineering investigation, you also have to list criteria for testing your design solution.
prepare	If you **prepare** for something, you get ready for it.
	Examples: You can prepare for severe weather after you hear a forecast from a weather reporter. Prepare for a tornado by seeking shelter in a basement. Prepare for a power outage by gathering a flashlight, a battery-operated radio, and canned food.

Transform (TRANS)

accommodate	If you **accommodate** something, you make changes to suit its specific needs.
	Examples: Revise your claim to accommodate new evidence if it does not fit with your current theory. If a classmate points out a factor that is keeping your design solution from working, accommodate his or her suggestions to improve the design.
affect	If you **affect** something, you make parts of it change.
	Examples: Affect the strength of the force between two magnets by changing the distance between them. Affect the direction of the force between two magnets by changing their orientation. When you change a population's habitat in some way, you affect the organisms living there.
apply	If you **apply** something, you use it for a specific purpose.
	Examples: You can often apply your knowledge from other subjects (such as mathematics) when you think about scientific questions. For instance, you might apply the concept of probability when you explain why living things tend to inherit certain traits in certain environments.
cause	If you **cause** something, you make it happen.
	Examples: Cause an object to have a larger change in motion by exerting a larger force on it. For instance, you can cause a ball to hit the ground faster by throwing it down instead of allowing it to drop from your hand.
change	If you **change** something, you make it different.
	Examples: Change the speed of a marble by using a ramp. Change your mind about something after discovering evidence that does not fit with what you thought before. Change your environment to meet your needs by planting and growing food.
impact	If you **impact** something, you have an effect on it.
	Example: You will impact the environment negatively if you use up too much water (by taking it out of lakes, rivers, and streams, building levees, and so on), land (by building cities, growing crops, and so on), or natural resources (by extracting fresh water, minerals, fossil fuels, and so on).
influence	If you **influence** something, you change it to a certain degree.
	Examples: Influence the field of science research by repeating other people's experiments and doing your own investigations. Use science knowledge to influence the development of new technologies, and use technology to influence the way people gather and build new science knowledge.

manipulate
If you **manipulate** something, you control it or move it around for a specific purpose.

Examples: Manipulate the force of a magnetic interaction by holding the magnets farther apart or changing their direction. Manipulate a set of materials to create a model of a cell.

modify
If you **modify** something, you change it a little, usually to make it better.

Examples: Modify an engineering solution when you test it and find flaws in its design. Modify your argument when you realize that some of your evidence is flawed.

reduce
If you **reduce** something, you take away from it to make it smaller.

Examples: You can reduce some of the widespread human impact on Earth systems using creative engineering designs such as windmills or solar panels. Reduce your own individual impact by making personal choices that do not harm the environment.

refine
If you **refine** something, you make it clearer, better, or more precise.

Examples: Refine a scientific theory based on new data or evidence. Refine a design solution based on the results of your tests.

revise
If you **revise** something, you change it to make it better or more accurate.

Example: Revise your explanation of a scientific phenomenon or concept based on new observations or knowledge.

shape
If you **shape** something, you make it look a particular way.

Examples: Shape materials to suit your engineering needs. You can shape different materials using different processes. For instance, you can shape glass, but only after it is heated to an extremely high temperature. You can shape clay, but only if it is kept moist.

PART III

Domain-Specific Vocabulary Terms

Part III contains domain-specific terms from the science standards. In our analysis, we sought to include every important word that appeared in the grade-level NGSS. Additionally, we included science terms that appeared in an earlier compilation of vocabulary from standards documents (Marzano, 2004). Readers can use the appendix (page 179) to locate specific words in parts II and III. Please visit **marzanoresearch.com/reproducibles** for a complete alphabetical listing of the terms in parts II and III and the sources of each term. Unlike the words in part II, the words in part III are all domain-specific science terms, so they warranted an organizational scheme that situated each term firmly within a specific system of scientific ideas. Therefore, the terms in part III are organized into measurement topics rather than in interdisciplinary categories (as in part II). Measurement topics are categories of knowledge and skill found in a specific content area that extend across a range of grade levels. They are designed to highlight learning progressions from one grade level to the next. Consequently, measurement topics are used by researchers at Marzano Research to develop proficiency scales in different content areas. In this context, measurement topics are categories of related words that teachers can use to design units, create wordlists, and so on.

Since there are over five times as many terms in part III as in part II, providing descriptions and examples for each domain-specific term was beyond the scope of this work. In lieu of descriptions and examples for the part III terms, each term in part III is accompanied by a suggested grade-level range.

The grade-level range for each term is designated with Xs. For example, for the term *pull* in the Forces and Interactions measurement topic, there is an X in the kindergarten column and another X in the grade 1 column. This indicates our recommendation that the term be taught to students in kindergarten or grade 1. These ranges allow teachers to quickly locate appropriate words for their current topic of study at their assigned grade level.

Physical Science

1. Forces and Interactions

Term	Part of Speech	K	1	2	3	4	5	6–8	9–12
light	noun	X	X						
pull	noun	X	X						
push	noun	X	X						
roll	verb	X	X						
heat	noun	X	X	X					
heat	verb	X	X	X					
ramp	noun	X	X	X					
straight-line motion	noun	X	X	X					
rest	verb		X	X	X				
sound	noun		X	X	X				
speed	noun		X	X	X				
swing	verb		X	X	X				
zigzag motion	noun		X	X	X				
circular motion	noun			X	X				
change of direction	noun			X	X	X			
change of motion	noun			X	X	X			
change of speed	noun			X	X	X			
contact	verb			X	X	X			
flow	verb			X	X	X			
unit	noun			X	X	X			
device	noun				X	X			
surrounding	adjective				X	X			
applied force	noun				X	X	X		
balanced force	noun				X	X	X		
climate	noun				X	X	X		
collide	verb				X	X	X		
collision	noun				X	X	X		
controlled	adjective				X	X	X		
force	noun				X	X	X		
force strength	noun				X	X	X		
friction	noun				X	X	X		
future motion	noun				X	X	X		
past motion	noun				X	X	X		
position over time	noun				X	X	X		
sum	noun				X	X	X		
unbalanced force	noun				X	X	X		
independent	adjective					X	X		
measurement of motion	noun					X	X		
natural resource	noun					X	X		
conservation	noun					X	X	X	

continued →

Term	Part of Speech	K	1	2	3	4	5	6–8	9–12
electric current	noun					X	X	X	
exert	verb					X	X	X	
interaction	noun					X	X	X	
transfer	verb					X	X	X	
mass	noun						X	X	
relative position	noun						X	X	
constant speed	noun							X	
control [variable]	noun							X	
deceleration	noun							X	
dependent variable	noun							X	
direction of a force	noun							X	
direction of motion	noun							X	
economic	adjective							X	
impact	noun							X	
independent variable	noun							X	
inertia	noun							X	
Isaac Newton	noun							X	
Newton's first law of motion	noun							X	
Newton's second law of motion	noun							X	
Newton's third law of motion	noun							X	
nonlinear	adjective							X	
stationary	adjective							X	
frame of reference	noun							X	X
macroscopic	adjective							X	X
momentum	noun							X	X
net force	noun							X	X
optimal	adjective							X	X
systematic	adjective							X	X
acceleration	noun								X
constant force	noun								X
drag	noun								X
equal and opposite force	noun								X
fluid resistance	noun								X
initial	adjective								X
inverse square law	noun								X
Newtonian mechanics	noun								X
quantum of energy	noun								X
relative motion	noun								X
velocity	noun								X

2. Electric and Magnetic Forces

Term	Part of Speech	K	1	2	3	4	5	6–8	9–12
space	noun		X	X	X				
speed	noun		X	X	X				
contact	verb			X	X	X			
magnet	noun			X	X	X			
magnetic	adjective			X	X	X			
device	noun				X	X			
battery	noun				X	X	X		
charge attraction	noun				X	X	X		
electric	adjective				X	X	X		
electrically charged	adjective				X	X	X		
force	noun				X	X	X		
magnetic attraction	noun				X	X	X		
properties	noun				X	X	X		
wire	noun				X	X	X		
conductor	noun					X	X		
current	noun					X	X	X	
electric current	noun					X	X	X	
electrical energy	noun					X	X	X	
exert	verb					X	X	X	
gravitational	adjective					X	X	X	
interaction	noun					X	X	X	
magnetic force	noun					X	X	X	
magnetic repulsion	noun					X	X	X	
transfer	verb					X	X	X	
transmit	verb					X	X	X	
charged object	noun						X	X	
charged rod	noun						X	X	
attractive	adjective							X	
charge repulsion	noun							X	
electric force	noun							X	
electric motor	noun							X	
electromagnet	noun							X	
facility	noun							X	
field	noun							X	
generator	noun							X	
insulator	noun							X	
electromagnetic	adjective							X	X
orientation	noun							X	X
precision	noun							X	X
repulsive	adjective							X	X
Coulomb's law	noun								X
electric field	noun								X

continued →

Term	Part of Speech	K	1	2	3	4	5	6–8	9–12
electromagnetic force	noun								X
electrostatic force	noun								X
gravitational field	noun								X
magnetic field	noun								X
moving magnet	noun								X
permeate	verb								X
semiconductor	noun								X
superconductor	noun								X

3. Gravity

Term	Part of Speech	K	1	2	3	4	5	6–8	9–12
sun	noun	X							
Earth	noun	X	X	X					
Earth's gravity	noun		X	X	X				
gravity	noun		X	X	X				
space	noun		X	X	X				
flow	verb			X	X	X			
magnet	noun			X	X	X			
period [time]	noun			X	X	X			
planet	noun			X	X	X			
charge	noun				X	X	X		
Earth's rotation	noun				X	X	X		
Earth's surface	noun				X	X	X		
force	noun				X	X	X		
solar system	noun					X	X		
spherical	adjective					X	X		
exert	verb					X	X	X	
gravitational	adjective					X	X	X	
gravitational force	noun					X	X	X	
transfer	verb					X	X	X	
mass	noun						X	X	
orbital	adjective						X	X	
attractive	adjective							X	
direction of a force	noun							X	
direction of motion	noun							X	
field	noun							X	
Isaac Newton	noun							X	
linear	adjective							X	
Newton's law of gravitation	noun							X	
nonlinear	adjective							X	
Albert Einstein	noun								X
general theory of relativity	noun								X
gravitational energy	noun								X

Term	Part of Speech	K	1	2	3	4	5	6–8	9–12
gravitational field	noun								X
magnetic field	noun								X
permeate	verb								X

4. Energy and Forces

Term	Part of Speech	K	1	2	3	4	5	6–8	9–12
Earth	noun	X	X	X					
flow	verb			X	X	X			
lever arm	noun			X	X	X			
magnet	noun			X	X	X			
pulley	noun			X	X	X			
force	noun				X	X	X		
exert	verb					X	X	X	
store	verb					X	X	X	
transfer	verb					X	X	X	
relative	adjective						X	X	
static	adjective						X	X	
electrical charge	noun							X	
field	noun							X	
mechanical energy	noun							X	
potential energy	noun							X	
orientation	noun							X	X
Albert Einstein	noun								X
Bernoulli's principle	noun								X
buoyancy	noun								X
elasticity	noun								X
electric field	noun								X
inertial frame of reference	noun								X
magnetic field	noun								X
mass to energy conversion	noun								X
special theory of relativity	noun								X
speed of light	noun								X
torque	noun								X

5. Energy Definitions

Term	Part of Speech	K	1	2	3	4	5	6–8	9–12
roll	verb	X	X						
Earth	noun	X	X	X					
environment	noun	X	X	X					
grow	verb	X	X	X					
behavior	noun			X	X	X			

continued →

Term	Part of Speech	K	1	2	3	4	5	6–8	9–12
space	noun		X	X	X				
speed	noun		X	X	X				
flow	verb			X	X	X			
form	noun			X	X	X			
universe	noun			X	X	X			
electrical	adjective				X	X	X		
properties	noun				X	X	X		
spring [coil]	noun				X	X	X		
forms of energy	noun					X	X		
independent	adjective					X	X		
possess	verb					X	X		
transport	verb					X	X		
conservation	noun					X	X	X	
conversion	noun					X	X	X	
convert	verb					X	X	X	
microscopic scale	noun					X	X	X	
particle	noun					X	X	X	
renewable energy	noun					X	X	X	
store	verb					X	X	X	
transfer	verb					X	X	X	
combination	noun						X	X	
conserve	verb						X	X	
limited	adjective						X	X	
mass	noun						X	X	
relative	adjective						X	X	
field	noun							X	
generator	noun							X	
kinetic energy	noun							X	
magnitude	noun							X	
motion energy	noun							X	
proportional	adjective							X	
ratio	noun							X	
square root	noun							X	
thermal energy	noun							X	
chemical process	noun							X	X
macroscopic scale	noun							X	X
precision	noun							X	X
wind turbine	noun							X	X
approximation	noun								X
compression	noun								X
configuration	noun								X
efficient	adjective								X
entropy	noun								X
exponential	adjective								X

Term	Part of Speech	K	1	2	3	4	5	6–8	9–12
foot pound	noun								X
inherent	adjective								X
manifest	verb								X
manifestation	noun								X
mediate	verb								X
molecular energy	noun								X
radiation	noun								X
Rube Goldberg device	noun								X
solar cell	noun								X
solar oven	noun								X

6. Energy Conservation and Energy Transfer

Term	Part of Speech	K	1	2	3	4	5	6–8	9–12
cold	adjective	X							
hot	adjective	X							
sun	noun	X							
ice	noun	X	X						
life	noun	X	X						
light	noun	X	X						
soil	noun	X	X						
sunlight	noun	X	X						
canopy	noun	X	X	X					
cool	verb	X	X	X					
environment	noun	X	X	X					
heat	noun	X	X	X					
heat	verb	X	X	X					
human	noun	X	X	X					
nature	noun	X	X	X					
temperature	noun	X	X	X					
warm	verb	X	X	X					
liquid	noun		X	X	X				
melt	verb		X	X	X				
sound	noun		X	X	X				
speed	noun		X	X	X				
flow	verb			X	X	X			
form	noun			X	X	X			
state	noun			X	X	X			
region	noun				X	X			
surrounding	adjective				X	X			
volume	noun				X	X			
collide	verb				X	X	X		
collision	noun				X	X	X		
Earth's surface	noun				X	X	X		

continued →

Term	Part of Speech	K	1	2	3	4	5	6–8	9–12
electrical	adjective				X	X	X		
heat conduction	noun				X	X	X		
light absorption	noun				X	X	X		
properties	noun				X	X	X		
resource	noun				X	X	X		
sample	noun				X	X	X		
transform	verb				X	X	X		
vehicle	noun				X	X	X		
available	adjective					X	X		
transport	verb					X	X		
chemical	adjective					X	X	X	
conservation	noun					X	X	X	
conversion	noun					X	X	X	
convert	verb					X	X	X	
current	noun					X	X	X	
electric circuit	noun					X	X	X	
electric current	noun					X	X	X	
electrical energy	noun					X	X	X	
heat transfer	noun					X	X	X	
particle	noun					X	X	X	
passive	adjective					X	X	X	
solar heater	noun					X	X	X	
stored energy	noun					X	X	X	
transfer	verb					X	X	X	
average	adjective						X	X	
mass	noun						X	X	
thermal	adjective						X	X	
conservation of energy	noun							X	
control [variable]	noun							X	
dependent variable	noun							X	
design task	noun							X	
field	noun							X	
heat energy	noun							X	
heat radiation	noun							X	
heat retention	noun							X	
independent variable	noun							X	
insulate	verb							X	
kinetic energy	noun							X	
magnitude	noun							X	
mechanical motion	noun							X	
motion energy	noun							X	
precise	adjective							X	
proportional	adjective							X	
ratio	noun							X	

Term	Part of Speech	K	1	2	3	4	5	6–8	9–12
spontaneous	adjective							X	
thermal energy	noun							X	
uniform	adjective							X	
chemical process	noun							X	X
evolve	verb							X	X
heat convection	noun							X	X
precision	noun							X	X
systematic	adjective							X	X
closed system	noun								X
second law of thermodynamics	noun								X
stable	adjective								X
thermal equilibrium	noun								X
thermodynamics	noun								X
uncontrolled system	noun								X

7. Waves

Term	Part of Speech	K	1	2	3	4	5	6–8	9–12
color	noun	X	X						
light	noun	X	X						
straight line	noun	X	X						
Earth	noun	X	X	X					
reflect	verb		X	X	X				
sound	noun		X	X	X				
space	noun		X	X	X				
speed	noun		X	X	X				
tuning fork	noun		X	X	X				
vibrate	verb		X	X	X				
vibration	noun		X	X	X				
light reflection	noun			X	X	X			
surface	noun			X	X	X			
water wave	noun			X	X	X			
absorb	verb				X	X	X		
properties	noun				X	X	X		
properties of sound	noun				X	X	X		
sound wave	noun					X	X		
amplitude	noun					X	X	X	
dependent	adjective					X	X	X	
light emission	noun					X	X	X	
light refraction	noun					X	X	X	
net motion	noun					X	X	X	
transmit	verb					X	X	X	
wave	noun					X	X	X	

continued →

Term	Part of Speech	K	1	2	3	4	5	6–8	9–12
wavelength	noun					X	X	X	
wave peaks	noun					X	X	X	
brightness	noun						X	X	
transparent	adjective						X	X	
heat emission	noun							X	
light wave	noun							X	
linear	adjective							X	
matter wave	noun							X	
mechanical wave	noun							X	
nonlinear	adjective							X	
simple wave	noun							X	
electromagnetic	adjective							X	X
frequency	noun							X	X
Doppler effect	noun								X
electromagnetic radiation	noun								X
properties of waves	noun								X
radiation	noun								X
seismic wave	noun								X
vacuum	noun								X
wave packet	noun								X
wave source	noun								X

8. Electromagnetic Radiation

Term	Part of Speech	K	1	2	3	4	5	6–8	9–12
light	noun	X	X						
shadow	noun	X	X						
heat	noun	X	X	X					
living	adjective	X	X	X					
beam	noun		X	X	X				
light beam	noun		X	X	X				
light source	noun		X	X	X				
pinhole box	noun		X	X	X				
reflective	adjective		X	X	X				
flow	verb			X	X	X			
surface	noun			X	X	X			
X-ray	noun			X	X	X			
absorb	verb				X	X	X		
electric	adjective				X	X	X		
properties of light	noun				X	X	X		
convert	verb					X	X	X	
particle	noun					X	X	X	
wave	noun					X	X	X	
wavelength	noun					X	X	X	

Term	Part of Speech	K	1	2	3	4	5	6–8	9–12
atom	noun						X	X	
cell	noun						X	X	
phase	noun						X	X	
technical	adjective						X	X	
transparent	adjective						X	X	
color of light	noun							X	
field	noun							X	
illuminate	verb							X	
light scattering	noun							X	
light transmission	noun							X	
light wavelength	noun							X	
radio	adjective							X	
thermal energy	noun							X	
visible light	noun							X	
frequency	noun							X	X
opaque	adjective							X	X
peak	noun							X	X
tissue	noun							X	X
translucent	adjective							X	X
trough	noun							X	X
diffraction	noun								X
electrically neutral	adjective								X
electric potential	noun								X
electromagnetic field	noun								X
electromagnetic radiation	noun								X
electromagnetic spectrum	noun								X
electromagnetic wave	noun								X
gamma ray	noun								X
infrared radiation	noun								X
interference	noun								X
ionize	verb								X
magnetic field	noun								X
microwave	noun								X
ohm	noun								X
photoelectric	adjective								X
photon	noun								X
radiation	noun								X
resonance	noun								X
ultraviolet	adjective								X
ultraviolet radiation	noun								X

9. Information Technologies

Term	Part of Speech	K	1	2	3	4	5	6–8	9–12
computer	noun	X	X						
computer screen	noun	X	X						
light	noun	X	X						
human	noun	X	X	X					
machine	noun	X	X	X					
behavior	noun		X	X	X				
cell phone	noun		X	X	X				
human-made	adjective		X	X	X				
sound	noun		X	X	X				
communicate	verb			X	X	X			
communication	noun			X	X	X			
electricity	noun			X	X	X			
form	noun			X	X	X			
cost	noun				X	X			
device	noun				X	X			
advantage	noun				X	X	X		
coded	adjective				X	X	X		
cycle	noun				X	X	X		
decode	verb				X	X	X		
display	noun				X	X	X		
electrical	adjective				X	X	X		
exploration	noun				X	X	X		
medical	adjective				X	X	X		
Morse code	noun				X	X	X		
product	noun				X	X	X		
properties of light	noun				X	X	X		
digital	adjective					X	X		
high-tech	adjective					X	X		
sound wave	noun					X	X		
application	noun					X	X	X	
conversion	noun					X	X	X	
convert	verb					X	X	X	
digitize	verb					X	X	X	
memory	noun					X	X	X	
solar	adjective					X	X	X	
store	verb					X	X	X	
transfer	verb					X	X	X	
transmit	verb					X	X	X	
wave	noun					X	X	X	
cell	noun						X	X	
criteria	noun						X	X	
performance	noun						X	X	

Term	Part of Speech	K	1	2	3	4	5	6–8	9–12
scanner	noun						X	X	
technical	adjective						X	X	
advance	noun							X	
analog	adjective							X	
encode	verb							X	
format	noun							X	
instrumentation	noun							X	
light pulse	noun							X	
progress	noun							X	
radio wave	noun							X	
transmission	noun							X	
visual	adjective							X	
wave pulse	noun							X	
Wi-Fi device	noun							X	
binary	adjective							X	X
capacity	noun							X	X
chemical process	noun							X	X
civilization	noun							X	X
frequency	noun							X	X
interdependence	noun							X	X
degradation	noun								X
electron	noun								X
emit	verb								X
modern world	noun								X
photoelectric	adjective								X
pixel	noun								X
suitability	noun								X

10. States of Matter

Term	Part of Speech	K	1	2	3	4	5	6–8	9–12
cook	verb	X	X	X					
cool	verb	X	X	X					
heat	noun	X	X	X					
heat	verb	X	X	X					
temperature	noun	X	X	X					
gas	noun		X	X	X				
liquid	noun		X	X	X				
solid	noun		X	X	X				
vibrate	verb		X	X	X				
freeze	verb				X	X	X		
state	noun				X	X	X		
states of matter	noun				X	X	X		
change of state	noun				X	X	X		

continued →

Term	Part of Speech	K	1	2	3	4	5	6–8	9–12
collide	verb				X	X	X		
matter	noun				X	X	X		
particle	noun					X	X	X	
pressure	noun					X	X	X	
transfer	verb					X	X	X	
variation	noun					X	X	X	
atom	noun						X	X	
average	adjective						X	X	
building block	noun						X	X	
substance	noun						X	X	
helium	noun							X	
internal	adjective							X	
internal energy	noun							X	
kinetic energy	noun							X	
particle motion	noun							X	
potential energy	noun							X	
proportional	adjective							X	
pure substance	noun							X	
subunit	noun							X	
thermal energy	noun							X	
carbon dioxide	noun							X	X
inert atom	noun							X	X
molecular arrangement	noun							X	X
molecular motion	noun							X	X
molecular-level	adjective							X	X
molecule	noun							X	X
Avogadro's hypothesis	noun								X
reversible	adjective								X

11. Structure and Properties of Matter

Term	Part of Speech	K	1	2	3	4	5	6–8	9–12
color	noun	X	X						
temperature	noun	X	X	X					
exist	verb		X	X	X				
gas	noun		X	X	X				
human-made	adjective		X	X	X				
liquid	noun		X	X	X				
mixture	noun		X	X	X				
solid	noun		X	X	X				
space	noun		X	X	X				
flexibility	noun			X	X	X			
flexible	adjective			X	X	X			
hardness	noun			X	X	X			

Term	Part of Speech	K	1	2	3	4	5	6–8	9–12
magnetic	adjective			X	X	X			
powder	noun			X	X	X			
texture	noun			X	X	X			
unit	noun			X	X	X			
weight	noun			X	X	X			
cost	noun				X	X			
remove	verb				X	X			
volume	noun				X	X			
absorbency	noun				X	X	X		
attraction	noun				X	X	X		
electric	adjective				X	X	X		
electrical	adjective				X	X	X		
evaporate	verb				X	X	X		
force	noun				X	X	X		
matter	noun				X	X	X		
metal	noun				X	X	X		
product	noun				X	X	X		
properties	noun				X	X	X		
reflectivity	noun				X	X	X		
structure	noun				X	X	X		
transformation	noun				X	X	X		
baking soda	noun					X	X		
charged	adjective					X	X	X	
condensation	noun					X	X	X	
evaporation	noun					X	X	X	
matter particle	noun					X	X	X	
particle	noun					X	X	X	
pressure	noun					X	X	X	
vapor	noun					X	X	X	
atom	noun						X	X	
compress	verb						X	X	
conduction	noun						X	X	
conductivity	noun						X	X	
detect	verb						X	X	
dissolve	verb						X	X	
electrical conductivity	noun						X	X	
mineral	noun						X	X	
relative	adjective						X	X	
solubility	noun						X	X	
substance	noun						X	X	
actual mass	noun							X	
ammonia	noun							X	
attractive	adjective							X	
conductive	adjective							X	

continued →

Term	Part of Speech	K	1	2	3	4	5	6–8	9–12
electrical charge	noun							X	
element	noun							X	
extended structure	noun							X	
filtering	verb							X	
function	verb							X	
methanol	noun							X	
nucleus	noun							X	
properties of elements	noun							X	
reaction	noun							X	
receptor	noun							X	
separation method [for mixtures]	noun							X	
sodium chloride	noun							X	
thermal conductivity	noun							X	
atomic	adjective							X	X
atomic arrangement	noun							X	X
atomic theory	noun							X	X
atomic weight	noun							X	X
boiling point	noun							X	X
melting point	noun							X	X
molecular level	noun							X	X
molecule	noun							X	X
oxygen	noun							X	X
precision	noun							X	X
repulsive	adjective							X	X
simple molecule	noun							X	X
accelerator	noun								X
Antoine Lavoisier	noun								X
atomic energy	noun								X
atomic mass	noun								X
atomic motion	noun								X
atomic number	noun								X
atomic scale	noun								X
bond	noun								X
bulk scale	noun								X
catalyst	noun								X
chained molecules	noun								X
chemical bond	noun								X
chemical properties	noun								X
chromatography	noun								X
contact force	noun								X
derive	verb								X
durable	adjective								X
electron	noun								X
electron configuration	noun								X

Term	Part of Speech	K	1	2	3	4	5	6–8	9–12
electron sharing	noun								X
electron transfer	noun								X
elements of matter	noun								X
elementary particle	noun								X
element stability	noun								X
energy level	noun								X
formation of polymers	noun								X
graphite	noun								X
ion	noun								X
ionic motion	noun								X
isotope	noun								X
John Dalton	noun								X
molar volume	noun								X
networked material	noun								X
neutron	noun								X
outer electron state	noun								X
outermost	adjective								X
periodic table	noun								X
pharmaceutical	noun								X
proton	noun								X
radical reaction	noun								X
reactivity	noun								X
relative mass	noun								X
release of energy	noun								X
repulsion	noun								X
substructure	noun								X
surface tension	noun								X
synthetic polymer	noun								X
weight of subatomic particles	noun								X

12. Conservation of Matter

Term	Part of Speech	K	1	2	3	4	5	6–8	9–12
cool	verb	X	X	X					
heat	verb	X	X	X					
temperature	noun	X	X	X					
physical model	noun		X	X	X				
unit	noun				X	X	X		
universe	noun				X	X	X		
weight	noun				X	X	X		
volume	noun				X	X			
matter	noun				X	X	X		
product	noun				X	X	X		
properties	noun				X	X	X		

continued →

Term	Part of Speech	K	1	2	3	4	5	6–8	9–12
chemical	adjective					X	X	X	
conversion	noun					X	X	X	
phase change	noun					X	X	X	
atom	noun						X	X	
conservation of mass	noun						X	X	
conservation of matter	noun						X	X	
conserve	verb						X	X	
dissolve	verb						X	X	
mass	noun						X	X	
react	verb						X	X	
substance	noun						X	X	
transition	verb						X	X	
element	noun							X	
forms of matter	noun							X	
law of conservation of matter	noun							X	
proportional	adjective							X	
reactant	noun							X	
reaction	noun							X	
regularity	noun							X	
atomic	adjective							X	X
atomic-level	adjective							X	X
chemical process	noun							X	X
chemical reaction	noun							X	X
macroscopic	adjective							X	X
molecule	noun							X	X
chemical properties	noun								X
closed system	noun								X
mole	noun								X

13. Chemical Reactions

Term	Part of Speech	K	1	2	3	4	5	6–8	9–12
food	noun	X							
burn	verb	X	X						
environment	noun	X	X	X					
nature	noun	X	X	X					
sugar	noun	X	X	X					
temperature	noun	X	X	X					
thermometer	noun		X	X					
flow	verb			X	X	X			
medicine	noun			X	X	X			
release	verb			X	X	X			
region	noun				X	X			
absorb	verb				X	X	X		

Term	Part of Speech	K	1	2	3	4	5	6–8	9–12
climate	noun				X	X	X		
collision	noun				X	X	X		
controlled	adjective				X	X	X		
graduated cylinder	noun				X	X	X		
mixed	adjective				X	X	X		
product	noun				X	X	X		
properties	noun				X	X	X		
sum	noun				X	X	X		
fuel	noun					X	X		
natural resource	noun					X	X		
independent	adjective					X	X		
chemical	adjective					X	X	X	
microscopic	adjective					X	X	X	
particle	noun					X	X	X	
store	verb					X	X	X	
test results	noun					X	X	X	
transfer	verb				X	X	X		
accuracy	noun						X	X	
alternative	adjective						X	X	
atom	noun						X	X	
conserve	verb						X	X	
dissolve	verb						X	X	
Kelvin	adjective						X	X	
react	verb						X	X	
substance	noun						X	X	
ammonium chloride	noun							X	
calcium chloride	noun							X	
chemical compound	noun							X	
chemical element	noun							X	
chemical energy	noun							X	
chlorine	noun							X	
concentration of reactants	noun							X	
element	noun							X	
food oxidation	noun							X	
kinetic energy	noun							X	
metal reactivity	noun							X	
nonmetal reactivity	noun							X	
nonreactive gas	noun							X	
nucleus	noun							X	
physical properties	noun							X	
pure substance	noun							X	
reactant	noun							X	
reaction	noun							X	
reaction rate	noun							X	

continued →

Term	Part of Speech	K	1	2	3	4	5	6–8	9–12
refinement	noun							X	
sodium	noun							X	
sodium hydroxide	noun							X	
surface area of reactants	noun							X	
synthetic	adjective							X	
thermal energy	noun							X	
zinc	noun							X	
atomic-level	adjective							X	X
carbon	noun							X	X
chemical process	noun							X	X
chemical reaction	noun							X	X
dynamic	noun							X	X
interdependence	noun							X	X
iterative process	noun							X	X
macroscopic	adjective							X	X
macroscopic level	noun							X	X
molecular level	noun							X	X
molecule	noun							X	X
optimal	adjective							X	X
oxidation	noun							X	X
oxygen	noun							X	X
acid	noun								X
acid-base reactions	noun								X
atomic configuration	noun								X
atomic reaction	noun								X
base	noun								X
bond	noun								X
carbon atom	noun								X
catalyst	noun								X
chemical properties	noun								X
chemical reaction rate	noun								X
chemical reaction system	noun								X
chemical system	noun								X
concentration	noun								X
condition-dependent	adjective								X
electron state	noun								X
endothermic reaction	noun								X
exothermic reaction	noun								X
equilibrium	noun								X
hydrogen	noun								X
hydrogen ion	noun								X
Le Chatelier's principle	noun								X
metallic surface	noun								X
outer electron state	noun								X

Term	Part of Speech	K	1	2	3	4	5	6–8	9–12
outermost	adjective								X
oxidation-reduction reaction	noun								X
periodic table	noun								X
properties of reactants	noun								X
proton	noun								X
rearrangement	noun								X
recombination of chemical elements	noun								X
stable	adjective								X
unanticipated	adjective								X

14. Bonds

Term	Part of Speech	K	1	2	3	4	5	6–8	9–12
flow	verb			X	X	X			
release	verb			X	X	X			
absorption	noun				X	X	X		
collision	noun				X	X	X		
product	noun				X	X	X		
sum	noun				X	X	X		
store	verb					X	X	X	
atom	noun							X	X
conserve	verb							X	X
kinetic energy	noun							X	
reactant	noun							X	
reaction	noun							X	
chemical process	noun							X	X
chemical reaction	noun							X	X
molecular level	noun							X	X
molecule	noun							X	X
atomic bonding principles	noun								X
bond	noun								X
energy level	noun								X
rearrangement	noun								X
stable	adjective								X

15. Nuclear Processes

Term	Part of Speech	K	1	2	3	4	5	6–8	9–12
absorption	noun				X	X	X		
transformation	noun				X	X	X		
atom	noun						X	X	
Marie Curie	noun							X	
nuclear reaction	noun							X	

continued →

Term	Part of Speech	K	1	2	3	4	5	6–8	9–12
nucleus	noun							X	
Pierre Curie	noun							X	
atomic bomb	noun								X
decay rate	noun								X
Enrico Fermi	noun								X
Ernest Rutherford	noun								X
fission	noun								X
fusion	noun								X
hydrogen bomb	noun								X
Lise Meitner	noun								X
neutron	noun								X
nuclear	adjective								X
nuclear force	noun								X
nuclear mass	noun								X
nuclear process	noun								X
nuclear stability	noun								X
particle emission	noun								X
proton	noun								X
radioactive decay	noun								X
rate of nuclear decay	noun								X
spontaneous nuclear reaction	noun								X
unstable	adjective								X

Life Science

16. Growth and Development of Organisms

Term	Part of Speech	K	1	2	3	4	5	6–8	9–12
flower	noun	X							
food	noun	X							
life	noun	X	X						
light	noun	X	X						
plant	noun	X	X						
birth	noun	X	X	X					
death	noun	X	X	X					
grow	verb	X	X	X					
seed	noun	X	X	X					
survive	verb	X	X	X					
comfort	verb		X	X					
environmental	adjective		X	X					
insect	noun		X	X					
shell	noun		X	X					
adult	noun		X	X	X				

Term	Part of Speech	K	1	2	3	4	5	6–8	9–12
behavior	noun		X	X	X				
growth	noun		X	X	X				
life cycle	noun		X	X	X				
mate	noun		X	X	X				
nectar	noun		X	X	X				
parent	noun		X	X	X				
plant growth	noun		X	X	X				
pollen	noun		X	X	X				
predator	noun		X	X	X				
shelter	noun		X	X	X				
behavior patterns	noun			X	X	X			
characteristic	noun			X	X	X			
drought	noun			X	X	X			
herd	verb			X	X	X			
offspring	noun			X	X	X			
species	noun			X	X	X			
existence	noun				X	X	X		
reproduction	noun				X	X	X		
unique	adjective				X	X	X		
organism	noun					X	X		
breed	noun					X	X	X	
diverse	adjective					X	X	X	
transfer	verb					X	X	X	
development	noun						X	X	
attract	verb							X	
characteristics of life	noun							X	
germination	noun							X	
plant structure	noun							X	
plumage	noun							X	
reproductive system	noun							X	
soil fertility	noun							X	
vocalization	noun							X	
fertilizer	noun							X	X
genetic	adjective							X	X
specialized	adjective							X	X
reproductive capacity	noun								X

17. Matter and Energy in Organisms

Term	Part of Speech	K	1	2	3	4	5	6–8	9–12
food	noun	X							
sun	noun	X							
bone	noun	X	X						
light	noun	X	X						

continued →

Term	Part of Speech	K	1	2	3	4	5	6–8	9–12
plant	noun	X	X						
soil	noun	X	X						
sunlight	noun	X	X						
body	noun	X	X	X					
environment	noun	X	X	X					
grow	verb	X	X	X					
human	noun	X	X	X					
living	adjective	X	X	X					
living thing	noun	X	X	X					
nonliving	adjective	X	X	X					
recycle	verb	X	X	X					
requirements for life	noun	X	X	X					
sugar	noun	X	X	X					
survive	verb	X	X	X					
temperature	noun	X	X	X					
growth	noun		X	X	X				
ecosystem	noun			X	X	X			
flow	noun			X	X	X			
muscle	noun			X	X	X			
release	verb			X	X	X			
movement	noun				X	X			
algae	noun				X	X	X		
atmosphere	noun				X	X	X		
backbone	noun				X	X	X		
body repair	noun				X	X	X		
body warmth	noun				X	X	X		
consumer	noun				X	X	X		
cycle	noun				X	X	X		
food web	noun				X	X	X		
matter	noun				X	X	X		
organization	noun				X	X	X		
photosynthetic plants	noun				X	X	X		
plant matter	noun				X	X	X		
product	noun				X	X	X		
transform	verb				X	X	X		
transformation	noun				X	X	X		
independent	adjective					X	X		
organism	noun					X	X		
role	noun					X	X		
transport	verb					X	X		
chemical	adjective					X	X	X	
conservation	noun					X	X	X	
convert	verb					X	X	X	
store	verb					X	X	X	

Term	Part of Speech	K	1	2	3	4	5	6–8	9–12
transfer	noun					X	X	X	
atom	noun						X	X	
conserve	verb						X	X	
cycle	verb						X	X	
decomposer	noun						X	X	
energy flow	noun						X	X	
flow chart	noun						X	X	
react	verb						X	X	
aquatic	adjective							X	
element	noun							X	
Louis Pasteur	noun							X	
microorganism	noun							X	
organic	adjective							X	
phytoplankton	noun							X	
producer	noun							X	
reaction	noun							X	
terrestrial	adjective							X	
carbon	noun							X	X
carbon dioxide	noun							X	X
chemical process	noun							X	X
chemical reaction	noun							X	X
interdependent	adjective							X	X
molecule	noun							X	X
nutrient	noun							X	X
oxygen	noun							X	X
photosynthesis	noun							X	X
protein	noun							X	X
amino acid	noun								X
amino acid sequence	noun								X
biological molecule	noun								X
bond	noun								X
cellular respiration	noun								X
chemical equation	noun								X
compound	noun								X
DNA	noun								X
flow of matter	noun								X
germ theory	noun								X
hydrocarbon	noun								X
hydrogen	noun								X
living system	noun								X
net transfer	noun								X
photosynthesizing organism	noun								X
transfer system	noun								X

18. Ecosystem Dynamics

Term	Part of Speech	K	1	2	3	4	5	6–8	9–12
food	noun	X							
land	noun	X							
life	noun	X	X						
plant	noun	X	X						
environment	noun	X	X	X					
human	noun	X	X	X					
hunt	verb	X	X	X					
living thing	noun	X	X	X					
nonliving	adjective	X	X	X					
seasonal	adjective	X	X	X					
survive	verb	X	X	X					
temperature	noun	X	X	X					
environmental	adjective		X	X					
area	noun		X	X	X				
exist	verb		X	X	X				
growth	noun		X	X	X				
herbivore	noun		X	X	X				
omnivore	noun		X	X	X				
prey	noun		X	X	X				
flood	noun			X	X				
characteristic	noun			X	X	X			
ecosystem	noun			X	X	X			
food chain	noun			X	X	X			
habitat	noun			X	X	X			
period [time]	noun			X	X	X			
species	noun			X	X	X			
volcanic eruption	noun			X	X	X			
population	noun				X	X			
biodiversity	noun				X	X	X		
climate	noun				X	X	X		
competition	noun				X	X	X		
disease	noun				X	X	X		
environmental changes	noun				X	X	X		
environmental conditions	noun				X	X	X		
food web	noun				X	X	X		
physical characteristic	noun				X	X	X		
reproduce	verb				X	X	X		
reproduction	noun				X	X	X		
resource	noun				X	X	X		
resource availability	noun				X	X	X		
transform	verb				X	X	X		
available	adjective					X	X		
organism	noun					X	X		

Term	Part of Speech	K	1	2	3	4	5	6–8	9–12
population density	noun					X	X		
dependent	adjective					X	X	X	
diversity	noun					X	X	X	
diversity of life	noun					X	X	X	
extreme	adjective					X	X	X	
requirement	noun					X	X	X	
support	noun					X	X	X	
average	noun						X	X	
limited	adjective						X	X	
relative	adjective						X	X	
trend	noun						X	X	
predation	noun						X	X	X
resilient	adjective						X	X	X
constrain	verb							X	
disruption	noun							X	
abundance	noun							X	X
abundant	adjective							X	X
biological	adjective							X	X
capacity	noun							X	X
dynamic	adjective							X	X
interdependent	adjective							X	X
oxygen	noun							X	X
status	noun							X	X
carrying capacity	noun								X
chemical organization of organisms	noun								X
disturbance	noun								X
durable	adjective								X
equilibrium of ecosystems	noun								X
finite	adjective								X
fluctuation	noun								X
living system	noun								X
moderate	adjective								X
sea level	noun								X
stable	adjective								X
tension	noun								X

19. Interdependent Relationships in Ecosystems

Term	Part of Speech	K	1	2	3	4	5	6–8	9–12
food	noun	X							
plant	noun	X	X						
environment	noun	X	X	X					
living	adjective	X	X	X					

continued →

Term	Part of Speech	K	1	2	3	4	5	6–8	9–12
nonliving	adjective	X	X	X					
seed	noun	X	X	X					
survive	verb	X	X	X					
behavior	noun		X	X	X				
mimic	verb		X	X	X				
pollinate	verb		X	X	X				
pollination	noun		X	X	X				
predatory	adjective		X	X	X				
survival	noun		X	X	X				
migrate	verb			X	X				
ecosystem	noun			X	X	X			
flock	noun			X	X	X			
group behavior	noun			X	X	X			
herd	verb			X	X	X			
membership	noun			X	X	X			
species	noun			X	X	X			
swarm	verb			X	X	X			
population	noun				X	X			
competitive	adjective				X	X	X		
cooperative	adjective				X	X	X		
cope	verb				X	X	X		
reproduce	verb				X	X	X		
organism	noun					X	X		
role	noun					X	X		
social	adjective					X	X		
relative	adjective						X	X	
disperse	verb							X	
ecological role	noun							X	
host	noun							X	
infection	noun							X	
mutualism	noun							X	
mutually beneficial	adjective							X	
parasite	noun							X	
evolve	verb							X	X
genetic	adjective							X	X
interdependent	adjective							X	X
abiotic	adjective								X

20. Matter and Energy in Ecosystems

Term	Part of Speech	K	1	2	3	4	5	6–8	9–12
food	noun	X							
life	noun	X	X						
plant	noun	X	X						

Term	Part of Speech	K	1	2	3	4	5	6–8	9–12
soil	noun	X	X						
Earth	noun	X	X	X					
environment	noun	X	X	X					
recycle	verb	X	X	X					
survive	verb	X	X	X					
exist	verb		X	X	X				
gas	noun		X	X	X				
growth	noun		X	X	X				
liquid	noun		X	X	X				
solid	noun		X	X	X				
ecosystem	noun			X	X	X			
flow	verb			X	X	X			
ocean	noun			X	X	X			
release	verb			X	X	X			
species	noun			X	X	X			
movement	noun				X	X			
algae	noun				X	X	X		
atmosphere	noun				X	X	X		
bacteria	noun				X	X	X		
composition of matter	noun				X	X	X		
consume	verb				X	X	X		
cycle	noun				X	X	X		
food web	noun				X	X	X		
matter	noun				X	X	X		
plant part	noun				X	X	X		
independent	adjective					X	X		
organism	noun					X	X		
role	noun					X	X		
waste matter	noun					X	X		
chemical	adjective					X	X	X	
store	verb					X	X	X	
transfer	verb					X	X	X	
atom	noun						X	X	
biosphere	noun						X	X	
conserve	verb						X	X	
cycle	verb						X	X	
decompose	verb						X	X	
decomposer	noun						X	X	
decomposition	noun						X	X	
energy transfer	noun						X	X	
fungi	noun						X	X	
geosphere	noun						X	X	
hydrosphere	noun						X	X	
microbe	noun						X	X	

continued →

Term	Part of Speech	K	1	2	3	4	5	6–8	9–12
react	verb						X	X	
restore	verb						X	X	
aerobic	adjective							X	
anaerobic	adjective							X	
element	noun							X	
field	noun							X	
geological	adjective							X	
linear	adjective							X	
nonlinear	adjective							X	
recycling of matter	noun							X	
biological	adjective							X	X
carbon	noun							X	X
chemical process	noun							X	X
interdependent	adjective							X	X
molecule	noun							X	X
oxygen	noun							X	X
photosynthesis	noun							X	X
biomass	noun								X
carbon cycle	noun								X
cellular respiration	noun								X
durable	adjective								X
energy requirements of living systems	noun								X
hydrogen	noun								X
inefficient	adjective								X
nitrogen	noun								X
respiration	noun								X
solar energy	noun								X
stable	adjective								X
trophic level	noun								X

21. Humans, Biodiversity, and Ecosystems

Term	Part of Speech	K	1	2	3	4	5	6–8	9–12
food	noun	X							
life	noun	X	X						
soil	noun	X	X						
Earth	noun	X	X	X					
environment	noun	X	X	X					
human	noun	X	X	X					
living	adjective	X	X	X					
recycle	verb	X	X	X					
recycling	noun	X	X	X					
environmental	adjective		X	X					

Term	Part of Speech	K	1	2	3	4	5	6–8	9–12
safety	noun		X	X					
material	adjective		X	X	X				
survival	noun		X	X	X				
ecosystem	noun				X	X	X		
erosion	noun				X	X	X		
habitat	noun				X	X	X		
health	noun				X	X	X		
medicine	noun				X	X	X		
pollution	noun				X	X	X		
species	noun				X	X	X		
dam	noun					X	X		
extinction	noun					X	X		
population	noun					X	X		
region	noun					X	X		
biodiversity	noun					X	X	X	
climate	noun					X	X	X	
endangered species	noun					X	X	X	
resource	noun					X	X	X	
service	noun					X	X	X	
threatened species	noun				X	X	X		
independent	adjective						X	X	
landscape	noun						X	X	
natural resource	noun						X	X	
organism	noun						X	X	
overpopulation	noun						X	X	
oceanic	adjective						X	X	X
threaten	verb						X	X	X
consequence	noun							X	X
destruction	noun							X	X
humanity	noun							X	X
inspirational	adjective							X	X
naturalistic observation	noun							X	X
economic	adjective							X	
economical	adjective							X	
human activity	noun							X	
impact	noun							X	
linear	adjective							X	
nonlinear	adjective							X	
real-world	adjective							X	
terrestrial	adjective							X	
water purification	noun							X	
climate change	noun							X	X
cultural	adjective							X	X
distinct	adjective							X	X

continued →

Term	Part of Speech	K	1	2	3	4	5	6–8	9–12
emergence	noun							X	X
formation	noun							X	X
genetic variation	noun							X	X
integrity	noun							X	X
invasive species	noun							X	X
nutrient	noun							X	X
preserve	verb							X	X
sustain	verb							X	X
systematic	adjective							X	X
adverse	adjective								X
anthropogenic	adjective								X
diverge	verb								X
efficient	adjective								X
essential	adjective								X
human modification of ecosystems	noun								X
living system	noun								X
overexploitation	noun								X
productivity	noun								X
recreational	adjective								X
speciation	noun								X
stable	adjective								X
urbanization	noun								X

22. Structure and Function

Term	Part of Speech	K	1	2	3	4	5	6–8	9–12
flower	noun	X							
food	noun	X							
leaf	noun	X	X						
plant	noun	X	X						
body	noun	X	X	X					
branch	noun	X	X	X					
fruit	noun	X	X	X					
grow	verb	X	X	X					
hear	verb	X	X	X					
human	noun	X	X	X					
root	noun	X	X	X					
survive	verb	X	X	X					
temperature	noun	X	X	X					
shell	noun		X	X					
animal features	noun		X	X	X				
behavior	noun		X	X	X				
blood	noun		X	X	X				

Term	Part of Speech	K	1	2	3	4	5	6–8	9–12
equipment	noun		X	X	X				
growth	noun		X	X	X				
human-made	adjective		X	X	X				
mimic	verb		X	X	X				
petal	noun		X	X	X				
skin	noun		X	X	X				
stem	noun		X	X	X				
stomach	noun		X	X	X				
survival	noun		X	X	X				
thorn	noun		X	X	X				
brain	noun			X	X	X			
flow	verb			X	X	X			
heart	noun			X	X	X			
lung	noun			X	X	X			
muscle	noun			X	X	X			
movement	noun				X	X			
grasp	verb				X	X	X		
habit	noun				X	X	X		
intruder	noun				X	X	X		
moisture	noun				X	X	X		
organization	noun				X	X	X		
plant organ	noun				X	X	X		
plant product	noun				X	X	X		
product	noun				X	X	X		
reproduction	noun				X	X	X		
root development	noun				X	X	X		
structure	noun				X	X	X		
organism	noun					X	X		
organ	noun					X	X	X	
cell	noun						X	X	
detect	verb						X	X	
response	noun						X	X	
body plan	noun							X	
circulatory system	noun							X	
digestive system	noun							X	
elastic	adjective							X	
excretory system	noun							X	
external	adjective							X	
external cue	noun							X	
external feature	noun							X	
function	noun							X	
functional	adjective							X	
heart rate	noun							X	
intellectual	adjective							X	

continued →

Term	Part of Speech	K	1	2	3	4	5	6–8	9–12
internal	adjective							X	
internal cue	noun							X	
internal structure	noun							X	
invertebrate	noun							X	
life-sustaining functions	noun							X	
muscular system	noun							X	
nervous system	noun							X	
organ system	noun							X	
organism system failure	noun							X	
reproductive system	noun							X	
respiratory system	noun							X	
skeletal system	noun							X	
specialized organ	noun							X	
specialized tissue	noun							X	
subsystem	noun							X	
tolerance	noun							X	
vertebrate	noun							X	
conceptual	adjective							X	X
multicellular	adjective							X	X
nutrient	noun							X	X
organic matter	noun							X	X
precision	noun							X	X
specialized	adjective							X	X
stimulus	noun							X	X
structural	adjective							X	X
tissue	noun							X	X
anatomical characteristic	noun								X
breakdown of food molecules	noun								X
derive	verb								X
destabilize	verb								X
embryo formation	noun								X
enzyme	noun								X
excitatory molecule	noun								X
feedback mechanism	noun								X
hierarchical	adjective								X
homeostasis	noun								X
inhibitory molecule	noun								X
immune system	noun								X
living system	noun								X
mediate	verb								X
molecular synthesis	noun								X
neural	adjective								X
organic compound synthesis	noun								X
protein structure	noun								X
protein synthesis	noun								X

Term	Part of Speech	K	1	2	3	4	5	6–8	9–12
regulate	verb								X
stabilize	verb								X
stomate	noun								X
system level	noun								X
transform matter and/or energy	verb								X
transport matter and/or energy	verb								X

23. Information Processing

Term	Part of Speech	K	1	2	3	4	5	6–8	9–12
behavior	noun		X	X	X				
brain	noun			X	X	X			
senses	noun				X	X	X		
chemical	adjective					X	X	X	
mechanical	adjective					X	X	X	
memory	noun					X	X	X	
perception	noun					X	X	X	
process	verb					X	X	X	
storage	noun					X	X	X	
transfer	verb					X	X	X	
transmit	verb					X	X	X	
accuracy	noun						X	X	
cell	noun						X	X	
immediate	adjective							X	
nerve	noun							X	
receptor	noun							X	
sense receptor	noun							X	
sensory	adjective							X	
behavioral response to stimuli	noun							X	X
electromagnetic	adjective							X	X
stimulus	noun							X	X
neuron	noun								X
neurotransmitter	noun								X

24. Cell Theory

Term	Part of Speech	K	1	2	3	4	5	6–8	9–12
life	noun	X	X						
grow	verb	X	X	X					
living thing	noun	X	X	X					
nonliving	adjective	X	X	X					
magnification	noun		X	X					

continued →

Term	Part of Speech	K	1	2	3	4	5	6–8	9–12
magnifier	noun		X	X					
flow	verb			X	X	X			
unit	noun			X	X	X			
ability to support life	noun				X	X	X		
code	noun				X	X	X		
microscope	noun				X	X	X		
properties	noun				X	X	X		
independent	adjective					X	X		
organism	noun					X	X		
role	noun					X	X		
microscopic	adjective					X	X	X	
organ	noun					X	X	X	
cell	noun						X	X	
development	noun						X	X	
cell membrane	noun							X	
cell wall	noun							X	
chloroplast	noun							X	
fundamental unit of life	noun							X	
identical	adjective							X	
nucleus	noun							X	
mitochondria	noun							X	
cell growth	noun							X	X
cell organelle	noun							X	X
chromosome	noun							X	X
egg	noun							X	X
egg cell	noun							X	X
fertilize	verb							X	X
formation	noun							X	X
gene	noun							X	X
genetic	adjective							X	X
interdependence	noun							X	X
molecule	noun							X	X
multicellular	adjective							X	X
protein	noun							X	X
specialized	adjective							X	X
specialized cell	noun							X	X
sperm	noun							X	X
sperm cell	noun							X	X
tissue	noun							X	X
unicellular	adjective							X	X
variant	noun							X	X
atomic nucleus	noun								X
cell function	noun								X
cellular communication	noun								X
cellular differentiation	noun								X

Term	Part of Speech	K	1	2	3	4	5	6–8	9–12
cellular division	noun								X
cellular energy conversion	noun								X
cellular regulation	noun								X
cellular response	noun								X
cellular waste disposal	noun								X
cytoplasm	noun								X
daughter cell	noun								X
differentiation	noun								X
DNA	noun								X
Golgi apparatus	noun								X
mitosis	noun								X
nucleated cell	noun								X
parent cell	noun								X
successive	adjective								X
transport of cell materials	noun								X
vacuole	noun								X

25. Inheritance of Traits

Term	Part of Speech	K	1	2	3	4	5	6–8	9–12
plant	noun	X	X						
human	noun	X	X	X					
exact	adjective		X	X	X				
exist	verb		X	X	X				
growth	noun		X	X	X				
parent	noun		X	X	X				
sibling	noun		X	X	X				
characteristic	noun			X	X	X			
offspring	noun			X	X	X			
parent-offspring similarity	noun			X	X	X			
species	noun			X	X	X			
region	noun				X	X			
code	verb				X	X	X		
feature	noun				X	X	X		
inherit	verb				X	X	X		
inheritance	noun				X	X	X		
inherited characteristic	noun				X	X	X		
natural phenomenon	noun				X	X	X		
reproduce	verb				X	X	X		
trait	noun				X	X	X		
organism	noun					X	X		
role	noun					X	X		
breed	noun					X	X	X	
transfer	verb					X	X	X	
variation	noun					X	X	X	

continued →

Term	Part of Speech	K	1	2	3	4	5	6–8	9–12
cell	noun						X	X	
development	noun						X	X	
instruction	noun						X	X	
recognizable	adjective						X	X	
version	noun						X	X	
allele	noun							X	
contribute	verb							X	
hereditary information	noun							X	
identical	adjective							X	
Punnett square	noun							X	
random	adjective							X	
transmission	noun							X	
asexual reproduction	noun							X	X
chromosome	noun							X	X
formation	noun							X	X
gene	noun							X	X
genetic	adjective							X	X
genetic variation	noun							X	X
human genetics	noun							X	X
molecule	noun							X	X
protein	noun							X	X
sexual reproduction	noun							X	X
structural	adjective							X	X
subset	noun							X	X
arise	verb								X
chromosome pair	noun								X
derived characteristic	noun								X
DNA	noun								X
DNA molecule	noun								X
DNA structure	noun								X
DNA subunit	noun								X
dominant trait	noun								X
filial generation	noun								X
gene encoding	noun								X
gene expression	noun								X
Gregor Mendel	noun								X
Mendelian genetics	noun								X
new gene combinations	noun								X
parental generation	noun								X
polygenic trait	noun								X
recessive trait	noun								X
recombination of genetic material	noun								X
regulate	verb								X

Term	Part of Speech	K	1	2	3	4	5	6–8	9–12
regulatory	adjective								X
segment	noun								X
segregation	noun								X
sex cell	noun								X
sex chromosome	noun								X
sex-linked trait	noun								X
storage of genetic information	noun								X

26. Variation of Traits

Term	Part of Speech	K	1	2	3	4	5	6–8	9–12
plant	noun	X	X						
environment	noun	X	X	X					
human	noun	X	X	X					
similarities and differences among organisms	noun	X	X	X					
environmental	adjective		X	X					
growth	noun		X	X	X				
individual differences	noun		X	X	X				
characteristic	noun				X	X	X		
diet	noun				X	X	X		
population	noun				X	X			
inherit	verb				X	X	X		
inheritable	adjective				X	X	X		
inheritance	noun				X	X	X		
stunt	verb				X	X	X		
trait	noun				X	X	X		
harmful	adjective					X	X		
organism	noun					X	X		
microscopic	adjective					X	X	X	
variation	noun					X	X	X	
cell	noun						X	X	
combination	noun						X	X	
beneficial	adjective							X	
neutral	adjective							X	
probability	noun							X	
production	noun							X	
progress	noun							X	
species diversity	noun							X	
chromosome	noun							X	X
distinct	adjective							X	X
distribution	noun							X	X
gene	noun							X	X
genetic	adjective							X	X

continued →

Term	Part of Speech	K	1	2	3	4	5	6–8	9–12
genetic variation	noun							X	X
protein	noun							X	X
sexual reproduction	noun							X	X
structural	adjective							X	X
variant	noun							X	X
cell division	noun								X
DNA replication	noun								X
genetic diversity	noun								X
genetic mutation	noun								X
insufficient	adjective								X
meiosis	noun								X
mutation	noun								X
regulate	verb								X
replication	noun								X
selective gene expression	noun								X

27. Adaptation

Term	Part of Speech	K	1	2	3	4	5	6–8	9–12
environment	noun	X	X	X					
human	noun	X	X	X					
seasonal	adjective	X	X	X					
survive	verb	X	X	X					
temperature	noun	X	X	X					
environmental	adjective		X	X					
survival	noun		X	X	X				
survival of organisms	noun		X	X	X				
flood	noun				X	X			
characteristic	noun				X	X	X		
drought	noun				X	X	X		
ecosystem	noun				X	X	X		
habitat	noun				X	X	X		
species	noun				X	X	X		
extinct	adjective				X	X			
extinction	noun				X	X			
population	noun				X	X			
barrier	noun				X	X	X		
reproduce	verb				X	X	X		
reproduction	noun				X	X	X		
trait	noun				X	X	X		
independent	adjective					X	X		
organism	noun					X	X		
geographic	adjective					X	X	X	
trend	noun						X	X	

Term	Part of Speech	K	1	2	3	4	5	6–8	9–12
adaptation	noun						X	X	X
beneficial change	noun						X	X	X
detrimental change	noun						X	X	X
acquired trait	noun							X	
decrease	noun							X	
increase	noun							X	
life form change	noun							X	
proportional	adjective							X	
adaptive characteristics	noun							X	X
anatomical	adjective							X	X
behavioral	adjective							X	X
behavioral change in organisms	noun							X	X
climate change	noun							X	X
distinct	adjective							X	X
distribution	noun							X	X
emergence	noun							X	X
emergence of life forms	noun							X	X
evolution	noun							X	X
fertilizer	noun							X	X
frequency	noun							X	X
gene	noun							X	X
generation	noun							X	X
natural selection	noun							X	X
abiotic	adjective								X
acidity	noun								X
advantageous	adjective								X
biotic	adjective								X
deforestation	noun								X
diverge	verb								X
dominate	verb								X
heritable	adjective								X
physiological	adjective								X

28. Natural Selection

Term	Part of Speech	K	1	2	3	4	5	6–8	9–12
plant	noun	X	X						
environment	noun	X	X	X					
human	noun	X	X	X					
survive	verb	X	X	X					
behavior	noun		X	X	X				
mate	noun		X	X	X				
parent	noun		X	X	X				

continued →

Term	Part of Speech	K	1	2	3	4	5	6–8	9–12
predator	noun		X	X	X				
survival	noun		X	X	X				
camouflage	noun			X	X	X			
characteristic	noun			X	X	X			
coloration	noun			X	X	X			
offspring	noun			X	X	X			
species	noun			X	X	X			
population	noun				X	X			
advantage	noun				X	X	X		
competition	noun				X	X	X		
inheritance	noun				X	X	X		
reproduce	verb				X	X	X		
reproduction	noun				X	X	X		
resource	noun				X	X	X		
trait	noun				X	X	X		
variety	noun				X	X	X		
independent	adjective					X	X		
organism	noun					X	X		
shift	verb					X	X	X	
variation	noun					X	X	X	
consequence	noun						X	X	
development	noun						X	X	
adaptation	noun						X	X	X
animal husbandry	noun							X	
artificial selection	noun							X	
continuation of species	noun							X	
decrease	noun							X	
impact	noun							X	
potential	adjective							X	
probability	noun							X	
proportional	adjective							X	
selective breeding	noun							X	
suppression	noun							X	
taxonomy	noun							X	
anatomical	adjective							X	X
behavioral	adjective							X	X
capacity	noun							X	X
distribution	noun							X	X
evolution	noun							X	X
gene	noun							X	X
gene therapy	noun							X	X
generation	noun							X	X
genetic	adjective							X	X
genetic modification	noun							X	X

Term	Part of Speech	K	1	2	3	4	5	6–8	9–12
genetic variation	noun							X	X
interdependence	noun							X	X
natural selection	noun							X	X
predominance	noun							X	X
sexual reproduction	noun							X	X
advantageous	adjective								X
Charles Darwin	noun								X
correlation coefficient	noun								X
dominate	verb								X
expression	noun								X
heritable	adjective								X
morphology	noun								X
mutation	noun								X
physiological	adjective								X
physiological change	noun								X
physiology	noun								X
proliferation	noun								X
reproductive value of traits	noun								X
survival value of traits	noun								X

29. Fossils

Term	Part of Speech	K	1	2	3	4	5	6–8	9–12
plant	noun	X	X						
dinosaur	noun	X	X	X					
Earth	noun	X	X	X					
environment	noun	X	X	X					
nature	noun	X	X	X					
exist	verb		X	X	X				
time period	noun			X	X				
extinct	adjective				X	X			
extinction	noun				X	X			
fossil	noun				X	X			
layer	noun				X	X			
collection	noun				X	X	X		
existence	noun				X	X	X		
organism	noun					X	X		
rock layer	noun					X	X		
diversity	noun					X	X	X	
life form	noun					X	X	X	
sedimentary	adjective						X	X	
chronological order	noun							X	
fossil record	noun							X	
history of life	noun							X	

continued →

Term	Part of Speech	K	1	2	3	4	5	6–8	9–12
natural law	noun							X	
anatomical	adjective							X	X
ancestry	noun							X	X
radioactive dating	noun							X	X
radioactive isotope	noun								X

30. Evidence of Common Ancestry

Term	Part of Speech	K	1	2	3	4	5	6–8	9–12
body	noun	X	X	X					
history	noun			X	X	X			
species	noun			X	X	X			
fossil	noun				X	X			
fossil evidence	noun				X	X	X		
organism	noun					X	X		
role	noun					X	X		
diversity	noun					X	X	X	
development	noun						X	X	
anatomy	noun							X	
descent	noun							X	
embryo	noun							X	
fossil record	noun							X	
unity of life	noun							X	
anatomical	adjective							X	X
ancestry	noun							X	X
biological	adjective							X	X
biological evolution	noun							X	X
branch	verb							X	X
embryological	adjective							X	X
evolution	noun							X	X
evolutionary	adjective							X	X
genetic	adjective							X	X
macroscopic	adjective							X	X
modern	adjective							X	X
reconstruction	noun							X	X
amino acid	noun								X
biochemical characteristics	noun								X
common ancestry	noun								X
degree of kinship	noun								X
DNA sequence	noun								X
evidence for the unity among organisms	noun								X
origin of life	noun								X
phylogenetics	noun								X

Term	Part of Speech	K	1	2	3	4	5	6–8	9–12
sequence	noun								X
shared characteristic	noun								X

Earth and Space Science

31. The Solar System

Term	Part of Speech	K	1	2	3	4	5	6–8	9–12
fall [autumn]	noun	X							
moon	noun	X							
sky	noun	X							
spring [season]	noun	X							
summer	noun	X							
sun	noun	X							
winter	noun	X							
daylight	noun	X	X						
month	noun	X	X						
season	noun	X	X						
shadow	noun	X	X						
star	noun	X	X						
sunlight	noun	X	X						
week	noun	X	X						
year	noun	X	X						
Earth	noun	X	X	X					
seasonal	adjective	X	X	X					
sun's position	noun		X	X					
area	noun		X	X	X				
Earth's gravity	noun		X	X	X				
gas	noun		X	X	X				
gravity	noun		X	X	X				
human-made	adjective		X	X	X				
night sky	noun		X	X	X				
space	noun		X	X	X				
circular motion	noun				X	X			
photograph	noun				X	X	X		
planet	noun				X	X	X		
surface	noun				X	X	X		
universe	noun				X	X	X		
volcano	noun				X	X	X		
discovery	noun				X	X			
layer	noun				X	X			
atmosphere	noun				X	X	X		
attraction	noun				X	X	X		

continued →

Term	Part of Speech	K	1	2	3	4	5	6–8	9–12
collision	noun				X	X	X		
cycle	noun				X	X	X		
Earth's rotation	noun				X	X	X		
feature	noun				X	X	X		
force	noun				X	X	X		
galaxy	noun				X	X	X		
moon's phases	noun				X	X	X		
North Pole	noun				X	X	X		
pole	noun				X	X	X		
properties	noun				X	X	X		
rotation	noun				X	X	X		
South Pole	noun				X	X	X		
sun's size	noun				X	X	X		
telescope	noun				X	X	X		
tide	noun				X	X	X		
visible	adjective				X	X	X		
apparent movement of the planets	noun					X	X		
axis	noun					X	X		
Earth's axis	noun					X	X		
role	noun					X	X		
solar system	noun					X	X		
Earth's orbit	noun					X	X	X	
gravitational	adjective					X	X	X	
gravitational pull	noun					X	X	X	
Milky Way	noun					X	X	X	
development	noun						X	X	
orbit	noun						X	X	
orbital	adjective						X	X	
phase	noun						X	X	
relative	adjective						X	X	
spacecraft	noun						X	X	
tilted	adjective						X	X	
lunar phase	noun						X	X	X
asteroid	noun							X	
asteroid impact	noun							X	
asteroid movement patterns	noun							X	
disk	noun							X	
Earth-sun-moon system	noun							X	
eclipse	noun							X	
field	noun							X	
instrument	noun							X	
intensity	noun							X	
Isaac Newton	noun							X	

Term	Part of Speech	K	1	2	3	4	5	6–8	9–12
linear growth	noun							X	
meteor movement patterns	noun							X	
particle ring	noun							X	
physical change	noun							X	
planet composition	noun							X	
planet orbits	noun							X	
planet size	noun							X	
planet surface features	noun							X	
satellite	noun							X	
solar system formation	noun							X	
crust	noun							X	X
cyclic	adjective							X	X
elliptical orbit	noun							X	X
interdependence	noun							X	X
orbital radius	noun							X	X
Copernican revolution	noun								X
Copernicus	noun								X
Johannes Kepler	noun								X
Kepler's laws of motion	noun								X
logarithm	noun								X
Ptolemy	noun								X
space probe	noun								X
sun's radiation	noun								X

32. The Universe and Stars

Term	Part of Speech	K	1	2	3	4	5	6–8	9–12
moon	noun	X							
sky	noun	X							
sun	noun	X							
burn	verb	X	X						
light	noun	X	X						
star	noun	X	X						
Earth	noun	X	X	X					
gas	noun		X	X	X				
life cycle	noun		X	X	X				
rise	verb		X	X	X				
star age	noun		X	X	X				
star brightness	noun		X	X	X				
lifetime	noun			X	X				
form	noun			X	X	X			
life span	noun			X	X	X			
universe	noun			X	X	X			
movement	noun				X	X			

continued →

Term	Part of Speech	K	1	2	3	4	5	6–8	9–12
apparent movement of the stars	noun				X	X	X		
apparent movement of the sun	noun				X	X	X		
constellation	noun				X	X	X		
cycle	noun				X	X	X		
galaxy	noun				X	X	X		
visible	adjective				X	X	X		
independent	adjective					X	X		
role	noun					X	X		
dependent	adjective					X	X	X	
astronomical	adjective					X	X	X	
astronomical distance	noun					X	X	X	
astronomical object	noun					X	X	X	
astronomical size	noun					X	X	X	
astronomy	noun					X	X	X	
microscopic	adjective					X	X	X	
transfer	verb					X	X	X	
atom	noun						X	X	
brightness	noun						X	X	
development	noun						X	X	
immensely	adverb						X	X	
mass	noun						X	X	
relative	adjective						X	X	
vast	adjective						X	X	
celestial body	noun							X	
comet	noun							X	
comet impact	noun							X	
comet movement patterns	noun							X	
element	noun							X	
field	noun							X	
Galileo	noun							X	
helium	noun							X	
iron	noun							X	
light year	noun							X	
nucleus	noun							X	
atomic	adjective							X	X
chemical process	noun							X	X
frequency	noun							X	X
interdependence	noun							X	X
massive	adjective							X	X
age of the universe	noun								X
Big Bang theory	noun								X
composition of the universe	noun								X
core	noun								X
cosmic microwave background	noun								X

Term	Part of Speech	K	1	2	3	4	5	6–8	9–12
Doppler effect	noun								X
electromagnetic energy	noun								X
electromagnetic radiation	noun								X
emit	verb								X
evidence for the expansion of the universe	noun								X
Halley's comet	noun								X
history of the universe	noun								X
hydrogen	noun								X
interstellar	adjective								X
microwave	noun								X
neutron	noun								X
nuclear	adjective								X
nuclear fission	noun								X
nuclear fusion	noun								X
nucleosynthesis	noun								X
origin of the universe	noun								X
peer review	noun								X
primordial	adjective								X
proton	noun								X
radiation	noun								X
recede	verb								X
red shift	noun								X
solar flare	noun								X
space weather	noun								X
spectrum	noun								X
star composition	noun								X
star destruction	noun								X
star formation	noun								X
star size	noun								X
star system	noun								X
star temperature	noun								X
star types	noun								X
stellar	adjective								X
stellar energy	noun								X
sunspot	noun								X
supernova	noun								X

33. Weather and Climate

Term	Part of Speech	K	1	2	3	4	5	6–8	9–12
land	noun	X							
rain	noun	X							
snow	noun	X							

continued →

Term	Part of Speech	K	1	2	3	4	5	6–8	9–12
sun	noun	X							
ice	noun	X	X						
rainy	adjective	X	X						
season	noun	X	X						
sunlight	noun	X	X						
warm	adjective	X	X						
wind	noun	X	X						
cloudy	adjective	X	X	X					
cool	adjective	X	X	X					
daily weather pattern	noun	X	X	X					
Earth	noun	X	X	X					
heat	noun	X	X	X					
heat	verb	X	X	X					
living thing	noun	X	X	X					
seasonal changes	noun	X	X	X					
seasonal weather pattern	noun	X	X	X					
temperature	noun	X	X	X					
weather	noun	X	X	X					
weather patterns	noun	X	X	X					
area	noun		X	X	X				
prediction	noun		X	X	X				
space	noun		X	X	X				
precipitation	noun				X	X			
flow	noun				X	X	X		
glacier	noun				X	X	X		
ocean	noun				X	X	X		
planet	noun				X	X	X		
surface	noun				X	X	X		
volcanic eruption	noun				X	X	X		
continent	noun				X	X			
region	noun				X	X			
volume	noun				X	X			
air movement	noun				X	X	X		
atmosphere	noun				X	X	X		
Celsius	adjective				X	X	X		
characteristics of air	noun				X	X	X		
climate	noun				X	X	X		
collide	verb				X	X	X		
cycle	noun				X	X	X		
Fahrenheit	adjective				X	X	X		
glacial	adjective				X	X	X		
interconnected	adjective				X	X	X		
ocean current	noun				X	X	X		
rotation	noun				X	X	X		

Term	Part of Speech	K	1	2	3	4	5	6–8	9–12
typical	adjective				X	X	X		
weather condition	noun				X	X	X		
axis	noun					X	X		
global	adjective					X	X		
ice age	noun					X	X		
landform	noun					X	X		
local	adjective					X	X		
regional	adjective					X	X		
solar system	noun					X	X		
vegetation	noun					X	X		
condensation	noun					X	X	X	
geographic	adjective					X	X	X	
geography	noun					X	X	X	
latitude	noun					X	X	X	
longitude	noun					X	X	X	
oceanic	adjective					X	X	X	
pressure	noun					X	X	X	
solar	adjective					X	X	X	
store	verb					X	X	X	
transfer	verb					X	X	X	
weather map	noun					X	X	X	
accuracy	noun						X	X	
average	adjective						X	X	
biosphere	noun						X	X	
high pressure	adjective						X	X	
low pressure	adjective						X	X	
mass	noun						X	X	
orbit	noun						X	X	
tilt	noun						X	X	
air mass	noun							X	
air mass circulation	noun							X	
altitude	noun							X	
atmospheric	adjective							X	
atmospheric circulation	noun							X	
climatic pattern	noun							X	
constrain	verb							X	
convection cycle	noun							X	
Coriolis effect	noun							X	
density	noun							X	
geological	adjective							X	
gradual	adjective							X	
human activity	noun							X	
humidity	noun							X	
intensity	noun							X	

continued →

Term	Part of Speech	K	1	2	3	4	5	6–8	9–12
land distribution	noun							X	
ocean circulation	noun							X	
salinity	noun							X	
unequal heating of air	noun							X	
unequal heating of land masses	noun							X	
unequal heating of oceans	noun							X	
carbon dioxide	noun							X	X
climate change	noun							X	X
cyclical	adjective							X	X
determinant	noun							X	X
distribution	noun							X	X
latitudinal	adjective							X	X
longitudinal	adjective							X	X
orientation	noun							X	X
probabilistic	adjective							X	X
redistribute	verb							X	X
tectonic	adjective							X	X
tectonic cycle	noun							X	X
time scale	noun							X	X
volcanic ash cloud	noun							X	X
concentration	noun								X
electromagnetic radiation	noun								X
radiation	noun								X
sea level	noun								X

34. Natural Hazards

Term	Part of Speech	K	1	2	3	4	5	6–8	9–12
life	noun	X	X						
wind	noun	X	X						
Earth	noun	X	X	X					
human	noun	X	X	X					
severe weather	noun	X	X	X					
weather	noun	X	X	X					
weather scientist	noun	X	X	X					
forecast	noun		X	X					
weather forecasting	noun		X	X					
prediction	noun		X	X	X				
descriptive	adjective			X	X				
flood	noun			X	X				
drought	noun			X	X	X			
earthquake	noun			X	X	X			
existing	adjective			X	X	X			

Term	Part of Speech	K	1	2	3	4	5	6–8	9–12
forest fire	noun			X	X	X			
form	noun			X	X	X			
hurricane	noun			X	X	X			
surface	noun			X	X	X			
tornado	noun			X	X	X			
tsunami	noun			X	X	X			
volcanic eruption	noun			X	X	X			
everyday life	noun				X	X			
hazard	noun				X	X			
lightning rod	noun				X	X			
natural hazard	noun				X	X			
region	noun				X	X			
barrier	noun				X	X	X		
climate	noun				X	X	X		
designed world	noun				X	X	X		
force	noun				X	X	X		
global	adjective					X	X		
local	adjective					X	X		
natural resource	noun					X	X		
resistant	adjective					X	X		
natural process	noun					X	X	X	
development	noun						X	X	
reservoir	noun						X	X	
catastrophic	adjective							X	
debris	noun							X	
economic	adjective							X	
geologic	adjective							X	
impact	noun							X	
magnitude	noun							X	
satellite	noun							X	
frequency	noun							X	X
interdependence	noun							X	X
mass wasting	noun							X	X

35. Weathering and Erosion

Term	Part of Speech	K	1	2	3	4	5	6–8	9–12
grass	noun	X							
land	noun	X							
tree	noun	X							
ice	noun	X	X						
rock	noun	X	X						
soil	noun	X	X						
wind	noun	X	X						

continued →

Term	Part of Speech	K	1	2	3	4	5	6–8	9–12
cool	verb	X	X	X					
Earth	noun	X	X	X					
heat	verb	X	X	X					
living thing	noun	X	X	X					
gravity	noun		X	X	X				
material	noun		X	X	X				
rainfall	noun		X	X	X				
speed	noun		X	X	X				
windbreak	noun			X	X				
dike	noun			X	X	X			
erosion	noun			X	X	X			
freeze	verb			X	X	X			
shrub	noun			X	X	X			
thaw	verb			X	X	X			
movement	noun				X	X			
region	noun				X	X			
volume	noun				X	X			
cycle	noun				X	X	X		
physical characteristic	noun				X	X	X		
slope	noun				X	X	X		
weathered rock	noun				X	X	X		
weathering	noun				X	X	X		
living organism	noun					X	X		
sediment	noun					X	X		
vegetation	noun					X	X		
angle	noun					X	X	X	
particle	noun					X	X	X	
erosion resistance	noun						X		
deposition	noun							X	X
sediment deposition	noun							X	X
biogeology	noun								X

36. Water and Earth's Surface

Term	Part of Speech	K	1	2	3	4	5	6–8	9–12
land	noun	X							
sun	noun	X							
ice	noun	X	X						
rock	noun	X	X						
soil	noun	X	X						
sunlight	noun	X	X						
Earth	noun	X	X	X					
lake	noun	X	X	X					
river	noun	X	X	X					

Term	Part of Speech	K	1	2	3	4	5	6–8	9–12
temperature	noun	X	X	X					
area	noun		X	X	X				
exist	verb		X	X	X				
gravity	noun		X	X	X				
liquid	noun		X	X	X				
liquid water	noun		X	X	X				
melt	verb		X	X	X				
pond	noun		X	X	X				
solid	noun		X	X	X				
precipitation	noun				X	X			
stream	noun				X	X			
underground	adjective				X	X			
erosion	noun				X	X	X		
flow	noun				X	X	X		
form	noun				X	X	X		
freeze	verb				X	X	X		
frost	noun				X	X	X		
glacier	noun				X	X	X		
ocean	noun				X	X	X		
planet	noun				X	X	X		
salt water	noun				X	X	X		
state	noun				X	X	X		
surface	noun				X	X	X		
unit	noun				X	X	X		
weight	noun			X	X	X	X		
movement	noun				X	X			
volume	noun				X	X			
atmosphere	noun				X	X	X		
cycle	noun				X	X	X		
Earth's surface	noun				X	X	X		
force	noun				X	X	X		
forms of water	noun				X	X	X		
fresh water	noun				X	X	X		
glacial movement	noun				X	X	X		
moisture	noun				X	X	X		
properties of soil	noun				X	X	X		
properties of water	noun				X	X	X		
properties	noun				X	X	X		
rock breakage	noun				X	X	X		
rock composition	noun				X	X	X		
soil color	noun				X	X	X		
soil composition	noun				X	X	X		
soil texture	noun				X	X	X		
weathering	noun				X	X	X		

continued →

Term	Part of Speech	K	1	2	3	4	5	6–8	9–12
wedge	verb				X	X	X		
available	adjective					X	X		
global	adjective					X	X		
role	noun					X	X		
transportation	noun					X	X		
transport	verb					X	X		
water capacity	noun					X	X		
chemical	adjective					X	X	X	
condensation	noun					X	X	X	
evaporation	noun					X	X	X	
mechanical	adjective					X	X	X	
polar ice caps	noun					X	X	X	
store	verb					X	X	X	
transfer	verb					X	X	X	
transmit	verb					X	X	X	
wetland	noun					X	X	X	
alternative	adjective						X	X	
dissolve	verb						X	X	
groundwater	noun						X	X	
mineral	noun						X	X	
percentage	noun						X	X	
reservoir	noun						X	X	
rock cycle	noun						X	X	
water cycle	noun						X	X	
content	noun							X	
crystal	noun							X	
percolation	noun							X	
deposition	noun							X	X
distribution	noun							X	X
dynamic	noun							X	X
hydrologic cycle	noun							X	X
melting point	noun							X	X
molecular	adjective							X	X
transpiration	noun							X	X
universal solvent	noun							X	X
advection	noun								X
rock sequences	noun								X
soluble	adjective								X
substructure	noun								X
viscosity	noun								X

37. Earth's History

Term	Part of Speech	K	1	2	3	4	5	6–8	9–12
land	noun	X							
plant	noun	X	X						
rock	noun	X	X						
Earth	noun	X	X	X					
river	noun	X	X	X					
age	noun		X	X					
mammoth	noun		X	X					
shell	noun		X	X					
space	noun		X	X	X				
lifetime	noun			X	X				
prehistoric animals	noun			X	X				
time period	noun			X	X				
form	noun			X	X	X			
earthquake	noun			X	X	X			
erosion	noun			X	X	X			
history	noun			X	X	X			
planet	noun			X	X	X			
surface	noun			X	X	X			
volcanic eruption	noun			X	X	X			
canyon	noun				X	X			
fossil	noun				X	X			
layer	noun				X	X			
prehistoric organism	noun				X	X	X		
record	noun				X	X	X		
global	adjective					X	X		
ice age	noun					X	X		
landscape	noun					X	X		
local	adjective					X	X		
mountain chain	noun					X	X		
prehistoric environment	noun					X	X		
presence	noun					X	X		
regional	adjective					X	X		
rock layer	noun					X	X		
solar system	noun					X	X		
Earth force	noun					X	X	X	
plate tectonics	noun					X	X	X	
rock formation	noun					X	X	X	
ancient	adjective						X	X	
development	noun						X	X	
mineral	noun						X	X	
relative	adjective						X	X	
account	noun							X	

continued →

Term	Part of Speech	K	1	2	3	4	5	6–8	9–12
asteroid	noun							X	
crater	noun							X	
Earth's age	noun							X	
evidence from sedimentary rock	noun							X	
fossil record	noun							X	
geologic	adjective							X	
geologic evidence	noun							X	
Homo sapiens	noun							X	
meteorite	noun							X	
ocean basin	noun							X	
rock layer movement	noun							X	
spontaneous	adjective							X	
decay	noun							X	X
formation	noun							X	X
radioactive	adjective							X	X
rock strata	noun							X	X
time scale	noun							X	X
Earth's formation	noun								X
extent	noun								X
lunar rock	noun								X
moon rock	noun								X
nuclear	adjective								X
planetary	adjective								X
radiometric dating	noun								X
rock record	noun								X
stable	adjective								X

38. Plate Tectonics

Term	Part of Speech	K	1	2	3	4	5	6–8	9–12
hot	adjective	X							
land	noun	X							
sun	noun	X							
rock	noun	X	X						
Earth	noun	X	X	X					
heat	noun	X	X	X					
living	adjective	X	X	X					
age	noun		X	X					
boulder	noun		X	X					
Earth materials	noun		X	X					
solid rock	noun		X	X					
liquid	noun		X	X	X				
melt	verb		X	X	X				

Term	Part of Speech	K	1	2	3	4	5	6–8	9–12
solid	noun		X	X	X				
body of water	noun			X	X				
lifetime	noun			X	X				
earthquake	noun			X	X	X			
flow	noun			X	X	X			
history	noun			X	X	X			
mountain	noun			X	X	X			
ocean	noun			X	X	X			
planet	noun			X	X	X			
reflection	noun			X	X	X			
rock characteristics	noun			X	X	X			
surface	noun			X	X	X			
volcano	noun			X	X	X			
continent	noun				X	X			
fossil	noun				X	X			
layer	noun				X	X			
movement	noun				X	X			
sea floor	noun				X	X			
collide	verb				X	X	X		
cycle	noun				X	X	X		
Earth's surface	noun				X	X	X		
feature	noun				X	X	X		
properties	noun				X	X	X		
bedrock	noun					X	X		
mountain chain	noun					X	X		
mountain range	noun					X	X		
ocean floor	noun					X	X		
organism	noun					X	X		
plate	noun					X	X		
band	noun					X	X	X	
continental	adjective					X	X	X	
continental boundary	noun					X	X	X	
gravitational	adjective					X	X	X	
laboratory	noun					X	X	X	
ocean trench	noun					X	X	X	
plate tectonics	noun					X	X	X	
pressure	noun					X	X	X	
topographic map	noun					X	X	X	
wave	noun					X	X	X	
ancient	adjective						X	X	
cycle	verb						X	X	
outward	adjective						X	X	
physical replica	noun						X	X	
sedimentation	noun						X	X	

continued →

Term	Part of Speech	K	1	2	3	4	5	6–8	9–12
thermal	adjective						X	X	
chemical change	noun							X	
continental shelf	noun							X	
crustal deformation	noun							X	
crustal plate movement	noun							X	
crystalline solid	noun							X	
crystallization	noun							X	
crystallize	verb							X	
deform	verb							X	
density	noun							X	
Earth's crust	noun							X	
fracture zone	noun							X	
geologic	adjective							X	
geologic force	noun							X	
geological shift	noun							X	
geologist	noun							X	
lithosphere	noun							X	
physical change	noun							X	
recrystallization	noun							X	
rock layer movement	noun							X	
spontaneous	adjective							X	
tectonic process	noun							X	
atomic	adjective							X	X
chemical process	noun							X	X
continental crust	noun							X	X
convection	noun							X	X
crust	noun							X	X
decay	noun							X	X
distribution	noun							X	X
interdependence	noun							X	X
interior	noun							X	X
radioactive	adjective							X	X
reconstruction	noun							X	X
Alfred Wegener	noun								X
ancient core	noun								X
convection current	noun								X
historical	adjective								X
inner core	noun								X
interface	noun								X
isotope	noun								X
magnetic field	noun								X
mantle	noun								X
mountain building	noun								X
nuclear	adjective								X

Term	Part of Speech	K	1	2	3	4	5	6–8	9–12
ocean layers	noun								X
ocean ridge	noun								X
oceanic crust	noun								X
one-dimensional	adjective								X
outer core	noun								X
physical process	noun								X
plate boundary	noun								X
plate collision	noun								X
probe	noun								X
probe	verb								X
radial	adjective								X
radioactive decay	noun								X
radiometric dating	noun								X
sea-floor spreading	noun								X
seismic wave	noun								X

39. Earth Systems

Term	Part of Speech	K	1	2	3	4	5	6–8	9–12
land	noun	X							
ice	noun	X	X						
rock	noun	X	X						
soil	noun	X	X						
sunlight	noun	X	X						
wind	noun	X	X						
cloud	noun	X	X	X					
Earth	noun	X	X	X					
environment	noun	X	X	X					
human	noun	X	X	X					
living thing	noun	X	X	X					
nature	noun	X	X	X					
river	noun	X	X	X					
temperature	noun	X	X	X					
weather	noun	X	X	X					
Earth materials	noun		X	X					
pebble	noun		X	X					
melt	verb		X	X	X				
space	noun		X	X	X				
underground	adjective			X	X				
earthquake	noun			X	X	X			
ecosystem	noun			X	X	X			
erosion	noun			X	X	X			
mountain	noun			X	X	X			
ocean	noun			X	X	X			

continued →

Term	Part of Speech	K	1	2	3	4	5	6–8	9–12
period [time]	noun			X	X	X			
planet	noun			X	X	X			
surface	noun			X	X	X			
valley	noun			X	X	X			
volcano	noun			X	X	X			
dam	noun				X	X			
movement	noun				X	X			
atmosphere	noun				X	X	X		
changes in the Earth's surface	noun				X	X	X		
climate	noun				X	X	X		
Earth's surface	noun				X	X	X		
Earth's temperature	noun				X	X	X		
feature	noun				X	X	X		
force	noun				X	X	X		
gases of the atmosphere	noun				X	X	X		
glacial	adjective				X	X	X		
surface feature	noun				X	X	X		
weathering	noun				X	X	X		
wind patterns	noun				X	X	X		
global	adjective					X	X		
landform	noun					X	X		
local	adjective					X	X		
mountain range	noun					X	X		
ocean floor	noun					X	X		
organism	noun					X	X		
plate	noun					X	X		
plateau	noun					X	X		
sediment	noun					X	X		
transport	verb					X	X		
vegetation	noun					X	X		
continental	adjective					X	X	X	
microscopic	adjective					X	X	X	
ocean trench	noun					X	X	X	
plate tectonics	noun					X	X	X	
wetland	noun					X	X	X	
atmospheric composition	noun						X	X	
atmospheric layers	noun						X	X	
atmospheric pressure	noun						X	X	
biosphere	noun						X	X	
destructive	adjective						X	X	
geosphere	noun						X	X	
groundwater	noun						X	X	
hydrosphere	noun						X	X	
igneous rock	noun						X	X	

Term	Part of Speech	K	1	2	3	4	5	6–8	9–12
metamorphic rock	noun						X	X	
mineral	noun						X	X	
molten	adjective						X	X	
original	adjective						X	X	
sedimentation	noun						X	X	
sedimentary rock	noun						X	X	
water cycle	noun						X	X	
catastrophic	adjective							X	
Earth's atmosphere	noun							X	
Earth's climate	noun							X	
Earth's layers	noun							X	
Earth system	noun							X	
geologic	adjective							X	
humidity	noun							X	
impact	noun							X	
increase	noun							X	
internal	adjective							X	
landslide	noun							X	
meteor	noun							X	
meteor impact	noun							X	
negative	adjective							X	
positive	adjective							X	
runoff	noun							X	
coastal	adjective							X	X
crust	noun							X	X
deposition	noun							X	X
distribution	noun							X	X
dynamic	adjective							X	X
formation	noun							X	X
geochemical reaction	noun							X	X
geoscience	noun							X	X
greenhouse gas	noun							X	X
mass wasting	noun							X	X
molten rock	noun							X	X
optimal	adjective							X	X
spatial	adjective							X	X
surface runoff	noun							X	X
atmospheric change	noun								X
Charles Lyell	noun								X
destabilize	verb								X
Earth's elements	noun								X
Earth's external energy sources	noun								X

continued →

Term	Part of Speech	K	1	2	3	4	5	6–8	9–12
Earth's internal energy sources	noun								X
feedback effect	noun								X
geochemical cycle	noun								X
geologic time	noun								X
geologic time scale	noun								X
geological dating	noun								X
irreversible	adjective								X
ocean layers	noun								X
ocean ridge	noun								X
recharge	verb								X
seamount	noun								X
stabilize	verb								X
tectonic uplift	noun								X
temporal	adjective								X

40. Humans and Earth Systems

Term	Part of Speech	K	1	2	3	4	5	6–8	9–12
land	noun	X							
soil	noun	X	X						
Earth	noun	X	X	X					
environment	noun	X	X	X					
human	noun	X	X	X					
lake	noun	X	X	X					
living thing	noun	X	X	X					
recycle	verb	X	X	X					
reuse	verb	X	X	X					
river	noun	X	X	X					
severe weather	noun	X	X	X					
temperature	noun	X	X	X					
environmental	adjective		X	X					
safety	noun		X	X					
physical model	noun		X	X	X				
flood	noun			X	X				
migration	noun			X	X				
precipitation	noun			X	X				
stream	noun			X	X				
drought	noun			X	X	X			
earthquake	noun			X	X	X			
ecosystem	noun			X	X	X			
erosion	noun			X	X	X			
form	noun			X	X	X			
habitat	noun			X	X	X			

Term	Part of Speech	K	1	2	3	4	5	6–8	9–12
hurricane	noun			X	X	X			
ocean	noun			X	X	X			
pollution	noun			X	X	X			
species	noun			X	X	X			
surface	noun			X	X	X			
tsunami	noun			X	X	X			
volcanic eruption	noun			X	X	X			
dam	noun				X	X			
extinction	noun				X	X			
human population	noun				X	X			
natural hazard	noun				X	X			
population	noun				X	X			
region	noun				X	X			
atmosphere	noun				X	X	X		
climate	noun				X	X	X		
fresh water	noun				X	X	X		
resource	noun				X	X	X		
waste	noun				X	X	X		
construction	noun					X	X		
crops	noun					X	X		
effort	noun					X	X		
fossil fuel	noun					X	X		
global	adjective					X	X		
independent	adjective					X	X		
livestock	noun					X	X		
local	adjective					X	X		
mining	noun					X	X		
natural resource	noun					X	X		
regional	adjective					X	X		
vegetation	noun					X	X		
diversity	noun					X	X	X	
societal	adjective					X	X	X	
wetland	noun					X	X	X	
agriculture	noun						X	X	
biosphere	noun						X	X	
development	noun						X	X	
fertile	adjective						X	X	
groundwater	noun						X	X	
industry	noun						X	X	
material world	noun						X	X	
mineral	noun						X	X	
river delta	noun						X	X	
aquifer	noun							X	
Earth system	noun							X	

continued →

Term	Part of Speech	K	1	2	3	4	5	6–8	9–12
economic	adjective							X	
geologic	adjective							X	
human activity	noun							X	
human impact	noun							X	
impact	noun							X	
land usage	noun							X	
levee	noun							X	
negative	adjective							X	
positive	adjective							X	
water usage	noun							X	
civilization	noun							X	X
consumption	noun							X	X
cultural	adjective							X	X
interior	adjective							X	X
mass wasting	noun							X	X
modern	adjective							X	X
per-capita	adjective							X	X
urban development	noun							X	X
biomass	noun								X
degradation	noun								X
destabilize	verb								X
geoengineering	noun								X
mass migration	noun								X
ozone	noun								X
pollutant	noun								X
sea level	noun								X
stabilize	verb								X

41. Biogeology

Term	Part of Speech	K	1	2	3	4	5	6–8	9–12
food	noun	X							
land	noun	X							
tree	noun	X							
life	noun	X	X						
plant	noun	X	X						
soil	noun	X	X						
Earth	noun	X	X	X					
environment	noun	X	X	X					
human	noun	X	X	X					
living thing	noun	X	X	X					
root	noun	X	X	X					
exist	verb		X	X	X				
erosion	noun			X	X	X			

Term	Part of Speech	K	1	2	3	4	5	6–8	9–12
form	noun			X	X	X			
habitat	noun			X	X	X			
atmosphere	noun				X	X	X		
coral reef	noun				X	X	X		
Earth's surface	noun				X	X	X		
weathering	noun				X	X	X		
organism	noun					X	X		
biosphere	noun						X	X	
impact	noun							X	
carbon dioxide	noun							X	X
deposition	noun							X	X
dynamic	adjective							X	X
evolution	noun							X	X
formation	noun							X	X
geoscience	noun							X	X
oxygen	noun							X	X
photosynthesis	noun							X	X
abiotic components of ecosystems	noun								X
biogeology	noun								X
coastline	noun								X
coevolution	noun								X
microbial	adjective								X
stable	adjective								X

42. Natural Resources

Term	Part of Speech	K	1	2	3	4	5	6–8	9–12
food	noun	X							
grass	noun	X							
land	noun	X							
burn	verb	X	X						
rock	noun	X	X						
soil	noun	X	X						
sunlight	noun	X	X						
wind	noun	X	X						
Earth	noun	X	X	X					
environment	noun	X	X	X					
forested	adjective	X	X	X					
human	noun	X	X	X					
living thing	noun	X	X	X					
recycle	verb	X	X	X					
reuse	verb	X	X	X					
environmental	adjective		X	X					

continued →

Term	Part of Speech	K	1	2	3	4	5	6–8	9–12
safety	noun		X	X					
material	adjective		X	X	X				
coal	noun			X	X	X			
form	noun			X	X	X			
habitat	noun			X	X	X			
health	noun			X	X	X			
ocean	noun			X	X	X			
period [time]	noun			X	X	X			
pollution	noun			X	X	X			
dam	noun				X	X			
human population	noun				X	X			
population	noun				X	X			
surrounding	adjective				X	X			
animal product	noun				X	X	X		
atmosphere	noun				X	X	X		
biodiversity	noun				X	X	X		
designed world	noun				X	X	X		
fresh water	noun				X	X	X		
improved	adjective				X	X	X		
metal	noun				X	X	X		
oil	noun				X	X	X		
resource	noun				X	X	X		
resource availability	noun				X	X	X		
weathering	noun				X	X	X		
fissile material	noun					X	X		
fossil fuel	noun					X	X		
fuel	noun					X	X		
mining	noun					X	X		
natural resource	noun					X	X		
nonrenewable	adjective					X	X		
renewable	adjective					X	X		
renewable resource	noun					X	X		
surface mining	noun					X	X		
conservation	noun					X	X	X	
nonrenewable energy	noun					X	X	X	
renewable energy	noun					X	X	X	
agricultural	adjective						X	X	
biosphere	noun						X	X	
development	noun						X	X	
groundwater	noun						X	X	
material world	noun						X	X	
mineral	noun						X	X	
physical replica	noun						X	X	
economic	adjective							X	

Term	Part of Speech	K	1	2	3	4	5	6–8	9–12
energy source	noun							X	
geologic process	noun							X	
geologic trap	noun							X	
hydrothermal	adjective							X	
impact	noun							X	
issue	noun							X	
long-term	adjective							X	
management	noun							X	
marine sediment	noun							X	
metal ore	noun							X	
negative	adjective							X	
organic	adjective							X	
positive	adjective							X	
short-term	adjective							X	
subduction zone	noun							X	
civilization	noun							X	X
consumption	noun							X	X
deposition	noun							X	X
distribution	noun							X	X
geoscience	noun							X	X
human decision	noun							X	X
interdependence	noun							X	X
modern	adjective							X	X
per-capita	adjective							X	X
petroleum	noun							X	X
best practice	noun								X
cost-benefit	adjective								X
derive	verb								X
efficient	adjective								X
ethical	adjective								X
extract	verb								X
geopolitical	adjective								X
harvesting of resources	noun								X
irreversible	adjective								X
natural gas	noun								X
oil shale	noun								X
regulation	noun								X
sustainability	noun								X
tar sand	noun								X
urban planning	noun								X
waste management	noun								X

43. Global Climate Change

Term	Part of Speech	K	1	2	3	4	5	6–8	9–12
ice	noun	X	X						
Earth	noun	X	X	X					
human	noun	X	X	X					
temperature	noun	X	X	X					
weather	noun	X	X	X					
forecast	noun		X	X					
gas	noun		X	X	X				
precipitation	noun			X	X				
health	noun			X	X	X			
ocean	noun			X	X	X			
period [time]	noun			X	X	X			
population	noun				X	X			
volume	noun				X	X			
absorb	verb				X	X	X		
atmosphere	noun				X	X	X		
climate	noun				X	X	X		
glacial	adjective				X	X	X		
fossil fuel	noun					X	X		
global	adjective					X	X		
organism	noun					X	X		
regional	adjective					X	X		
role	noun					X	X		
diverse	adjective					X	X	X	
natural process	noun					X	X	X	
agriculture	noun						X	X	
average	adjective						X	X	
biosphere	noun						X	X	
geosphere	noun						X	X	
hydrosphere	noun						X	X	
advance	noun							X	
atmospheric	adjective							X	
capability	noun							X	
climate science	noun							X	
combustion	noun							X	
consistency	noun							X	
disturb	verb							X	
global temperature	noun							X	
global warming	noun							X	
gradual	adjective							X	
human activity	noun							X	
human behavior	noun							X	
impact	noun							X	

Term	Part of Speech	K	1	2	3	4	5	6–8	9–12
marine	adjective							X	
mean surface temperature	noun							X	
methane	noun							X	
solar radiation	noun							X	
volcanic activity	noun							X	
vulnerability	noun							X	
carbon dioxide	noun							X	X
climate change	noun							X	X
geoscience	noun							X	X
global climate change	noun							X	X
greenhouse gas	noun							X	X
photosynthetic	adjective							X	X
acidification	noun								X
biomass	noun								X
cryosphere	noun								X
initial	adjective								X
irreversible	adjective								X
sea level	noun								X

44. Carbon Cycle

Term	Part of Speech	K	1	2	3	4	5	6–8	9–12
plant	noun	X	X						
soil	noun	X	X						
living	adjective	X	X	X					
ocean	noun				X	X	X		
atmosphere	noun				X	X	X		
climate	noun				X	X	X		
cycle	noun				X	X	X		
organism	noun					X	X		
biosphere	noun							X	X
conserve	verb							X	X
cycle	verb							X	X
geosphere	noun							X	X
hydrosphere	noun							X	X
human activity	noun							X	
carbon	noun							X	X
carbon dioxide	noun							X	X
oxygen	noun							X	X
biogeochemical	adjective								X
closed system	noun								X
concentration	noun								X
foundation	noun								X
nitrogen cycle	noun								X

Engineering

45. Defining Problems

Term	Part of Speech	K	1	2	3	4	5	6–8	9–12
design	noun	X	X	X					
environment	noun	X	X	X					
human	noun	X	X	X					
engineer	noun		X	X	X				
engineering	noun		X	X	X				
material	noun		X	X	X				
challenge	noun				X	X	X		
health	noun				X	X	X		
pollution	noun			X	X	X			
cost	noun				X	X			
situation	noun				X	X			
climate	noun				X	X	X		
design problem	noun				X	X	X		
design solution	noun				X	X	X		
designed world	noun				X	X	X		
feature	noun				X	X	X		
improved	adjective				X	X	X		
operate	verb				X	X	X		
proposal	noun				X	X	X		
question formulation	noun				X	X	X		
resource	noun				X	X	X		
success	noun				X	X	X		
successful	adjective				X	X	X		
global	adjective					X	X		
local	adjective					X	X		
natural resource	noun					X	X		
requirement	noun					X	X	X	
societal	adjective					X	X	X	
supply	noun					X	X	X	
testable	adjective					X	X	X	
consequence	noun						X	X	
criteria	noun						X	X	
development	noun						X	X	
humanity	noun						X	X	
limitation	noun						X	X	
design task	noun							X	
economic	adjective							X	
impact	noun							X	
long-term	adjective							X	
negative	adjective							X	

Term	Part of Speech	K	1	2	3	4	5	6–8	9–12
positive	adjective							X	
potential	noun							X	
precise	adjective							X	
real-world	adjective							X	
short-term	adjective							X	
consideration	noun							X	X
qualitative	adjective							X	X
quantitative	adjective							X	X
specification	noun							X	X
aspect	noun								X
critical	adjective								X
manifestation	noun								X
mitigation	noun								X

46. Designing Solutions

Term	Part of Speech	K	1	2	3	4	5	6–8	9–12
design	noun	X	X	X					
machine	noun	X	X	X					
teamwork	noun	X	X	X					
sketch	noun		X	X					
storyboard	noun		X	X					
diagram	noun		X	X	X				
engineer	noun		X	X	X				
engineering	noun		X	X	X				
physical model	noun		X	X	X				
diorama	noun				X	X	X		
existing	adjective				X	X	X		
design problem	noun				X	X	X		
design process	noun				X	X	X		
design solution	noun				X	X	X		
designed	adjective				X	X	X		
operate	verb				X	X	X		
peers	noun				X	X	X		
replicable experiment	noun				X	X	X		
reproducible result	noun				X	X	X		
independent	adjective					X	X		
societal	adjective					X	X	X	
break down	verb						X	X	
convincing	adjective						X	X	
criteria	noun						X	X	
physical replica	noun						X	X	
priority	noun						X	X	
abstract	adjective							X	

continued →

Term	Part of Speech	K	1	2	3	4	5	6–8	9–12
agreed-upon	adjective							X	
concrete	adjective							X	
jointly	adverb							X	
mathematical model	noun							X	
real-world	adjective							X	
theoretical model	noun							X	
consideration	noun							X	X
representation	noun							X	X
systematic	adjective							X	X
dramatization	noun								X
tradeoff	noun								X

47. Evaluating and Testing Solutions

Term	Part of Speech	K	1	2	3	4	5	6–8	9–12
best	adjective	X	X	X					
environment	noun	X	X	X					
balance	noun		X	X					
calculator	noun		X	X					
ruler	noun		X	X					
safety	noun		X	X					
engineering	noun		X	X	X				
characteristic	noun			X	X	X			
flow	verb			X	X	X			
cost	noun				X	X			
design solution	noun				X	X	X		
designed	adjective				X	X	X		
difficulty	noun				X	X	X		
operate	verb				X	X	X		
presentation	noun				X	X	X		
successful	adjective				X	X	X		
failure point	noun					X	X		
independent	adjective					X	X		
perform	verb					X	X		
collaboratively	adverb					X	X	X	
prototype	noun					X	X	X	
test results	noun					X	X	X	
trial	noun					X	X	X	
control of variables	noun						X	X	
controlled experiment	noun						X	X	
criteria	noun						X	X	
data analysis	noun						X	X	
data interpretation	noun						X	X	
data presentation	noun						X	X	

Term	Part of Speech	K	1	2	3	4	5	6–8	9–12
redesign process	noun						X	X	
abstract	adjective							X	
concrete	adjective							X	
design system	noun							X	
element	noun							X	
impact	noun							X	
linear	adjective							X	
nonlinear	adjective							X	
real-world	adjective							X	
computational	adjective							X	X
consideration	noun							X	X
cultural	adjective							X	X
iterative process	noun							X	X
optimal	adjective							X	X
quantitative	adjective							X	X
statistical	adjective							X	X
systematic	adjective							X	X
aesthetics	noun								X
algebraic	adjective								X
aspect	noun								X
critical	adjective								X
exponential	adjective								X
logarithm	noun								X
revision of scientific theories	noun								X
tradeoff	noun								X
trigonometric	adjective								X

Appendix
Master List of Terms

This appendix lists all of the words from parts II and III in alphabetical order. Teachers looking for a specific word can use this listing to find it quickly. Each term is followed by initials or numbers that indicate where the term can be found in the book. If a word is followed by initials such as EVAL, which represent a category (Evaluation), it is found in part II. If a word is followed by a number, which represents a measurement topic, it is found in part III.

Part II Categories

Crosscutting Practices and Concepts

ARG   Engaging in argument from evidence

C/E   Cause and effect

DATA Analyzing and interpreting data

E/M   Energy and matter

E/S   Constructing explanations and designing solutions

INFL Influence of engineering, technology, and science on society and the natural world

INFO Obtaining, evaluating, and communicating information

INT   Interdependence of science, engineering, and technology

INV   Planning and carrying out investigations

MCT   Using mathematics and computational thinking

MOD   Developing and using models

PAT   Patterns

Q/P   Asking questions and defining problems

S/C   Stability and change

S/F   Structure and function

SPQ   Scale, proportion, and quantity

SYS   Systems and system models

Cognitive Verbs

ADD	Add To	EXEC	Execute	REDO	Redo
ARR	Arrange	EXP	Explain	SBP	See the Big Picture
C/C	Compare/Contrast	HYP	Hypothesize	SI	Seek Information
COLL	Collaborate	INF	Infer	SYM	Symbolize
CRE	Create	MEAS	Measure	TM	Think Metacognitively
DEC	Decide	P/A	Prove/Argue	TRANS	Transform
DEF	Define	PS	Problem Solve		
EVAL	Evaluate	PULL	Pull Apart		

Part III Measurement Topics

Physical Science

1. Forces and Interactions
2. Electric and Magnetic Forces
3. Gravity
4. Energy and Forces
5. Energy Definitions
6. Energy Conservation and Energy Transfer
7. Waves
8. Electromagnetic Radiation
9. Information Technologies
10. States of Matter
11. Structure and Properties of Matter
12. Conservation of Matter
13. Chemical Reactions
14. Bonds
15. Nuclear Processes

Life Science

16. Growth and Development of Organisms
17. Matter and Energy in Organisms
18. Ecosystem Dynamics
19. Interdependent Relationships in Ecosystems
20. Matter and Energy in Ecosystems
21. Humans, Biodiversity, and Ecosystems
22. Structure and Function
23. Information Processing
24. Cell Theory
25. Inheritance of Traits
26. Variation of Traits
27. Adaptation
28. Natural Selection
29. Fossils
30. Evidence of Common Ancestry

Earth and Space Science

Engineering

Terms

A

ability to support life, 24

abiotic, 19, 27

abiotic components of ecosystems, 41

absorb, 7, 8, 13, 43

absorbency, 11

absorption, 14, 15

abstract, MOD, 46, 47

abundance, 18

abundant, 18

acceleration, 1

accelerator, 11

accept, DEC

accommodate, TRANS

account (noun), 37

account (verb), EXP

accumulate, ADD

accuracy, 13, 23, 33

accurate, DATA

achieve, EXEC

acid, 13

acid-base reactions, 13

acidification, 43

acidity, 27

acquire, SI

acquired trait, 27

activity, SYS

actual mass, 11

adaptation, 27, 28

adaptive characteristics, 27

address, PS

adult, 16

advance, 9, 43

advantage, 9, 28

advantageous, 27, 28

advection, 36

adverse, 21

aerobic, 20

aesthetics, 47

affect, TRANS

age, 37, 38

age of the universe, 32

agreed-upon, 46

agricultural, 42

agriculture, 40, 43

air mass, 33

air mass circulation, 33

air movement, 33

Albert Einstein, 3, 4

Alfred Wegener, 38

algae, 17, 20

algebraic, MCT, 47

allele, 25

allow, P/A

alternative, 13, 36

altitude, 33

amino acid, 17, 30

amino acid sequence, 17

ammonia, 11

ammonium chloride, 13

amount, SPQ

amplitude, 7

anaerobic, 20

analog, 9

analysis, DATA

analyze, PULL

anatomical, 27, 28, 29, 30

anatomical characteristic, 22

difference, PAT

differentiate, C/C

differentiation, 24

difficulty, 47

diffraction, 8

digestive system, 22

digital, INFO, 9

digitize, 9

dike, 35

dinosaur, 29

diorama, 46

direction of a force, 1, 3

direction of motion, 1, 3

disassemble, PULL

discovery, INV, 31

disease, 18

disk, 31

disperse, 19

display (noun), 9

display (verb), SYM

disruption, 18

dissolve, 11, 12, 13, 36

distance, SPQ

distinct, 21, 26, 27

distinguish, C/C

distribute, ARR

distribution, 26, 27, 28, 33, 36, 38, 39, 42

disturb, 43

disturbance, 18

diverge, 21, 27

diverse, 16, 43

diversity, 18, 29, 30, 40

diversity of life, 18

DNA, 17, 24, 25

DNA molecule, 25

DNA replication, 26

DNA sequence, 30

DNA structure, 25

DNA subunit, 25

dominant trait, 25

dominate, 27, 28

Doppler effect, 7, 32

drag, 1

dramatization, 46

drought, 16, 27, 34, 40

durable, 11, 18, 20

dynamic (adjective), 18, 39, 41

dynamic (noun), 13, 36

E

Earth, 3, 4, 5, 7, 20, 21, 29, 31, 32, 33, 34, 35, 36, 37, 38, 39, 40, 41, 42, 43

Earth force, 37

Earth materials, 38, 39

earthquake, 34, 37, 38, 39, 40

Earth's age, 37

Earth's atmosphere, 39

Earth's axis, 31

Earth's climate, 39

Earth's crust, 38

Earth's elements, 39

Earth's external energy sources, 39

Earth's formation, 37

Earth's gravity, 3, 31

Earth's internal energy sources, 39

Earth's layers, 39

Earth's orbit, 31

Earth's rotation, 3, 31

Earth's surface, 3, 6, 36, 38, 39, 41

Earth's temperature, 39

Earth-sun-moon system, 31

Earth system, 39, 40

eclipse, 31

F

H

I

land distribution, 33

land usage, 40

landform, 33, 39

landscape, 21, 37

landslide, 39

latitude, 33

latitudinal, 33

law of conservation of matter, 12

layer, 29, 31, 37, 38

Le Chatelier's principle, 13

lead, COLL

leaf, 22

learn, TM

levee, 40

lever arm, 4

life, 6, 16, 18, 20, 21, 24, 34, 41

life cycle, 16, 32

life form, 29

life form change, 27

life span, 32

life-sustaining functions, 22

lifetime, 32, 37, 38

light, 1, 6, 7, 8, 9, 16, 17, 32

light absorption, 6

light beam, 8

light emission, 7

light pulse, 9

light reflection, 7

light refraction, 7

light scattering, 8

light source, 8

light transmission, 8

light wave, 7

light wavelength, 8

light year, 32

lightning rod, 34

limit, PS

limitation, 45

limited, 5, 18

linear, DATA, 3, 7, 20, 21, 47

linear growth, 31

link, ADD

liquid, 6, 10, 11, 20, 36, 38

liquid water, 36

Lise Meitner, 15

lithosphere, 38

livestock, 40

living, 8, 17, 19, 21, 38, 44

living organism, 35

living system, 17, 18, 21, 22

living thing, 17, 18, 24, 33, 35, 39, 40, 41, 42

local, 33, 34, 37, 39, 40, 45

locate, DEF

logarithm, MCT, 31, 47

logical, ARG

longitude, 33

longitudinal, 33

long-term, 42, 45

Louis Pasteur, 17

low pressure, 33

lunar phase, 31

lunar rock, 37

lung, 22

M

machine, 9, 46

macroscopic, 1, 12, 13, 30

macroscopic level, 13

macroscopic scale, 5

magnet, 2, 3, 4

magnetic, 2, 11

magnetic attraction, 2

magnetic field, 2, 3, 4, 8, 38

N

O

S

T

References and Resources

Achieve. (2014). *Three dimensions.* Accessed at www.nextgenscience.org/three-dimensions on May 30, 2014.

Adams, M. J. (1990). *Beginning to read: Thinking and learning about print.* Cambridge, MA: MIT Press.

Amaral, O. M., Garrison, L., & Klentschy, M. (2002). Helping English learners increase achievement through inquiry-based science instruction. *Bilingual Research Journal, 26*(2), 213–239.

Anderson, J. R., & Reder, L. M. (1979). An elaborative processing explanation of depth of processing. In L. S. Cermak & F. I. M. Craik (Eds.), *Levels of processing in human memory* (pp. 385–404). Hillsdale, NJ: Erlbaum.

Anderson, R. C., & Freebody, P. (1979). *Vocabulary knowledge* (Tech. Rep. No. 136). Urbana-Champaign: University of Illinois, Center for the Study of Reading.

Anderson, R. C., & Freebody, P. (1985). Vocabulary knowledge. In H. Singer & R. B. Ruddell (Eds.), *Theoretical models and processes of reading* (3rd ed., pp. 343–371). Newark, DE: International Reading Association.

Anderson, R. C., & Pearson, P. D. (1984). A scheme-theoretic view of basic processes in reading. In P. D. Pearson (Ed.), *Handbook of reading research* (pp. 255–291). New York: Longman.

Baumann, J. F., & Kame'enui, E. J. (1991). Research on vocabulary instruction: Ode to Voltaire. In J. Flood, J. M. Jensen, D. Lapp, & J. R. Squire (Eds.), *Handbook of research on teaching the English language arts* (pp. 604–632). New York: Macmillan.

Beck, I. L., & McKeown, M. G. (1991). Conditions of vocabulary acquisition. In R. Barr, M. L. Kamil, P. Mosenthal, & P. D. Pearson (Eds.), *Handbook of reading research* (Vol. 2, pp. 789–814). Mahwah, NJ: Erlbaum.

Beck, I. L., & McKeown, M. G. (2007). Increasing young low-income children's oral vocabulary repertoires through rich and focused instruction. *The Elementary School Journal, 107*(3), 251–271.

Beck, I. L., McKeown, M. G., & Kucan, L. (2002). *Bringing words to life: Robust vocabulary instruction.* New York: Guilford Press.

Beck, I. L., Perfetti, C. A., & McKeown, M. G. (1982). Effects of long-term vocabulary instruction on lexical access and reading comprehension. *Journal of Educational Psychology, 74*(4), 506–521.

Becker, W. C. (1977). Teaching reading and language to the disadvantaged: What we have learned from field research. *Harvard Educational Review, 47*(4), 518–543.

Berne, J. I., & Blachowicz, C. L. Z. (2008). What reading teachers say about vocabulary instruction: Voices from the classroom. *The Reading Teacher, 62*(4), 314–323.

Beyersdorfer, J. M. (1991). *Middle school students' strategies for selection of vocabulary in science texts.* Unpublished doctoral dissertation, National-Louis University, Evanston, IL.

Biemiller, A. (1999, April). *Estimating vocabulary growth for ESL children with and without listening comprehension instruction.* Paper presented at the annual conference of the American Educational Research Association, Montreal, Quebec, Canada.

Biemiller, A. (2001). Teaching vocabulary: Early, direct, and sequential. *American Educator, 25*(1), 24–28, 47.

Biemiller, A. (2005). Size and sequence in vocabulary development: Implications for choosing words for primary grade vocabulary instruction. In E. H. Hiebert & M. L. Kamil (Eds.), *Teaching and learning vocabulary: Bringing research to practice* (pp. 223–242). Mahwah, NJ: Erlbaum.

Biemiller, A. (2006). Vocabulary development and instruction: A prerequisite for school learning. In D. K. Dickinson & S. B. Neuman (Eds.), *Handbook of early literacy research* (Vol. 2, pp. 41–51). New York: Guilford Press.

Biemiller, A. (2012). Teaching vocabulary in the primary grades: Vocabulary instruction needed. In E. J. Kame'enui & J. F. Baumann (Eds.), *Vocabulary instruction: Research to practice* (2nd ed., pp. 34–50). New York: Guilford Press.

Biemiller, A., & Boote, C. (2006). An effective method for building meaning vocabulary in primary grades. *Journal of Educational Psychology, 98*(1), 44–62.

Biemiller, A., & Slonim, N. (2001). Estimating root word vocabulary growth in normative and advantaged populations: Evidence for a common sequence of vocabulary acquisition. *Journal of Educational Psychology, 93*(3), 498–520.

Blachowicz, C. L. Z., & Fisher, P. (2000). Vocabulary instruction. In M. L. Kamil, P. B. Mosenthal, P. D. Pearson, & R. Barr (Eds.), *Handbook of reading research* (Vol. 3, pp. 503–523). Mahwah, NJ: Erlbaum.

Blachowicz, C. L. Z., & Fisher, P. (2008). Attentional vocabulary instruction: Read-alouds, word play, and other motivating strategies for fostering informal word learning. In A. E. Farstrup & S. J. Samuels (Eds.), *What research has to say about vocabulary instruction* (pp. 32–55). Newark, DE: International Reading Association.

Blachowicz, C. L. Z., & Fisher, P. (2012). Keep the "fun" in fundamental: Encouraging word consciousness and incidental word learning in the classroom through word play. In E. J. Kame'enui & J. F. Baumann (Eds.), *Vocabulary instruction: Research to practice* (2nd ed., pp. 189–209). New York: Guilford Press.

Blachowicz, C. L. Z., Fisher, P. J. L., Costa, M., & Pozzi, M. (1993, November). *Researching vocabulary learning in middle school cooperative reading groups: A teacher-researcher collaboration.* Paper presented at the tenth Great Lakes Regional Reading Conference, Chicago.

Blachowicz, C. L. Z., Fisher, P. J. L., Ogle, D., & Watts-Taffe, S. (2006). Vocabulary: Questions from the classroom. *Reading Research Quarterly, 41*(4), 524–539.

Booth, A. E. (2009). Causal supports for early word learning. *Child Development, 80*(4), 1243–1250.

Bowman, B., Donovan, S., & Burns, M. S. (2000). *Eager to learn: Educating our preschoolers.* Washington, DC: National Academy Press.

Bravo, M. A., & Cervetti, G. N. (2008). Teaching vocabulary through text and experience in content areas. In A. E. Farstrup & S. J. Samuels (Eds.), *What research has to say about vocabulary instruction* (pp. 130–149). Newark, DE: International Reading Association.

Breland, H. M., Jones, R. J., & Jenkins, L. (1994). *The College Board vocabulary study.* New York: College Entrance Examination Board.

Brophy, J. E., & Good, T. L. (1986). Teacher behavior and student achievement. In M. C. Wittrock (Ed.), *Handbook of research on teaching* (3rd ed., pp. 328–375). New York: Macmillan.

Cain, K., Oakhill, J. V., Barnes, M. A., & Bryant, P. E. (2001). Comprehension skill, inference-making ability, and their relation to knowledge. *Memory and Cognition, 29*(6), 850–859.

Calderón, M., Hertz-Lazarowitz, R., & Slavin, R. (1998). Effects of Bilingual Cooperative Integrated Reading and Composition on students making the transition from Spanish to English reading. *The Elementary School Journal, 99*(2), 153–165.

Carey, S. (1978). The child as word learner. In M. Halle, J. Bresnan, & G. A. Miller (Eds.), *Linguistic theory and psychological reality* (pp. 264–293). Cambridge, MA: MIT Press.

Carey, S. (1988). Conceptual differences between children and adults. *Mind and Language, 3*(3), 167–181.

Carleton, L., & Marzano, R. J. (2010). *Vocabulary games for the classroom.* Bloomington, IN: Marzano Research.

Carlo, M. S., August, D., McLaughlin, B., Snow, C. E., Dressler, C., Lippman, D. N., et al. (2004). Closing the gap: Addressing the vocabulary needs of English-language learners in bilingual and mainstream classrooms. *Reading Research Quarterly, 39*(2), 188–215.

Casale, U. P. (1985). Motor imaging: A reading-vocabulary strategy. *Journal of Reading, 28*(7), 619–621.

Castek, J., Dalton, B., & Grisham, D. L. (2012). Using multimedia to support generative vocabulary learning. In E. J. Kame'enui & J. F. Baumann (Eds.), *Vocabulary instruction: Research to practice* (2nd ed., pp. 303–321). New York: Guilford Press.

Cervetti, G. N., Hiebert, E. H., & Pearson, P. D. (2010). *Factors that influence the difficulty of science words.* Santa Cruz, CA: TextProject.

Chall, J. S., & Jacobs, V. A. (2003). The classic study on poor children's fourth-grade slump. *American Educator, 27*(1), 14–15, 44.

Chi, M. T., & Koeske, R. D. (1983). Network representation of a child's dinosaur knowledge. *Developmental Psychology, 19*(1), 29–39.

Clark, E. V. (1993). *The lexicon in acquisition.* New York: Cambridge University Press.

Coyne, M. D., Capozzoli-Oldham, A., & Simmons, D. C. (2012). Vocabulary instruction for young children at risk of reading difficulties: Teaching word meanings during shared storybook reading. In E. J. Kame'enui & J. F. Baumann (Eds.), *Vocabulary instruction: Research to practice* (pp. 51–71). New York: Guilford Press.

Coyne, M. D., Simmons, D. C., & Kame'enui, E. J. (2004). Vocabulary instruction for young children at risk of experiencing reading difficulties: Teaching word meanings during shared storybook reading. In J. F. Baumann & E. J. Kame'enui (Eds.), *Vocabulary instruction: Research to practice* (pp. 41–58). New York: Guilford Press.

Cunningham, A. E., & Stanovich, K. E. (1997). Early reading acquisition and its relation to reading experience and ability 10 years later. *Developmental Psychology, 33*(6), 934–945.

Curtis, M. E., & Longo, A. M. (2001). Teaching vocabulary to adolescents to improve comprehension. *Reading Online, 5*(4). Accessed at www.readingonline.org/articles/curtis on May 27, 2014.

Dale, E. (1965). Vocabulary measurement: Techniques and major findings. *Elementary English, 42*(8), 895–901.

Dalton, B., & Grisham, D. L. (2011). eVoc strategies: 10 ways to use technology to build vocabulary. *The Reading Teacher, 64*(5), 306–317.

Daniels, M. (1994). The effect of sign language on hearing children's language development. *Communication Education, 43*(4), 291–298.

Daniels, M. (1996). Bilingual, bimodal education for hearing kindergarten students. *Sign Language Studies, 90,* 25–37.

Davis, F. B. (1942). Two new measures of reading ability. *Journal of Educational Psychology, 33*(5), 365–372.

Davis, F. B. (1944). Fundamental factors of comprehension in reading. *Psychometrika, 9*(3), 185–197.

Davis, F. B. (1968). Research in comprehension in reading. *Reading Research Quarterly, 3*(4), 499–545.

Davis, F. B. (1972). Psychometric research on comprehension in reading. *Reading Research Quarterly, 7*(4), 628–678.

Dole, J. A., Sloan, C., & Trathen, W. (1995). Teaching vocabulary within the context of literature. *Journal of Reading, 38*(6), 452–460.

Dunn, M., Bonner, B., & Huske, L. (2007). *Developing a systems process for improving instruction in vocabulary: Lessons learned.* Alexandria, VA: Association for Supervision and Curriculum Development.

Durso, F. T., & Shore, W. J. (1991). Partial knowledge of word meanings. *Journal of Experimental Psychology: General, 120*(2), 190–202.

Elleman, A. M., Lindo, E. J., Morphy, P., & Compton, D. L. (2009). The impact of vocabulary instruction on passage-level comprehension of school-age children: A meta-analysis. *Journal of Research on Educational Effectiveness, 2*(1), 1–44.

Entwisle, D. R. (1966). *Word associations of young children.* Baltimore: Johns Hopkins University Press.

Farkas, G., & Beron, K. (2004). The detailed age trajectory of oral vocabulary knowledge: Differences by class and race. *Social Science Research, 33*(3), 464–497.

Fisher, P. J. L., Blachowicz, C. L. Z., & Smith, J. C. (1991). Vocabulary learning in literature discussion groups. In J. Zutell & S. McCormick (Eds.), *Learner factors/teacher factors: Issues in literacy research and instruction (40th yearbook of the National Reading Conference)* (pp. 201–209). Chicago: National Reading Conference.

Fisher, P. J. L., & Danielsen, D. (1998). When fourth-graders select their own words for spelling and vocabulary. In L. Wedwick & R. K. Moss (Eds.), *Conversations: Teacher research in literacy learning* (pp. 23–27). Bloomington, IL: Illinois Reading Council.

Fry, E. B., Kress, J. E., & Fountoukidis, D. L. (2000). *The reading teacher's book of lists* (4th ed.). San Francisco: Jossey-Bass.

Gershkoff-Stowe, L., & Hahn, E. R. (2007). Fast mapping skills in the developing lexicon. *Journal of Speech, Language, and Hearing Research, 50*(3), 682–697.

Gifford, M., & Gore, S. (2008). *The effects of focused academic vocabulary instruction on underperforming math students.* Alexandria, VA: Association for Supervision and Curriculum Development.

Glaser, R. (1984). Education and thinking: The role of knowledge. *American Psychologist, 39*(2), 93–104.

Graves, M. F. (2000). A vocabulary program to complement and bolster a middle-grade comprehension program. In B. M. Taylor, M. F. Graves, & P. van den Broek (Eds.), *Reading for meaning: Fostering comprehension in the middle grades* (pp. 116–135). Newark, DE: International Reading Association.

Graves, M. F., Juel, C., & Graves, B. B. (1998). *Teaching reading in the 21st century.* Boston: Allyn & Bacon.

Haggard, M. R. (1982). The vocabulary self-selection strategy: An active approach to word learning. *Journal of Reading, 26*(3), 203–207.

Haggard, M. R. (1985). An interactive strategies approach to content reading. *Journal of Reading, 29*(3), 204–210.

Harmon, J. M., Hedrick, W. B., Wood, K. D., & Gress, M. (2005). Vocabulary self-selection: A study of middle-school students' word selections from expository texts. *Reading Psychology, 26*(3), 313–333.

Hart, B., & Risley, T. R. (1995). *Meaningful differences in the everyday experience of young American children.* Baltimore: Brookes.

Hart, B., & Risley, T. R. (2003). The early catastrophe: The 30 million word gap by age 3. *American Educator, 27*(1), 4–9.

Hattie, J. A. C. (2009). *Visible learning: A synthesis of over 800 meta-analyses relating to achievement.* New York: Routledge.

Haystead, M. W., & Marzano, R. J. (2009). *Meta-analytic synthesis of studies conducted at Marzano Research on instructional strategies.* Englewood, CO: Marzano Research. Accessed at www.marzanoresearch.com /research/reports/meta-analytic-synthesis-of-studies on May 27, 2014.

Hiebert, E. H., & Cervetti, G. N. (2012). What differences in narrative and informational texts mean for the learning and instruction of vocabulary. In E. J. Kame'enui & J. F. Baumann (Eds.), *Vocabulary instruction: Research to practice* (2nd ed., pp. 322–344). New York: Guilford Press.

Hoffman, J. V. (1991). Teacher and school effects in learning to read. In R. Barr, M. L. Kamil, P. Mosenthal, & P. D. Pearson (Eds.), *Handbook of reading research* (Vol. 2, pp. 911–950). Mahwah, NJ: Erlbaum.

Jenkins, J. R., & Dixon, R. (1983). Vocabulary learning. *Contemporary Educational Psychology, 8*(3), 237–260.

Jimenez, R. T. (1997). The strategic reading abilities and potential of five low-literacy Latina/o readers in middle school. *Reading Research Quarterly, 32*(3), 224–243.

Johnson, D. D., & Pearson, P. D. (1984). *Teaching reading vocabulary.* New York: Holt, Rinehart and Winston.

Juel, C., Biancarosa, G., Coker, D., & Deffes, R. (2003). Walking with Rosie: A cautionary tale of early reading instruction. *Educational Leadership, 60*(7), 12–18.

Just, M. A., & Carpenter, P. A. (1987). *The psychology of reading and language comprehension.* Boston: Allyn & Bacon.

Kagan, S., & Kagan, M. (2009). *Kagan cooperative learning.* San Clemente, CA: Kagan.

Kame'enui, E. J., Carnine, D. W., & Freschi, R. (1982). Effects of text construction and instructional procedures for teaching word meanings on comprehension and recall. *Reading Research Quarterly, 17*(3), 367–388.

Kelley, J. G., Lesaux, N. K., Kieffer, M. J., & Faller, S. E. (2010). Effective academic vocabulary instruction in the urban middle school. *The Reading Teacher, 64*(1), 5–14.

Klesius, J. P., & Searls, E. F. (1990). A meta-analysis of recent research in meaning vocabulary instruction. *Journal of Research and Development in Education, 23*(4), 226–235.

Leung, C. B. (1992). Effects of word-related variables on vocabulary growth repeated read-aloud events. In C. K. Kinzer & D. J. Leu (Eds.), *Literacy research, theory, and practice: Views from many perspectives (Forty-first yearbook of the National Reading Conference)* (pp. 491–498). Chicago: National Reading Conference.

Levelt, W. J. M., Roelofs, A., & Meyer, A. S. (1999). A theory of lexical access in speech production. *Behavioral and Brain Sciences, 22*(1), 1–38.

Manzo, U. C., & Manzo, A. V. (2008). Teaching vocabulary-learning strategies: Word consciousness, word connection, and word prediction. In A. E. Farstrup & S. J. Samuels (Eds.), *What research has to say about vocabulary instruction* (pp. 80–105). Newark, DE: International Reading Association.

Marmolejo, A. (1990). *The effects of vocabulary instruction with poor readers: A meta-analysis.* Unpublished master's thesis, Columbia University Teachers College, New York.

Marulis, L. M., & Neuman, S. B. (2010). The effects of vocabulary intervention on young children's word learning: A meta-analysis. *Review of Educational Research, 80*(3), 300–335.

Marzano, R. J. (2002). *Identifying the primary instructional concepts in mathematics: A linguistic approach*. Accessed at www.marzanoresearch.com/research/recommended-reading/identifying-the-primary-instructional-concepts-in-mathematics-a-linguistic-approach on October 20, 2014.

Marzano, R. J. (2004). *Building background knowledge for academic achievement: Research on what works in schools*. Alexandria, VA: Association for Supervision and Curriculum Development.

Marzano, R. J. (2005). *Marzano program for building academic vocabulary: Preliminary report of the 2004–2005 evaluation study*. Accessed at www.marzanoresearch.com/vocabulary/marzano-program-for-building-academic-vocabulary-preliminary-report-of-the-2004-2005-evaluation-study on May 27, 2014.

Marzano, R. J. (2006). *Marzano program for building academic vocabulary: Supplemental report of effects on specific subgroups (FRL & ELL students)*. Accessed at www.marzanoresearch.com/vocabulary/marzano-program-for-building-academic-vocabulary-supplemental-report-of-effects-on-specific-subgroups-frl-ell-students on May 27, 2014.

Marzano, R. J. (2007). *The art and science of teaching: A comprehensive framework for effective instruction*. Alexandria, VA: Association for Supervision and Curriculum Development.

Marzano, R. J. (2010). *Teaching basic and advanced vocabulary: A framework for direct instruction*. Boston: Cengage ELT.

Marzano, R. J., Brandt, R. S., Hughes, C. S., Jones, B. F., Presseisen, B. Z., Rankin, S. C., et al. (1988). *Dimensions of thinking: A framework for curriculum and instruction*. Alexandria, VA: Association for Supervision and Curriculum Development.

Marzano, R. J., & Pickering, D. J. (2005). *Building academic vocabulary: Teacher's manual*. Alexandria, VA: Association for Supervision and Curriculum Development.

Marzano, R. J., & Simms, J. A. (2013). *Vocabulary for the Common Core*. Bloomington, IN: Marzano Research.

Mayer, R. E. (2001). *Multimedia learning*. New York: Cambridge University Press.

Mayer, R. E., & Moreno, R. (2002). Animation as an aid to multimedia learning. *Educational Psychology Review, 14*(1), 87–99.

McKeown, M. G. (1991). Learning word meanings from definitions: Problems and potential. In P. J. Schwanenflugel (Ed.), *The psychology of word meanings* (pp. 137–156). Hillsdale, NJ: Erlbaum.

McKeown, M. G. (1993). Creating effective definitions for young word learners. *Reading Research Quarterly, 28*(1), 16–31.

McKeown, M. G., Beck, I. L., Omanson, R. C., & Perfetti, C. A. (1983). The effects of long-term vocabulary instruction on reading comprehension: A replication. *Journal of Reading Behavior, 15*(1), 3–18.

McKeown, M. G., Beck, I. L., Omanson, R. C., & Pople, M. T. (1985). Some effects of the nature and frequency of vocabulary instruction on the knowledge and use of words. *Reading Research Quarterly, 20*(5), 522–535.

McKeown, M. G., Beck, I. L., & Sandora, C. (2012). Direct and rich vocabulary instruction needs to start early. In E. J. Kame'enui & J. F. Baumann (Eds.), *Vocabulary instruction: Research to practice* (2nd ed., pp. 17–33). New York: Guilford Press.

McKeown, M. G., & Curtis, M. E. (Eds.). (1987). *The nature of vocabulary acquisition*. Hillsdale, NJ: Erlbaum.

Merriam-Webster's collegiate dictionary (11th ed.). (2012). Springfield, MA: Merriam-Webster.

Mezynski, K. (1983). Issues concerning the acquisition of knowledge: Effects of vocabulary training on reading comprehension. *Review of Educational Research, 53*(2), 253–279.

Miller, G. A., & Gildea, P. M. (1987). How children learn words. *Scientific American, 257*(3), 94–99.

Mol, S. E., Bus, A. G., & de Jong, M. T. (2009). Interactive book reading in early education: A tool to stimulate print knowledge as well as oral language. *Review of Educational Research, 79*(2), 979–1007.

Mol, S. E., Bus, A. G., de Jong, M. T., & Smeets, D. J. H. (2008). Added value of dialogic parent-child book readings: A meta-analysis. *Early Education and Development, 19*(1), 7–26.

Nagy, W. (2005). Why vocabulary instruction needs to be long-term and comprehensive. In E. H. Hiebert & M. L. Kamil (Eds.), *Teaching and learning vocabulary: Bringing research to practice* (pp. 27–44). Mahwah, NJ: Erlbaum.

Nagy, W., Berninger, V., Abbott, R., Vaughan, K., & Vermeulen, K. (2003). Relationship of morphology and other language skills to literacy skills in at-risk second-grade readers and at-risk fourth-grade writers. *Journal of Educational Psychology, 95*(4), 730–742.

Nagy, W. E., & Anderson, R. C. (1984). How many words are there in printed school English? *Reading Research Quarterly, 19*(3), 304–330.

Nagy, W. E., Herman, P. A., & Anderson, R. C. (1985). Learning words from context. *Reading Research Quarterly, 20*(2), 233–253.

Nagy, W. E., & Scott, J. A. (2000). Vocabulary processes. In M. L. Kamil, P. B. Mosenthal, P. D. Pearson, & R. Barr (Eds.), *Handbook of reading research* (Vol. 3, pp. 269–284). Mahwah, NJ: Erlbaum.

National Early Literacy Panel. (2008). *Developing early literacy: Report of the National Early Literacy Panel.* Washington, DC: National Institute for Literacy.

National Reading Panel. (2000). *Teaching children to read: An evidence-based assessment of the scientific research literature on reading and its implications for reading instruction: Reports of the subgroups.* Bethesda, MD: National Institute of Child Health and Human Development.

National Research Council. (2012). *A framework for K–12 science education: Practices, crosscutting concepts, and core ideas.* Washington, DC: National Academies Press.

Neuman, S. B., & Dwyer, J. (2009). Missing in action: Vocabulary instruction in pre-K. *The Reading Teacher, 62*(5), 384–392.

Neuman, S. B., & Dwyer, J. (2011). Developing vocabulary and conceptual knowledge for low-income preschoolers: A design experiment. *Journal of Literacy Research, 43*(2), 103–129.

Neuman, S. B., Newman, E. H., & Dwyer, J. (2011). Educational effects of a vocabulary intervention on preschoolers' word knowledge and conceptual development: A cluster-randomized trial. *Reading Research Quarterly, 46*(3), 249–272.

Neuman, S. B., & Roskos, K. (2005). The state of state pre-kindergarten standards. *Early Childhood Research Quarterly, 20*(2), 125–145.

NGSS Lead States. (2013). *Next Generation Science Standards: For states, by states.* Washington, DC: National Academies Press.

Nye, C., Foster, S. H., & Seaman, D. (1987). Effectiveness of language intervention with the language/learning disabled. *Journal of Speech and Hearing Disorders, 52*(4), 348–357.

Padak, N., Newton, E., Rasinski, T., & Newton, R. M. (2008). Getting to the root of word study: Teaching Latin and Greek word roots in elementary and middle grades. In A. E. Farstrup & S. J. Samuels (Eds.), *What research has to say about vocabulary instruction* (pp. 6–31). Newark, DE: International Reading Association.

Paribakht, T. S., & Wesche, M. (1996). Enhancing vocabulary acquisition through reading: A hierarchy of text-related exercise types. *Canadian Modern Language Review, 52*(2), 155–178.

Pearson, P. D., Hiebert, E. H., & Kamil, M. L. (2007). Vocabulary assessment: What we know and what we need to learn. *Reading Research Quarterly, 42*(2), 282–296.

Poirier, B. M. (1989). *The effectiveness of language intervention with preschool handicapped children: An integrative review.* Unpublished doctoral dissertation, Utah State University, Logan.

Pressley, M., Allington, R. L., Wharton-McDonald, R., Block, C. C., & Morrow, L. M. (2001). *Learning to read: Lessons from exemplary first-grade classrooms.* New York: Guilford Press.

Rasinski, T., Padak, N., Newton, R. M., & Newton, E. (2007). *Building vocabulary from word roots.* Huntington Beach, CA: Teacher Created Materials.

Read, J. (2000). *Assessing vocabulary.* New York: Cambridge University Press.

Roehr, S., & Carroll, K. (Eds.). (2010). *Collins COBUILD illustrated basic dictionary of American English.* Boston: Heinle Cengage Learning.

Rosenshine, B. V. (1986). Synthesis of research on explicit teaching. *Educational Leadership, 43*(7), 60–69.

Sadoski, M., & Paivio, A. (2001). *Imagery and text: A dual coding theory of reading and writing.* Mahwah, NJ: Erlbaum.

Scarborough, H. S. (1998). Early identification of children at risk for reading disabilities: Phonological awareness and some other promising predictors. In B. K. Shapiro, P. J. Accardo, & A. J. Capute (Eds.), *Specific reading disability: A view of the spectrum* (pp. 75–119). Timonium, MD: York Press.

Scarborough, H. S. (2002). Connecting early language and literacy to later reading (dis)abilities: Evidence, theory, and practice. In S. B. Neuman & D. K. Dickinson (Eds.), *Handbook of early literacy research* (Vol. 1, pp. 97–110). New York: Guilford Press.

Scott, J. A., Jamieson-Noel, D., & Asselin, M. (2003). Vocabulary instruction throughout the day in twenty-three Canadian upper-elementary classrooms. *The Elementary School Journal, 103*(3), 269–286.

Scott, J. A., Miller, T. F., & Flinspach, S. L. (2012). Developing word consciousness: Lessons from highly diverse fourth-grade classrooms. In E. J. Kame'enui & J. F. Baumann (Eds.), *Vocabulary instruction: Research to practice* (2nd ed., pp. 169–188). New York: Guilford Press.

Scott, J. A., & Nagy, W. E. (1997). Understanding the definitions of unfamiliar verbs. *Reading Research Quarterly, 32*(2), 184–200.

Sénéchal, M. (1997). The differential effect of storybook reading on preschoolers' acquisition of expressive and receptive vocabulary. *Child Language, 24*(1), 123–138.

Shapiro, B. J. (1969). The subjective estimation of relative word frequency. *Journal of Verbal Learning and Verbal Behavior, 8*(2), 248–251.

Singer, H. (1965). A developmental model of speed of reading in grades 3 through 6. *Reading Research Quarterly, 1*(1), 29–49.

Snow, C., Burns, M. S., & Griffin, P. (1998). *Preventing reading difficulties in young children.* Washington, DC: National Academy Press.

Stahl, K. A. D., & Bravo, M. A. (2010). Contemporary classroom vocabulary assessment for content areas. *Reading Teacher, 63*(7), 566–578.

Stahl, K. A. D., & Stahl, S. A. (2012). Young word wizards!: Fostering vocabulary development in preschool and primary education. In E. J. Kame'enui & J. F. Baumann (Eds.), *Vocabulary instruction: Research to practice* (2nd ed., pp. 72–92). New York: Guilford Press.

Stahl, S. (1983). Differential word knowledge and reading comprehension. *Journal of Reading Behavior, 15*(4), 33–50.

Stahl, S. A. (1999). *Vocabulary development.* Cambridge, MA: Brookline Books.

Stahl, S. A. (2005). Four problems with teaching word meanings (and what to do to make vocabulary an integral part of instruction). In E. H. Hiebert & M. L. Kamil (Eds.), *Teaching and learning vocabulary: Bringing research to practice* (pp. 95–114). Mahwah, NJ: Erlbaum.

Stahl, S. A., & Clark, C. H. (1987). The effects of participatory expectations in classroom discussion on the learning of science vocabulary. *American Educational Research Journal, 24*(4), 541–555.

Stahl, S. A., & Fairbanks, M. M. (1986). The effects of vocabulary instruction: A model-based meta-analysis. *Review of Educational Research, 56*(1), 72–110.

Stahl, S. A., & Murray, B. A. (1994). Defining phonological awareness and its relationship to early reading. *Journal of Educational Psychology, 86*(2), 221–234.

Stahl, S. A., & Nagy, W. E. (2006). *Teaching word meanings.* Mahwah, NJ: Erlbaum.

Stahl, S. A., & Vancil, S. J. (1986). Discussion is what makes semantic maps work in vocabulary instruction. *The Reading Teacher, 40*(1), 62–67.

Stanovich, K. E. (1986). Matthew effects in reading: Some consequences of individual differences in the acquisition of literacy. *Reading Research Quarterly, 21*(4), 360–407.

Stanovich, K. E., Cunningham, A. E., & Feeman, D. J. (1984). Intelligence, cognitive skills, and early reading progress. *Reading Research Quarterly, 19*(3), 278–303.

Sternberg, R. J. (1985). *Beyond IQ: A triarchic theory of human intelligence.* New York: Cambridge University Press.

Storch, S. A., & Whitehurst, G. J. (2002). Oral language and code-related precursors to reading: Evidence from a longitudinal structural model. *Developmental Psychology, 38*(6), 934–947.

Templin, M. (1957). *Certain language skills in children: Their development and interrelationships.* Minneapolis, MN: University of Minnesota Press.

Thurstone, L. L. (1946). Note on a reanalysis of Davis' reading tests. *Psychometrika, 11*(3), 185–188.

Tinkham, T. (1997). The effects of semantic and thematic clustering on the learning of second language vocabulary. *Second Language Research, 13*(2), 138–163.

Trueswell, J. C., Medina, T. N., Hafri, A., & Gleitman, L. R. (2013). Propose but verify: Fast mapping meets cross-situational word learning. *Cognitive Psychology, 66*(1), 126–156.

Vogel, E. (2003). Using informational text to build children's knowledge of the world around them. In N. K. Duke & V. S. Bennett-Armistead, *Reading and writing informational text in the primary grades: Research-based practices* (pp. 157–198). New York: Scholastic.

Watts, S. M. (1995). Vocabulary instruction during reading lessons in six classrooms. *Journal of Reading Behavior, 27*(3), 399–424.

Wharton-McDonald, R., Pressley, M., & Hampston, J. M. (1998). Literacy instruction in nine first-grade classrooms: Teacher characteristics and student achievement. *The Elementary School Journal, 99*(2), 101–128.

Whipple, G. (Ed.). (1925). *The 24th yearbook of the National Society for the Study of Education: Report of the National Committee on Reading*. Bloomington, IL: Public School.

White, T. G., Graves, M. F., & Slater, W. H. (1990). Growth of reading vocabulary in diverse elementary schools: Decoding and word meaning. *Journal of Educational Psychology, 82*(2), 281–290.

White, T. G., Sowell, J., & Yanagihara, A. (1989). Teaching elementary students to use word-part clues. *The Reading Teacher, 42*(4), 302–308.

Wilkinson, K. M., Ross, E., & Diamond, A. (2003). Fast mapping of multiple words: Insights into when "the information provided" does and does not equal "the information perceived." *Journal of Applied Developmental Psychology, 24*(6), 739–762.

Wright, T., & Neuman, S. B. (2010, April). *Explicit vocabulary instruction in kindergarten*. Paper presented at the annual meeting of the Michigan Reading Association, Grand Rapids.

Zwiers, J. (2008). *Building academic language: Essential practices for content classrooms, grades 5–12*. San Francisco: Jossey-Bass.

Index

MARZANO Research

Drive student success
in science

 Signature PD Service

Vocabulary for the New Science Standards Workshop

Boost your science and engineering instruction. This workshop guides your school or district through the process of creating and implementing a comprehensive vocabulary program for terms taken directly from the Next Generation Science Standards (NGSS).

Learning Outcomes

- Discover how vocabulary instruction can enhance students' understanding of science concepts.
- Acquire a six-step process for effective vocabulary instruction.
- Plan for teaching each of the six steps using descriptions and examples from the NGSS.
- Learn to develop systems for assessing and tracking student vocabulary knowledge.
- Take home a wealth of practical resources, including a process for creating a customized set of academic and content-area vocabulary terms to use in your classroom, school, or district.

Get started!
marzanoresearch.com/OnsitePD
888.849.0851